Full With Wills

My Life in My Music: A Memoir

Arthur Wills

Published in Great Britain by
Pen Press Publishers Ltd
39 Chesham road
The Old School House
Brighton
BN2 1NB

ISBN 1-905203-89-6
ISBN13 978-1-905203-89-5

Printed and bound in Great Britain by Cpod, Trowbridge, Wiltshire

'Ay, fill it full with wills'

Shakespeare (Sonnet 136)

Preface

In this book I have endeavoured to relate the story of my life with reference to the compositions which demonstrate the complex interweaving of the life and the work – full with Wills and the music that I willed. Thus I have adopted a somewhat 'stream of consciousness approach' rather than a simple and strict adherence to a 'diary' sequence of events. Nothing was published until my thirty-second year, naturally coinciding with my appointment as Organist and Master of the Choristers (or Director of Music as it is now called) at Ely Cathedral. This unique environment has continued to influence me since I first set eyes on it.

Contents

Photographs and illustrations:

In cot 1926 - 'Why am I here?'

My parents and MBM card: Basil Wills - (Uncle) - Sid Gibbs - A Wills (Father)

St. John's Baptist (Bablake) Church, Coventry c.1937

St Paul's Church, Warwick - Organist 1940-43

St Alban's Church, Leamington Spa - Organist 1943-46

St Mary's Collegiate Church, Warwick - Assistant Organist 1946-48

Canterbury Cathedral - No.17 The Precincts (SECM) Student 1948-49

Ely 'How rise thy towers, serene and bright'

Paintings of Ely Cathedral by John Titterton (Mary's Grandfather)

The Harrison Organ at Ely Cathedral

Mary - pupil; Arthur - teacher. 1949

Marriage - Dinner at Warldorf Hotel, London. 1953

No.2, The Almonry - (Drawing by Owen Rees, 2nd Verger)

Colin and Rachel

King's School Orchestra at rehearsal in Porta

The Royal Academy of Music

The Duke's Hall, Royal Academy of Music

At the Organ console, Ely Cathedral 1986

Choristers in the Lady Chapel with myself, James Tilly (Housemaster) and Peter North (Assistant Housemaster) c. 1985

Rehearsal of Guitar Concerto – Lethbridge, Canada. 1996

Rome, 1990

Receiving OBE 1990

At the Study in Paradise House 2006 – 'Still here!'

Chapter 1

About Us in Our Infancy

I was born in Coventry on the 19th September 1926. It was the year of the General Strike, which was of course a reaction to the high level of unemployment countrywide. My father worked in the motor industry and was 'on the dole' at the time when I was born. He played the piano but his main instrument was the mandolin-banjo (also known as the banjolin), and he was a member of the MBM Trio which played in the Working Men's Clubs of the Coventry area. Their business card records the names of Sid Gibbs, my father Archibald and my uncle Basil. Apparently money was so short at that time that it was necessary for him to pawn his mandolin in order to be able to buy what was immediately required for my coming into the world. I of course knew nothing about money problems, either then, or at any other time in my childhood. It was quite idyllic, and I have only the happiest memories of my home life – 'Heaven lies about us…'

We lived at 13 Norfolk Street (in the Spon End district) throughout most of my childhood, and I assume that I was born in that house with its outside toilet – absolutely necessary if you are destined to eventually 'get on in life'! After the Second World War, that street, along with much of the surrounding area, was demolished in order to make way for the Coventry Ringroad – a thoroughly hideous attempt to improve traffic flow. My grandmother was a midwife and she and her husband lived with us – an extended family in one house, and I imagine that she would have delivered me and my sisters at birth. This mode of life hardly exists now, but it was in very many ways a most happy, useful and generally satisfactory arrangement. I had two sisters, Joan and Vera, so the seven of us had to get along with each other as amicably as possible. It must have helped that I had an intense interior life, nurtured by books, music, and my own imagination. *Grimm's Fairy Tales* both fascinated and terrified me, especially the vivid page-size illustrations. As the only boy, and the youngest child, doubtless I was thoroughly spoiled.

It was my great good fortune to be educated at St John's School, a short walk away from where we lived. This was a Church School, attached to St John the Baptist Church which stands at the juncture with Smith Street and Corporation Street, both leading to the City centre. This schooling, which finished at the age of fourteen in 1940, was the only formal general education I had. I failed to get into the Grammar School, but this did not appear to worry me unduly – from an early age I instinctively felt that things would always turn out well in the end. I was in a school play which required me to sing a short solo, and that led to the suggestion that I should audition for the Church Choir. I was successful, and of course it proved to be one of the best and most useful experiences of my life – perhaps crucial sums it up even more adequately.

In 1989 David Salter commissioned me to write an anthem for the baptism of his daughter, Alice, at St John the Baptist Church, Knaresborough, where he was Director of Music. For the text I chose the words of the appealing hymn by Bishop How – 'It is a thing most wonderful' and entitled the piece 'A Child Like Me.' In the English Hymnal it is set to an 'English traditional melody' and I quoted this in the course of my piece, giving it to be hummed by the tenors and basses. I think that it resonates with my own childhood as a chorister very potently. The John Ireland setting of these words for treble voices is a wonderfully expressive and moving piece – ever a favourite of mine for the anthem at Boy's Voices Evensongs at Ely.

The churchmanship at St John the Baptist Church, Coventry was Anglo-Catholic, which initiated me into the ritual and colour of the Sunday Eucharist. Music is an essential part of this Service and grows out of it quite naturally – it is really a kind of music-theatre experience and the repertoire covers the whole gamut from plainchant to the most exuberant 19th/21st century settings. The Organist and Choirmaster was also the Headmaster of St John's School – George Parker, an innately kind man, though often too sarcastic for more than my just liking – my tendency to daydream often infuriated him. When I visited him in his retirement I was both taken aback and slightly disillusioned by his vehemently expressed dislike of High Church Services! Nevertheless, my future was already presaged for me by those early choirboy years.

My sister Joan had started piano lessons with Mrs Pearson – a local piano teacher – but had quickly lost interest in them. She wanted to give up and was greatly relieved when I said that I wanted to learn, as she felt less awkward about telling her teacher of her own wish to give up music lessons. So I took over Joan's lesson time and quickly began to make progress. I liked the piano, but of course the organ was of greater interest – all that colour and volume! And it was a necessary music, not just for fun or entertainment but to be listened to in church or the concert hall and opera house – it surely had to mean something.

After a year or two of piano lessons I needed to be able to make a sound like an organ at home. I had heard, I'm not sure from what source, that someone had a harmonium for sale for five shillings (twenty-five pence in today's money!). With my parent's gift of the money and the loan of a pushcart from somewhere, I, with the willing help of friends pushed this quite heavy burden through the streets of Coventry to my home. The houses in Norfolk Street and in much of the surrounding area were built with a watchmaker's workshop on the second floor - known locally as the 'top shop' - (it was a three-storey house). This commodious room had long been a playground for me and was the ideal situation for my harmonium. Having installed it I decided that I wanted stop jambs on each side of the keyboard, rather than the row of stops above. We were taught woodwork as part of the school timetable (we had to go to another school for the lessons, and I cordially disliked the teacher, as much as he equally disapproved of my daydreaming propensity). Nevertheless, I had learnt enough to be able to change my harmonium around to suit my imagination of actually playing a proper organ. All this activity won approval from my parents. But when I decided that the organ alone was not sufficient to create the atmosphere I wanted for my musical dreams, and decided to build an altar with candle sticks, they began to worry somewhat. "Isn't it mocking the Church?" I heard my mother comment with obvious perplexity. "No, nothing like that." I was able to reassure her. And of course it wasn't – what I was after was atmosphere – an evocative setting for the music.

As the thirties went on times changed, the economy improved and soon the motor industry was transformed into aircraft production. My father had to work night shifts as required, and acquired an addiction to cigarettes which first led to an irritating cough – both for him and the family – and eventually to his death from lung cancer at the early age of fifty-six. I have never attempted to smoke – the very thought used to sicken me. Some Sunday evenings after Evensong I would go to one of the Working Men's Clubs with my parents when the MBM Trio was on the programme – what an atmosphere of beer and cigarettes! But now money was no longer so tight, and without really analysing the situation, I realised that I was being more than usually indulged, in that Christmas presents would include Meccano and model aircraft construction sets. I loved all of this, and I think that construction fascinated me from that period onwards, until I began to study music techniques and eventually compose.

4

The family acquired a wireless set, and at family agreeable times I would listen to concerts – the music of Elgar and Vaughan Williams I found especially attractive, and I began to try to reproduce those sounds on the piano. Talk of the likelihood of war was increasingly present, and my grandfather frequently expressed some irritation at my choice of the model aircraft I built – more often than not German rather than English. I can't explain why this was, except that possibly the German aeroplanes gave a more enticing atmosphere of power and excitement in their design, as well as a sense of toying with something of menace and danger. Most Saturday evenings my parents would take me out for a supper in town (pigs-feet!) and then on to a play at the Opera House, as it was grandly called. In fact it was a Playhouse with a repertory company and a change of play each week – essential experience for me of a world outside – with such people in it! I remember only one day out at the seaside – Rhyl, and it rained so incessantly that we went to the cinema to see 'Red Sails in the Sunset'. Apparently I went to sleep, and also lost my cap.

War was clearly imminent, and I remember filling sandbags in the Memorial Park – 1939 was a gloriously hot summer holiday time. When the war finally arrived, in company with most other school-children I was evacuated – in my case to Kenilworth, five miles away. The first few days were idyllic with a shop and a very congenial family including a most attractive daughter, but after a few days I was moved to a much less attractive household, though still very welcoming and caring, and home-sickness quickly set in. At my urgent request I was fetched back home and completed the final school year in the summer of 1940 at the age of fourteen.

I obtained my first job at a piano workshop in the city centre. Ever since, if I smell glue, I am transported in my mind at once back to that place. There was one young co-worker who, when he was not extolling the delights of his girlfriend attired in a swimming costume, talked about the Organist of the Cathedral – a Mr Alan Stephenson. "He plays a great piece by Mozart – Fantasia in F minor. You should hear it." I did eventually hear it, though not in Coventry (the Cathedral was destroyed in the air raids of November 1940) and it has remained one of my favourite pieces – an organ masterpiece – composed for an organ in a clock?!

But the air-raids long foretold had begun, and the city centre often showed signs of increasing devastation when I arrived for work in the morning. Sometime before, as a result of our increasing affluence, we had moved to a nicer house in Northumberland Road – a Hall with stained glass in the front door – even a set of bells for servants, what could they have been paid! – just off the Holyhead Road. But most nights now were spent in the garden Andersen shelter. In early November the house was hit by an incendiary bomb – not a great deal of damage resulted, but we had relatives in Warwick, ten miles away and it was decided that we should move there for the time being.

I vividly remember the family arriving at the railway station late one evening. There was an air raid in progress and of course everything was blacked out. Bombs were falling quite near the Station as we boarded the train, which left late, but we journeyed to Warwick without incident. It was to prove one of the defining changes in my life and future prospects.

My Organ Suite – 'Remembrance of Things Past: November Fourteenth' was composed in 1991 and commemorates the significance of that date in three crucial episodes in my early career. The autumn air-raids culminated in the 'blitz' of that date and the destruction of Coventry Cathedral. 'Threnody (Coventry, 1940)' is based upon three hymn tunes – 'Austrian Hymn' (Deutchland uber alles), 'Michael' and 'Winchester New'. Coventry Cathedral is dedicated to St Michael, and Winchester New (On Jordan's bank the Baptist's cry) commemorates my association with St John Baptist Church.

We were to stay with Uncle George and his family. Their house was in Market Street and he worked at a bakery in the town centre, and sang bass in St Paul's Church Choir. I naturally found a place there singing tenor, and when the organist retired early in 1941 I offered to play. I had no organ experience apart from my harmonium, but the legato touch which comes from playing a keyboard wind instrument I found quite naturally transferable to this two-manual tracker-action organ placed in a quite large building. Uncle George also found me a job delivering bread. Within a month of our move from Coventry, St Michael's Cathedral was to be destroyed – I had sung in several of the annual Church Choir Festivals held at Michaelmastide, but as a child the wartime disasters seemed of little moment – there were so many of them.

Eventually, my parents decided to stay in Warwick and took over a little general shop further down Market Street. Warwick was only ten miles away from Coventry but we never heard the sound of a bomb falling. It's hard now to think back over sixty years to those early days of playing the organ as a teenager. Presumably I learned all kinds of bad habits, but it's also true that in none of the lessons that I did have subsequently did any teacher ever impart any specific technical instruction – with regard to pedalling, for example. What was self-taught stayed that way. (In conversation with Sir William McKie years later, when I was at Westminster Abbey to play an organ concert, I was amused to hear him say that he also had never received any lessons on correct pedalling technique!) But I knew that I needed some good teaching, and I had heard of Stanley Vann, the Organist of Holy Trinity Church, Leamington Spa. He heard me play the Holy Trinity organ – an electric action instrument which I found hard to manage after the tracker organ I was used to. We did some work on the Eight Short Preludes and Fugues

7

of J.S. Bach, but Stanley then suggested that I should improve my piano technique with the Two-Part Inventions and other piano pieces that Mrs Pearson had not used. There were blackout restrictions of course, and Holy Trinity was not readily available for evening lessons – another disincentive for organ tuition. Stanley was a fine teacher, but within a year he was called up for military service.

I went on with lessons with local teachers, but by now had given up delivering bread in favour of a job in the record department of the Dale Forty music shop in the Parade, Leamington Spa. Though still not a great career move, it was at least related to music, and that in a much more interesting way than was the piano repair workshop. My task was to persuade the potential customers of the merits of the latest record releases, whether it was Beecham, Toscanini, or Duke Ellington. I had a wind-up gramophone in my bedroom and gradually acquired the shellac recordings that especially appealed to me through hearing them at the shop.

I thought that Wilhelm Furtwängler's Beethoven and Wagner was magnificent – especially Beethoven's Fifth Symphony and the Prelude and Leibestod from Wagner's Tristan and Isolde. My transcription for organ of the Prelude to Act 3 of Die Meistersinger is dedicated to Furtwängler's memory. And also Elgar conducting his own music – the Violin Concerto played by the 16-year-old Menuhin, also the Symphonic Study: Falstaff and the 2nd Symphony.

At work I was a sort of DJ, and through my attempts at marketing I also got to know a great amount of music and the latest recordings of it, and in addition made the acquaintance of many of the most musically interested – and interesting – townsfolk. I was fortunate enough to be blessed with one of these as my Assistant – a most helpful and attractive girl named Zena, of about the same age as myself. The Record Department was situated on the first floor, and fortunately the stairs were not carpeted. Amongst the clientele was Donald Perkins, the organist of St Alban's Church, and he, on learning that I played the organ, asked me if I would be able to deputise occasionally for him. St Alban's was the Daughter Church of All Saint's, the Parish Church of Leamington, and was Anglo-Catholic in churchmanship as of course all such establishments tended to be. This of course was what I had been brought up on in Coventry, and I relished the idea of using the English Hymnal again, rather than the (to me) somewhat tedious diet of Hymns Ancient and Modern at St Paul's. After showing me the organ – three manuals! – he went through Nicholson in C with me. On my apologising for my frequent mistakes, he always put me at my ease with "It's sight-reading, and a strange organ for you, isn't it?!" So I deputised for a week or so and then he was offered a position elsewhere in South London, and I was offered the post shortly before my seventeenth birthday. I think that it was quite likely that he knew that his time was nearly up, and wanted to find someone that he was happy with to take over from him.

But life was beginning to accelerate away for me and by this time I was an employee of Warwickshire County Council in the Weights and Measures Department. Why? Well, a Lay Reader at St Paul's – a Mr Spooner – was an Inspector in this department, and he offered the job to me. It was more money than selling records, and involved being driven round leafy Warwickshire, visiting shops and petrol stations and testing their equipment. It was not without interest and included many opportunities for conversation with the Inspector I was allotted to on the daily round of visits covering the County – if it was Mr Spooner either religion or politics was the usual topic. If a Court case resulted I would be called upon to give evidence – quite fun, I thought – clearly already a taste for drama and the limelight! But ironically it was also my first encounter with corruption in local government. In 1944 a young inspector was appointed who was somewhat cavalier in his interpretation of his duties, and thought nothing of taking an afternoon off at the Cinema if he felt like it, or filling up his tank with petrol at some garage we were testing without paying. But as a 17-year-old junior employee what could I do?

At St Alban's the observance of Feasts and Festivals on weekdays meant playing the organ at 6.30 in the morning. Quite a discipline! But it could be managed. I was continually learning new organ pieces to play as voluntaries and became especially interested in the French School. Continental organ sound and composition fascinated me from the time I heard a recording of Albert Schweitzer playing Cesar Franck's Choral in E major on the organ of Strasbourg Cathedral. While still at St Paul's I bought the music and tried to make the two-manual Warwick organ produce the right sounds. In my enthusiasm I even entered for a Scholarship at the Royal College of Music. All this without a teacher to help me prepare for such an ordeal, and of course I didn't get it. Never mind – I was simply avid for experience and a sense of progress in life, and it was a thrill to have to play to Sir George Dyson and have the opportunity to talk to him.

At the age of 16 at St Alban's I was in charge of a choir of men and boys, and in spite of wartime conditions we managed to keep a worthwhile repertoire going, but I was more than a little apprehensive when I heard that Sir Sydney Nicholson was removing his School of English Church Music from Tenbury Wells to Leamington (October 1943). One lady in the congregation commented to me (rather darkly, I thought) "The Choirs around here are going to have to smarten-up now!" In due course I invited the great man to attend a Boys' rehearsal which didn't go too badly, but he did suggest that I took the trouble to read more carefully his preface to the Parish Psalter. (Apparently I was already unknowingly putting into practice Boris Ord's famous dictum "The Parish Psalter is the easiest Psalter to alter".)

I also took the opportunity to ask the great man about the courses of study at the School and he was very ready to give me time to tell him about my interests and ambitions. He appeared to treat me as an equal. I found this to be just as true of Cathedral Organists when at every Bank holiday I would take the train to perhaps Oxford, Lichfield or York, and boldly ask to be allowed in the Organ loft for the Service. "Are you the FULL organist at your church?!" Sir Thomas Armstrong demanded dubiously when once I turned up at Christ Church Cathedral – nevertheless my requests were not ever refused. Not even by the famously crusty Sir Edward Bairstow when I arrived in York one Easter Monday in time for a 10.30 a.m. Sung Eucharist (Stanford in A). In fact I thought that his assistant (might it have been Francis Jackson?) was more irritated by my presence than was the Great Man himself. I remember Bairstow exclaiming "What on earth are they doing down there!" when something in the Choir went awry.

One memorable event at home was a performance of part of Bach's Christmas Oratorio by the Leamington Spa Bach Choir under Martindale Sidwell. He had taken on Vann's post at Holy Trinity until Stanley's return from active service and thereby inherited the Bach Choir also. For various good reasons no doubt there was no orchestra, and the great organist G.D. Cunningham from Birmingham Town Hall played the extremely taxing keyboard reduction brilliantly, albeit with an occasional slip of the finger. Sydney Nicholson was in the audience and commented on the "wizardry" of Cunningham's playing. The Priest-in-Charge at St Alban's was also present and he was less forgiving of the finger fallibility. The typical contrast between the sympathy and understanding of the professional and the critical nit-picking of a dilettante?!

In retrospect, William Blake's insight into the child growing into the man rings increasingly true with the passing years. My Concerto for Organ and Guitar is entitled 'Of

Innocence and Experience' and attempts to portray life with all its pains and problems as an unavoidable passage for the (at any rate partial) development of the character and soul. It was composed in 1988 and first performed at the Harrogate Festival in 1990 by myself and Fiona Richardson. Fiona had studied my Guitar Sonata with me at the RAM at the suggestion of her teacher Hector Quine. It wasn't well received by the critics, who I think found the title provocative. The three movements suggest a progress from a fairly untroubled simplicity through intense stress (the second movement is based on the plainchant Dies Irae) to the acceptance and resolution of the finale. Of course the guitar has to be amplified, but this is usually done in the concerto repertoire for the instrument generally. In 1996 I played it in Lethbridge, Alberta with Dale Ketcheson, a teacher of guitar at the University. And then a few years earlier in 1992 Michael Dudman had commissioned me to compose a song cycle for Contralto and Organ and again I turned to Blake for my text, entitling the three movement work 'Eternity's Sunrise' – another work about growth and life's experiences. Three of Blake's astonishing poems make this point with consummate ease – The Lamb, The Tyger, and Eternity. Katharine Capewell was the soloist, and her collaboration with Michael was a partnership which promised much for the future, only to be dashed by Michael's untimely death of a heart attack at the early age of fifty. This commission was for the bi-annual Keyboard Festival at Newcastle University, NSW, Australia.

I became eligible for military service when I reached the age of eighteen in September 1944, but on account of weak eyesight was graded C4, thereby not having to leave my musical pursuits. That same year a friend, Jim MacChesney, one of the basses in the St Alban's Choir, was called up to join the Royal Marines. He had already been offered a place at Gonville and Caius College, Cambridge, and had just begun a six-month Short Course there before beginning his

War Service. Knowing that the Cambridge organ and choral scene would be of the greatest interest to me he suggested that I should spend a week's holiday with him and explore as many as possible of the most interesting musical venues. Towards the end of my stay – I think it was the Thursday, Jim suggested that we should take a trip to Ely. We set off after an early lunch, took the train across the Fens, and walked up the hill from the station. On that dim November afternoon the experience of the cathedral was truly magical. I don't recall seeing any other visitors until the Evensong Service, which was sung unaccompanied in the Lady Chapel. The setting was Causton's Short Service and the anthem was Purcell's 'Remember not, Lord, our offences'. Dr Marmaduke Conway directed.

In the course of time I gradually became aware of a 'tug' pulling me towards Ely. I suppose that I must have seen books with accounts of the Cathedral, and the character of Cromwell always fascinated me. Much later I discovered that even St John the Baptist Church in Coventry had Cromwellian associations, the Royalist captives being imprisoned there in order to prevent any conspiracy to escape – in other words they were 'Sent to Coventry'. I must have read every book on Cromwell to be found in Warwick Library. And reading *The Musical Times* one day I noticed an advertisement for a Tenor Lay Clerk at Ely Cathedral. I was still in my late teens and foolishly decided to apply for it. I was invited to an audition, and I remember that the Precentor (whose address was Powcher's Hall in those days) suggested that of the two hotels I would probably prefer 'The Lamb' to 'The Bell'. But I 'chickened out' in today's inelegant expression, and I'm sure that it was for the best – for me and for Ely! But can life be such a random affair as some would have us believe? I think not. Jim and I went to a rehearsal in King's College Chapel and heard Dr Harold Darke rehearsing Stanford's 'Glorious and powerful God'. Darke was in charge at King's while Boris Ord was away on war service. Altogether the whole week was a fascinating experience for me, and although I was of course already aware that I would not ever be able to attend University as a student, I also knew that somehow or other I would have to circumvent this disadvantage.

Chapter 2

More Understanding

The Diplomas of the Royal College of Organists were my next objective, and I knew that the Paperwork Section of these examinations were more rigorous in their requirements than any other performance based diplomas. Where to find a teacher who could guide me? Talks with other musicians in Warwick drew me to the conclusion that there was only one – Dr Allen K. Blackall, who was Organist of St Mary's Collegiate Church, and Principal of the Birmingham School of Music (now the Birmingham Conservatoire). He was indeed a remarkable teacher, unremitting in his attention to detail, yet inspiring in his imparting of the essentials of the technique of composition. He often talked about the students at Birmingham chafing at the "academic keeping of the rules" required for the examinations. "Vaughan Williams writes consecutive fifths – why shouldn't I" was one of the most frequent questions he had to counter. He told me that his answer was always "That's fine – if you can write like Vaughan Williams!" In fact I enjoyed the exercises in species counterpoint in which all dissonances were strictly prepared and resolved – and even more so when I learned that Mozart was trained in precisely this way also. I worked with him until he left Warwick in 1946 to join the staff of The College of St Nicholas (the teaching base of the School of English Church Music) which was in the process of moving from Chislehurst to Canterbury. In that year I entered for ARCO and passed the Paperwork Section – a testimony to Dr Blackall's teaching. He also taught me a lesson when he wanted to illustrate a point from Chopin's Etude in G flat,

Opus 25. He went to the piano to play a section – "I used to be able to play that so beautifully," he lamented – a useful illustration of the necessity of keeping up one's technique in spite of all the other claims on the time available – and the ravages of increasing age.

In my retirement year from Ely in 1990 I was sent a copy of 'A Shepherd Boy' a carol – just the words and melody – which Dr Blackall wrote in 1938. He sent it as a Christmas card to his Head Chorister at St Mary's – George Coombes – who sang it at the Christmas Day Service that year, and then found the card on his return home. So then in 1990 I arranged it for SATB and organ and it was published by the RSCM – appropriately enough given Dr Blackall's tenure as a Lecturer at the SECM at Canterbury.

The War over, I was now 19, and I realised that if I was to realise my ambition and enter the profession I needed to meet more musicians, widen my experience and obtain useful qualifications – all that kind of thing. So back to Warwick I went – this time to become an underling instead of the Boss, working as his Assistant with Peter Burton, who had just been appointed fresh from Oxford to St Mary's Collegiate Church. Peter was a very engaging character who took the greatest interest in me and my future over the next two years (1946–48). He also deserved to have a great future, and in due course was appointed to St Alban's Abbey. There he was working with tremendous enjoyment and fulfilment until a tragic accident cut short his career. Always devoted to his Choristers he took them to the swimming baths on an occasion when one of them got into difficulties. Peter at once went to his assistance – the boy survived – but Peter drowned.

I also sang in the Choir when not needed on the organ stool. Leonard Harbour, a long serving alto in the Choir, took a great interest in me, and gave me every encouragement. I have every reason to be grateful to him and the many other people who thought me worthy of encouragement. I wish that

I had shown very much more gratitude to them – I am now, to my regret, very well aware of my many character deficiencies.

I must mention here a most useful educative experience – attendance at orchestral concerts, mainly in Birmingham at the Town Hall. One especially lingers in the mind. The London Philharmonic Orchestra was touring in the Midlands area with various guest conductors and I was able to be present at two of their concerts. The first was in Leamington and included Beethoven's Seventh Symphony. I was suitably impressed, but a week or so later the same orchestra was at Birmingham with Wilhelm Furtwängler – he had recently been 'de-Nazified' and this was one of his first appearances in the United Kingdom. I well remember every item in the programme – Mendelssohn's Overture 'Fingal's Cave', Beethoven's Seventh Symphony and Brahms' First. I was astonished to hear that the orchestra made a quite different sound, quite apart from the intensity of the interpretations, which riveted the attention from the first note to the last. Quite extraordinary! This was my first lesson in the concept of interpretation – as opposed to mere 'presentation' – not equalled until I heard Sir Thomas Beecham also with a variety of orchestras.

My organ lessons for the RCO Diplomas were free, but more importantly I was now in close contact with a man who seemed to know everybody worth knowing in the profession. Peter expected me to gain an Oxbridge Organ Scholarship, not realising at that time that my abbreviated schooling barred me from this normal entree into the world of academic music. (I was often tortured by questions about my academic past which required me to evade answering if at all possible. These days I come straight out with it!) It was then that my thoughts once again turned to the SECM. Nicholson had died, Gerald Knight had succeeded him as Warden and had also moved the School to the Precincts of Canterbury Cathedral, where he was Organist. The proud possessor of still only half an ARCO I went for an interview and was requested to try again after further study (or some similar admonition!). A little more than six months later I heard from Gerald that he had seen my name on the list of FRCO passes and would I now like to compete for the Society of the Faith Scholarship which would fund a year's study at the College of St Nicholas during the academic year 1948/49? Of course I would! Len Harbour commented "You've shaken him!"

I competed, and the Sub-Warden of the College recommended that I be awarded the Scholarship – he was Dr Sidney Campbell – himself poised on the starting line of an extraordinary career, and destined to exercise a cataclysmic influence on my future. I played the Bach G major Prelude and Fugue BWV541 and at the end Sidney asked me what I thought of my performance. I remember replying "Perhaps more the spirit than the letter!" but he seemed quite pleased, both with my reply and my performance. Before I could accept the Award I needed to find additional funds to pay for a year's keep in Canterbury. Praise be to the Labour Government of 1945! – Warwickshire County Council gave me £100, and that sum was quite adequate in those days for a year's subsistence away from home. Len Harbour took me out to dinner at the Warwick Arms Hotel, and as a finishing touch introduced me to the delights of Green Chatreuse! I was also to miss the delightful company of Sonia, a girl friend who also worked in the Weights and Measures Office.

After years of uncertainty (but full of interest and enjoyment) I could now focus fully on becoming a professional musician. It quickly became clear to me that the value of further education, however lengthy or abbreviated, lay mainly in the people one encountered, rather than in the (no doubt useful!) training of the mind. For instance, all students had to sing in the College Choir and take singing lessons from Robert Poole, and I did sufficiently well to be asked to deputise in the Cathedral Choir – this experience was to prove a most useful asset in my career prospects.

Amongst the students in my year Michael Fleming became a firm friend, and eventually a committed advocate of my music, not least as a reviewer for the RSCM magazine *Church Music Quarterly*. Stanley Jackson from Wellington Cathedral, New Zealand, was one of several mature overseas students, and a truly delightful man. The same was true of John (Jack) Barrett from Australia. In many ways, though, the most promising of the students was Peter Whitehouse, who had come from Wolverhampton with Sidney Campbell. Among the students they were sometimes referred to as 'the Wolverhampton Wanderers'! He was equally good on both piano and organ, and a performance I heard him do of Debussy's 'L'Isle Joyeuse' has stayed vividly in my mind. Although Peter obtained a place at Oxford he never really seemed to establish himself as at all notable in the profession. Even great ability is sometimes insufficient for long lasting success. I remember one lengthy discussion we had on his thesis that a composer's early works are the best. I wasn't entirely convinced, but had to agree that early works were usually the most immediately attractive and popular with the general public. In my case two instances of this theory are my 'Ave verum corpus' from Two Latin Motets for two-part trebles and organ (1960), and the Carillon on 'Orientis Partibus' for solo organ (1972). Both pieces have now been recorded three times – a reasonable index of their popularity.

Edred Wright was the Choirmaster – a very gifted musician and forthright critic of my choir-training abilities! He conducted a Ladies Choir in the town and asked me to be its accompanist, which I gladly did. He entered the Choir for the Canterbury Competitive Festival and it duly won with the greatest of ease. During the Summer Term there was a Cathedral Festival which included several performances of *The Zeal of thy House* – Dorothy L. Sayers' striking play on the building of Canterbury Cathedral. Gerald Knight had composed the incidental music for this, and we students were involved in the performance as a hidden choir. At one point

Peter Whitehouse and I were required to sing the plainchant Dies Irae with our faces turned to the wall so as to give an effect of distance. At one performance we unfortunately had a fit of the giggles and almost broke down. I heard Edred utter an outraged and despairing "My God!" but we managed to recover, and nothing was said afterwards. We were all invited to the party after the last night, and it was a very worthwhile experience meeting the author and the starry cast. Autographs in my copy of the play include Dorothy L. Sayers, Jill Balcon, Joseph O'Connor, Christopher Hassall and Michael Goodliffe. Ms Sayers was prevailed upon to make a speech in which she noted that all the situations and tensions in her play would be as equally matched by the present day Chapter of Canterbury as in that of the 12th century. I have to say that my own observations in Ely fully bear this opinion out, and added very considerably to the pleasure and interest of my being a member of the Cathedral Foundation.

Joseph Poole, the Precentor of the Cathedral, lectured on Liturgiology. He was a fascinating character, eventually going to the new Coventry Cathedral as Canon Precentor, and devising many of the Service Books for the rapidly developing Royal School of Church Music, as it eventually became. I didn't foresee then that I would eventually be involved as a composer in a good number of these productions. I remember many of his lectures, and especially one where he discussed the poetry of John Donne, eventually to become Dean of St Paul's Cathedral – 'a great visitor of ladies in his young days' as he engagingly put it. Gerald Knight took an Improvisation Class on the piano. I seemed to be the most adept in this class – after all, I had scraped an FRCO! He insisted that I should enter for the Piano Improvisation in the Canterbury Festival, because there was normally only one entry, a youngish lady who naturally always came First. Well, I entered and she still came first – on the grounds that her effort was more pianistic than mine, although mine was commended for its more interesting bass part. It's strange how one remembers these things! I sketched out my first composition (now lost) that year – a three-minute organ piece. It was described by the most mature of the students – and I think that it was meant to be a compliment – as 'a little Whitlock'. At any rate I took the comment to be understood as something like a commendation.

A more significant outcome of my knowing Sidney Campbell was his informed advice on my academic work. He made it his business to consider my more long-term future and advised me to matriculate in the University of Durham as a necessary preliminary to my obtaining the B.Mus. degree. I must have worked fast since I matriculated during July in English Language, Modern History, Religious Knowledge, Music and English Literature. What a good thing that I loved reading from childhood onwards!

As a student already possessing an FRCO Diploma I did not have any organ tuition at The College of St Nicholas. All students had to take their turn at accompanying Services, either in the College Chapel or in the Undercroft at the Cathedral. My final voluntaries usually aroused some comment – "What witches' brew was that!?" greeted me after an Evensong when I had played Vierne's Cortège from the Twenty-Four Pieces. Towards the end of the academic year three of us were asked to play a recital on the College Chapel organ. It was a large converted drawing room, quite dead acoustically. I opted to play Dupré's Prelude and Fugue in B major on the two-manual organ – a ridiculous choice really, but the piece fascinated me and I had been working at it for some time. "Like some great factory going full tilt" was the comment of one student, Timothy Lawford, and it was quite an apt description I think.

The second movement of 'Remembrance of Things Past' – November Fourteenth is 'Skirl' (Canterbury, 1948). I well remember Gerald Knight telling the students before the early Service "We have a little Prince!" Skirl is based on a Scottish melody 'Charlie is my darling', and a Welsh tune 'On this day our King was born'.

Sidney Campbell was the Organist at Sandwich Parish Church, and he occasionally asked me to deputise for him. On his appointment to Ely Cathedral in the course of that year he decided to resign that post, and suggested that I should take over from him, which I did in the Spring of 1949. Then, a few months later, he asked me whether I would like to go with him to Ely as his Assistant Organist and Tenor Lay Clerk. Those singing lessons had obviously proved useful! I realised that this move would transform my prospects and immediately accepted. The 'tug' to Ely was at last complete. What a good thing that I did not go ahead with my previous Tenor Lay Clerk application!

In addition to the Fellowship Diploma it was also necessary to have passed the Choir-training examination of the RCO in order to enter for the Archbishop's Diploma, and this I did in the Summer of 1949. Dr Harold Rhodes, of Winchester Cathedral, was the Examiner. The Society of the Faith Scholarship, although but a year in duration, had transformed my life and prospects. At last the concept of 'a career in music' was about to be attempted and realised.

Chapter 3

Make a Cheerful Noise

As I recall, the combined post of Assistant Organist and Tenor Lay Clerk brought in a salary of £200 and this could be augmented by piano teaching and other work at the King's School, where Dr Campbell was to be Director of Music. The connection with the Cathedral Foundation goes back to monastic times, the School being refounded by Henry VIII at the Reformation. In those days the School numbered around two hundred boys – the boys and teaching staff could all be readily accommodated in the wonderful Lady Chapel of the Cathedral for the daily Services. There was a piano in a side chapel which I played for Morning Assembly. On our arrival for the start of the Michaelmas Term I remember Sidney saying breezily "It's a tenth rate School!" and also "It's virgin territory!" He meant musically speaking of course – now it's a mixed school numbering nigh on a thousand pupils, and I'm quite sure that neither of Sidney's appellations is remotely accurate. But it was surprisingly true that previously there had not been any systematic teaching of music in the School, though one far-reaching step had already been decided upon – the Cathedral Choristers were now to be educated at the King's School instead of the tiny Cathedral Choir School which had been relying solely upon finding local boys of sufficient ability to sing in the Choir.

The appointment of Sidney Campbell as the first post-War Organist was the obvious time at which to make the change, though it's unlikely that the Chapter had tried to foresee the devastating effect that inflation would eventually wreak upon their limited finances. But that was some distance away and those concerned with the Choir were elated to contemplate the improvement in the standard of singing that might now be expected. And of course this innovation would in due course completely change the musical ethos of the School, as it was expected that many of the Choristers would go on into the Senior School and develop into useful altos, tenors and basses.

So term began with my introduction to the six Lay Clerks, of which I was to be an extra Tenor on Decani – the side of the Dean's Stall. Cantoris was the side where the Precentor had his seat, and to slightly complicate matters these two positions were in fact the opposite of that obtaining in most other cathedrals.

My role was to sing and direct the Choir from my place amongst the Lay Clerks, and be prepared to play the organ instead only if Sidney was absent or wanted to direct the Choir himself. If the music was unaccompanied it was the norm for the Organist to direct, but if not then the Choir was expected to 'look across' at each other, and 'sing to the organ.' This procedure meant of course that the ensemble was not always tidy, and that the concept of an 'interpretation' was hardly considered. Dynamics and tempo modifications were not easy to control and this resulted in renditions which were 'presented' rather than communicated to the listener. Much of the Canticle repertoire of the 17th, 18th and 19th centuries was composed with organ parts designed to help the Choir to commence phrases together without a director (known irreverently as 'the Anglican thump'), and inevitably this was eventually seen to be both a crude and somewhat irritating way of securing this. At King's College, Cambridge two Choral Scholars on each side were responsible for securing a tidy ensemble, and the results were also immeasurably improved through the benefit of a rehearsal for the full choir in the stalls before every Service. Historically, solo or 'verse' sections were allotted to each side in turn on a weekly basis. At Ely, Sidney soon adopted the practice of only using Decani for this, as he found it difficult to find singers of sufficient quality for both sides. At this point I remember that Jack Barrett came to sing with the choir for a time, before he returned to Australia. Furthermore, there was only one full practice each week, on Fridays after Evensong which of course meant that the Lay Clerks were required to sing much of the repertoire unrehearsed. I remember very clearly that verses were always given to Decani after one episode in which Stanford in G was listed on a Cantoris Verse week in error. The Bass who would have had to sing the solo in the Nunc Dimittis was considered impossible by Sidney, so he resorted to the stratagem of claiming that he couldn't manage the organ part of the Magnificat due to a strained wrist – definitely something here for tears! – therefore another setting would have to be substituted.

Sidney delighted in being a 'personality' and making his presence felt. Problems which others would have managed to massage into a tolerable outcome he would delight in 'rubbing it in'. Picture this – the anthem at a Monday Evensong was 'I will arise, and go to my Father' by Creighton, which begins with imitative entries in the three lower voices followed by the Trebles. No doubt it had not been possible to include this in the previous Friday rehearsal. There was some uncertainty amongst the lower voices as to the interval of a fourth or fifth in the appropriately rising phrase with which this piece begins. After three attempts at 'I will arise' Sidney barked "Sit down!" and returned to the Loft, leaving many red faces behind! Clearly this experience as a Lay Clerk was most useful in learning the business from the inside as it were. I stood next to a Bass of a somewhat humorous cast of mind, and he often produced mis-quotes from the Scriptures, of which two have stayed in my mind. On the Residentary Canons – "They toil not, neither do they sing." And – "Who can find a virtuous woman – her price is above rubies. What a pity they don't tell us what Ruby's price was!"

One vital task laid upon us was to introduce the English Hymnal, which was to replace Hymns Ancient and Modern, and thereby to sing the Office Hymns at Evensong before the Magnificat to the proper plainchant melodies. This was quite a task as some tunes were quite elaborate, and totally unfamiliar to the Choir. So for some Office Hymns we had to use the so-called 'modern' tunes provided as an alternative. But eventually we covered the whole repertoire and I'm glad to say that this still goes on today, half a century later. They are marvellous melodies, and the texts do give a specific character to each Service throughout the liturgical year. I am inclined to think that Ely is still the only cathedral to use this repertoire as a matter of daily routine. Sidney's experience of plainchant was somewhat limited, and the Psalms were given the same full-blooded accompaniment as when they were sung to Anglican chants, including Full Swell when he considered the text merited it. It was left to his successor, Michael Howard, to demonstrate a more appropriate style in this technique, and one which has left its mark firmly on today's practice.

My singing ability appeared to be generally appreciated, but there was some discomfort in pieces such as Gibbon's anthem 'This is the record of John'. We used the original E.H. Fellowes edition which is laid out for tenor solo verses, and in the key of F. This never felt entirely comfortable and it was a great relief to eventually discover that it was intended for counter-tenor (alto) in the key of A flat, where it lies quite easily in the range of the intended voice. Likewise, Sidney appeared to be happy with my choir direction, only making the comment that Decani (my side) sounded like King's College, Cambridge, and Cantoris like Westminster Abbey!

Dean Blackburn retired early in 1950, and we awaited the appointment of his successor with some trepidation – this is always the case, as 'the right man' can colour the total ethos of the Foundation. Sidney's predecessor, Marmaduke Conway had ended his term of office with an Assistant named Mr Bean. Unfortunately for him, Sidney had decided on me to replace Bean, and the Cathedral had to let him go.

Fortunately for me, though, I inherited a piano pupil he was now unable to take on – one Mary Titterton. Having no piano of my own, I had to visit in their houses any pupils I gradually acquired, and thus became acquainted with an excellent Rogers upright piano that eventually was to pass into joint ownership with Mary and myself on our marriage in 1953. Our developing friendship became a focus of feverish interest to the Choristers, who, as we learned much later, used to follow us around on our walks in Ely as much as their timetable allowed. Besides all the practical work absorbing most of my time I still needed to pursue the academic studies I knew to be essential to the career that was opening up before me. Obviously I should sit the ADCM examination, as I now had the FRCO and the choir-training diploma (CHM). My year at Canterbury had equipped me with 'the understanding' and all that was now required was a thorough grasp of the Syllabus for the year in question, which I decided would be 1951. This would enable me to finish my first year at Ely, and prepare for the examination with plenty of time in hand.

Back in Warwick though, catastrophy struck – after a brief illness my father died of lung cancer. It was not entirely a surprise – as mentioned earlier he had long been a heavy smoker, in company with many men (and women) of that epoch, and especially perhaps during the strains and stresses of the 1930's Recession and then the wartime years which ensued. It was a blow to all the family, but especially of course to my mother, who never really recovered from its shattering effects. Though it was at least some consolation to know that he had lived to see me embark on the career that he knew I wanted and had worked for. Mother eventually decided to move to Stratford-upon-Avon, and this change was also to have a considerable effect on my artistic interests. The funeral was in late January 1950, and I needed to be released from my cathedral duties. It was on a Saturday and I had been expected to play for a massed choral rehearsal in the afternoon; however Sidney quickly found a more than satisfactory substitute – Peter Hurford, who at that time was still in Cambridge but soon to move to Holy Trinity Church, Leamington Spa in succession to Stanley Vann, who was about to be appointed to Chelmsford Cathedral.

I was of course gauche, but Sidney was usually sympathetic to the difficulties I encountered. As a school leaver at 14, I had to try to give the impression of a wisdom, maturity and general ability that was hardly formed at the time. People often commented on the 'dulcet tones' of my speaking voice. I wasn't aware of this, but instinctively I suppose I must have realised that if I did not actually possess an 'Oxbridge' education then at the very least I needed to sound as if I had this useful qualification. A degree in music was the next goal, and Sidney suggested that the simplest course of action would be a correspondence course as this would not interfere with my many duties at the Cathedral and School. The man he suggested was Dr Frederick Wood, Organist at Blackpool Parish Church. Sidney had himself used him and found him very thorough, and I did so in my turn – to the point where I was able to sit the Durham First B.Mus. examination on March 16th, 1950 and pass at the first attempt. Flushed with success I attempted the Second Examination in the September following, but this was too soon and I failed. Always a useful experience, though, and I took pains to improve my handwriting (which Professor Arthur Hutchings pronounced often indecipherable) and also my knowledge of history and analysis. It worked, and I passed the Second B.Mus. examination in September 1951. Only the Exercise (either a History Dissertation or a Composition) stood between me and a university degree. Of course I knew that I would choose the composition option. I already knew 'in my bones' that this activity was to become of increasing importance to me, but little guessed then how this was to eventually dominate my various interests in the profession.

The year 1951 was to prove significant in many other ways, but January stands out in my mind as a portent when Patrick Hankey was Installed as Dean of Ely. As usual it was scheduled for a Saturday Evensong, and I was expecting to sing and direct the choir as normal. Sidney's health though was never completely reliable, especially in winter, and I received a message before the Choristers' morning practice informing me that his doctor would not allow him to get up that day, so would I please take the rehearsals and play for the Service. The Canticle setting was Stanford in C and the anthem Charles Wood's 'This sanctuary of my soul'. All went well, and the new Dean's only comment was that he wished we had chosen another anthem, as he found both the text and music of the Wood 'embarrassing'. Although at first I was slightly taken aback at this critique, with an increasing knowledge of the new Dean's character I came to realise that, as in religious matters, art could also be assessed from a more severe and austere standpoint than that of simple attractiveness. Hankey could be direct in his manner – I remember him waiting his turn to have his hair cut in Gutteridge's salon in St Mary's Street. When I vacated the chair for him he remarked dryly, "I thought that the anthem yesterday would have profited from a little more rehearsal." Fortunately I wasn't the one directing it, and gave as I thought, an adequate reply saying merely, "Yes, indeed!"

My domestic arrangements varied somewhat in these early years. At first I had an attic bedsit at The Old Sacristy – the time-honoured Organist's House on the North Side of the College (as the Cathedral Close was named in Ely). Sidney at first employed a housekeeper – Mrs Bligh, whose son was a Chorister. There was also another lodger helping to make ends meet. Mrs Bligh was recently widowed, and naturally at this time not of the sunniest disposition, so that Sidney's artistic temperament and somewhat intolerant stance on occasion did not make for the smoothest of household relationships. After a year or so there was a parting of the ways, and Sidney then took his main meal at the 'The Bell' hotel and I looked elsewhere for board and lodging. No. 11, Broad Street was recommended and there I fetched up next – with a Mrs Gotobed. This was a common Ely name – Bishop Wynn's gardener was probably a relation, and on walking down the College passing the Bishop's House one quickly grew accustomed to hearing the summons – "Gotobed!"

The accommodation was agreeable enough – though two disadvantages stay in mind. In the late summer there was a plague of spiders in my bedroom – I had never seen quite so many in one room and I remember lying in bed with great trepidation, watching them crawling around the picture rail and hoping that none would decide to join me in bed. The other was my landlady's interest in not just emptying my wastepaper basket, but also in reading any letters I deposited there, lacking the foresight at my tender age to destroy them. On the occasions of my visits to Durham for examination purposes, a certain amount of socialising with the other candidates was both natural and enjoyable, and in one of these carousals a girl named Peggy played a prominent role. We decided to correspond when she returned to London and I to Ely, resulting in a few meetings in London. It was one of her letters referring to these occasions that Mrs Gotobed passed on to Mary. Ely was a tiny town of 10,000 souls in those days, and it was assumed to be quite natural that everyone should know everything there was to know about everyone else. Come what may though, Mary and I were engaged to be married on Shakespeare's birthday, 23rd April 1952.

Mrs Gotobed now seemed rather less desirable as a landlady (and the spiders even less so) so I moved to

Cambridge Road where Miss Muriel Ambrose welcomed me to a very pleasant redbrick house. She was a chiropodist by profession, and I settled in there until Mary and I married in 1953. I decided to compose a String Quartet for the Exercise, and under the skilful guidance of Dr Wood this was accepted, and the degree of Bachelor of Music was conferred on me at a Congregation held 28th June 1952. A statutory five years had to elapse before I would be eligible to sit for the D.Mus. examination, but this was now firmly in my sights and made all the more desirable as I was aware that after that examination date an M.Mus. degree was to be substituted for the Doctorate, which was then to become a purely honorary degree. An M.Mus. seemed to be a poor substitute, to my way of thinking, so I decided that I would do my utmost to gain this final academic goal. Now in my third year at Ely, my feet were getting decidedly 'itchy' and a vacancy at Oakham Parish Church beckoned. The adjudicator was Dr Douglas Hopkins, Organist of Peterborough Cathedral and of course he knew me from the annual Three Choirs Festival of Ely, Norwich and Peterborough. I think he was minded to recommend me, but in a very useful conversation it emerged that neither he or myself thought Oakham to be necessarily the right move for me at that time, and I left quite happily without securing that appointment.

My experience in the preparation for the Durham B.Mus. was leading quite naturally towards a desire to compose. My first effort was for Men's Voices, a Sanctus, Benedictus and Agnus Dei. I decided to leave the Kyrie Eleison and Gloria in Excelsis Deo to Merbecke. The setting was agreeably received, the style being in a quite inoffensive Charles Wood idiom, and I had the excitement of hearing my work in the cathedral acoustic. Incidentally Dr Wood advised me to study the String Quartets of Charles Wood for my B.Mus. Exercise, and I was encouraged to discover later that both Vaughan Williams and Sir Thomas Beecham had found his teachings at Cambridge of the highest usefulness. David Willcocks once described Wood's Canticle settings to me as 'workaday' music – perhaps, but against this view must be set anthems such as 'Glory and honour and laud' for Palm Sunday – a piece both moving and exciting. When it became the custom not to have the Choristers back until the beginning of Holy Week, that anthem was a real loss to me. Until the mid-sixties it was unthinkable not to have the Choristers in residence for all the major Feasts in the Church Year. Indeed, the Boys were always on hand until the Sunday after Christmas, when the Carol Service was held. Ah, those days when the Feast of Christmas was really celebrated, and the commercial Christmas had not even been dreamt of. Today's celebration of the Nativity season is but a poor thing by comparison with those heady days of the fifties. It probably seems a spartan regime to 'modern' thinking, but the Choristers of those days would arrive in the third week of September and not see their homes again until after the Sunday after Christmas. No half-term holidays interrupted the routine, and 'Visiting Choirs' had not yet reared their useful heads. I remember what I am inclined to think would have been the first visiting choir at Ely. It was in Michael Howard's time and he happened to be away. It was Ascension Day, and on his return I told him that the choir was from Uppingham School – "How appropriate!" was Michael's only comment.

Ely in those days had a wonderfully 'monastic' character. Apart from diocesan services the worship was on behalf of the world and carried out by the Chapter and Choir whether or not there was anyone else present or not. In this simple fact lies the whole point of the 'Cathedral Tradition'. In our age, obsessed with TV 'ratings' and consumerism, cathedral worship still(?) stands like a lone beacon of sanity for the development of global spirituality. In those Services nothing was announced and the result was an uninterrupted momentum which carried one along very naturally. I remember a chorister parent attending Evensong and then waiting for me at the entrance to the organ stairway – "What wisdom!" was his first remark.

Returning to my early years in Ely at this point, there were of course musical interests in the town in addition to the main focus on the Cathedral and the King's School. I had a fair number of private piano pupils and there was some pleasure in accompanying Mary's Aunt – a Miss Titterton, who was a proficient violinist – for two hours each week in Sonatas ranging from Mozart to Brahms. The Ely and District Music Club arranged three concerts in the Autumn Season and I was frequently asked to act as Piano Accompanist. One such event included Ronald Smith playing Beethoven, Ravel, Chopin and Liszt, while I featured as accompanist to the soprano Irene Eisinger in songs by Mozart, Beethoven, Schubert and Brahms.

There was also a choral group based on an weekly Evening Class meeting which Dr Campbell directed, and which I inherited on his departure. More surprisingly perhaps, there was also an ad hoc operatic group inspired by Mr Slatopolsky, who held a senior position at the Sugar-Beet factory. He also conducted the Ely Male Voice Choir, and a programme dated Sunday 22nd February featured that Choir, the Soham Comrades Band, and myself as accompanist to the soprano soloist Loda Bielicka. The venue was the Rex Theatre (then in use as a Cinema) and the concert was in aid of 'The Ely Cathedral Death Watch Beetle Fund' – the Appeal recently launched by Dean Hankey. The Soham Comrades Band was a remarkably successful organisation for such a small population as Soham, being Eight Times Champions, East Anglia, and Second Section Winners at the Westminster Hall, London, 1952. Slatopolsky's musical enthusiasms were shared by his wife, who invariably took the leading soprano roles in his productions. He always enlisted me as pianist and also added other instrumentalists – 'for colour' – when they were available. His enthusiasm for music was admirable and boundless, and eventually led to his suggestion that the Ely Evening Class should form the nucleus of a choral group to be augmented by similar groups from the Fen area with the aim of performing some of the great classic choral works in the Cathedral. He made it clear that the soloists would be established professionals and the orchestral players of a similar standard. It was clear that he was ready, able, and willing to underwrite these undertakings, and so the project went ahead – in 1955 with the 'Messiah' by Handel, and the following year with Haydn's 'The Creation'. The orchestra for this was led by Emmanuel Hurwitz, who I imagine assembled the 'Band' for the performance. They of course were professional players of the highest standard, and I was not a little daunted by my task of directing a chorus with an orchestra of this size and expertise. After the rehearsal I told 'Manny' that this was my first experience of directing an orchestra 'of this size'. "You should do it again!" he exclaimed with his usual enthusiasm.

Mr Slatapolsky's enthusiasm and his financial support were greatly missed when he was promoted the following year and had to move away from the Ely Factory. My accompanist for the Ely Evening Class at this time was Joan Brown, who was the Music Mistress at the Girls High School, fresh from the RAM. As many remarked, she was a girl of striking attractiveness, and we did a few concerts as piano duetists at the King's School and elsewhere. Discussions with her about the Academy and its Professors no doubt turned my attention to the enticing possibility of some work in that field eventually.

Another notable figure in the amateur music world of that time was Tom Harris, a Miller by trade and a most enthusiastic organist and conductor by inclination. He had a two-manual and pedal organ by Arthur Harrison in his house, and conducted the Downham Choral Society in concerts held in St Edmund's Church, Downham Market. He used my services for his concerts until he retired in the late 60s, and on his death left me the first option on several items of furniture which I was delighted to acquire, and still possess and usefully enjoy with happy memories to this day.

I have already mentioned my Mother's decision to move to Stratford-upon-Avon after the death of my Father. Holidays spent there were of tremendous interest and delight from Easter 1950 onwards. Of course I attended Holy Trinity Church (Shakespeare's Burial Place) and got to know very well the two Organists there during my many visits. John Cooke wasn't entirely happy in that position, though his interests in the Memorial Theatre and its music were greatly stimulated. He found the local chorister situation not at all easy to handle, and was greatly relieved when he was appointed to the Cathedral in London, Ontario. This proved a useful stepping stone to his eventual appointment to the prestigious Church of the Advent, Boston, USA. His interest in composition began to bear fruit in Stratford with the publication of his most popular organ piece 'Fanfare' and an anthem for the annual Shakespeare Service – 'Fear no more the heat of the Sun'. He was succeeded by John Strickson, who had studied at the RAM and been Sub-Organist at Peterborough Cathedral with Stanley Vann. At this point I began to realise ever more clearly what a small world the musical firmament was proving to be.

John Strickson's work with the Church Choir was highly successful, and no less so with the Town Choral Society and the Warwickshire Orchestral Society – this last was largely made up of players local to the County, augmented by London professionals as needed, such as Paul Beard as Leader. During the 1960s I played the organ for many of their concerts in Stratford, Warwick, and Coventry, but the most interesting and certainly most important appearance was in the still newly-built Coventry Cathedral with the Warwickshire Orchestra on May 25th 1963. John had scheduled the Organ Concerto in E minor of Marcel Dupré and had naturally engaged the resident Organist David Lepine to perform this work. But with only a few weeks to go before the performance, David felt it necessary to withdraw, presumably through pressure of other commitments, and John turned to me to perform instead. Of course I agreed to do this. It was an exciting prospect – my first opportunity to play a concerto with a full symphony orchestra, and an opportunity to get to know the rarely performed Dupré Concerto – and also to play the new Harrison organ designed by Sidney Campbell! All went well and I found the experience very rewarding. In performance though, the work struck me as somewhat academic, and less interesting than some of Dupré's solo pieces, such as the 'Variations sur a Noel'. M.M.L. in the *Coventry Evening Telegraph* wrote thus about the Concerto:

"A large gathering listened on Saturday night in Coventry Cathedral to an organ concerto, the first, I think, to be played upon the instrument. It was a highly professional, electrifying piece, typically French in its clarity and keen edges – not surprising as it was written by Marcel Dupré, doyen of French organists, who by coincidence gives a recital in the cathedral on June 8.

Arthur Wills, organist of Ely Cathedral, playing with the Warwickshire Symphony Orchestra, under John Strickson, made the concerto sound brilliant but not showy. Conductor and soloist had obviously considered it very carefully. They brought out with complete unanimity the themes of the first movement, judged with perfection the balance needed to give all those contrasted sonorities in the orchestra and organ their chance in the second movement and attacked the stinging rhythms of the last movement with confidence – a movement in which the composer's inspiration only just holds out."

Exactly my opinion! Nevertheless the resultant outcome on my second visit to Paris a week or so later fully justified to an even greater extent my decision to perform the Concerto.

I attended the Sunday High Mass at St Sulpice and decided to see if I could obtain admission to the organ loft – just as I did as a teenager in cathedrals back home all those years ago – habits die hard! I mounted the stairs, only to find my way blocked by a considerable group of Dupré's admirers, and all kept firmly in hand by the redoubtable Madame Dupré. I decided to play my trump card, and said, "I am the Organist of Ely Cathedral, and last Saturday week I played your husband's Concerto in Coventry Cathedral." This did the trick, as I had expected. "You must come and sit with him on the bench!" – which proved to be as enjoyable and illuminating experience as I had anticipated. All was improvised, and at the Communion the Master informed me "Now I improvise a Ricecare in six voices!" I had heard that this was frequently the case, and it was certainly an absorbing example of the Master's art. It clarified for me the various strands – old and new – that played their part in the resultant artistry of this great musician. Dupré's harmonic language in his Toccatas and Finals is frequently exploratory in its chromaticsm and dissonance and might be considered as a link between that of Widor and Vierne and that of Messiaen. Messiaen's first organ piece – Diptyque – certainly recalls the idiom of the mid-period Dupré. But Dupré's editions and his approach to the Baroque repertoire are usually considered passé by the musicologists of a later generation, and critics were quick to point to deficiencies in the performances of his later years when some technical problems began to surface. But on this Sunday-morning visit to St Sulpice there was the Master – the embodiment of the French organ tradition – uniting the polyphony of the Baroque masters in his Communion with the near-atonal language of Messiaen in his tempestuous closing Sortie.

Apart from Stratford music-making the opportunity to enjoy productions of Shakespeare at their best were there for the taking. In 1951 – the Festival of Britain Year – the Memorial Theatre productions centred on the historical sequence *Richard II* to *Henry V*. Anthony Quayle was the newly appointed Director, and for this season he engaged the brightest stars in the theatrical firmament. Stratford had certainly not witnessed anything like this array of brilliance before. Interest though centred on the 21-year-old Richard Burton as Henry V and I doubt if he did anything later in his career more riveting than that performance. Many other performances stay in my mind – one such being *Titus Andronicus* with Laurence Olivier and Vivien Leigh. This play, with its many gruesome episodes anticipating the Jacobean School, is certainly not one of Shakespeare's greatest, and its performance roused the audience to much hardly suppressed mirth at times. I was sitting quite close to Peter Hall the producer, and one of the unanticipated highlights of the evening was to witness his obvious discomfiture at the reception of his production at the close of the performance.

In that year I attended a lecture by Anthony Quayle – 'The Actor and the Theatre'. A pretty comprehensive topic! The two points I remember from the elapse of half-a-century were (actor) 'Voice!' And (theatre) 'We English no longer know what and where we are since the collapse of our Imperial heritage.' Thinking of the stress Quayle placed on voice brings back to mind my opinion (then and since) that Robert Schofield was and is the finest actor of our time.

But back to Ely – Sidney Campbell's career may truly be described as meteoric. On his appointment to Ely in 1949 he was 40 years of age – seemingly quite late for a cathedral appointment. But after four years London beckoned, and in 1953 he was appointed to Southwark Cathedral. Three years later he moved to Canterbury and then in 1961 to St George's Chapel, Windsor Castle – a truly dazzling career for such a late starter. I have heard him dismissed as 'That eccentric!' but there was far more to his character and abilities than that summary commentary allows. My own career was founded on his offering the Assistantship at Ely to me, and his advice and encouragement was crucial throughout my career until his death at the age of 65 in 1974. In his last term at Ely in a concert with the Alexandra Choir, his solo organ contribution was my 'Rhapsody', a piece that I first submitted to Novellos (unsuccessfully), then later revised and used (this time successfully) as the 'Sortie' in my Eucharistic Suite – which Novellos readily published. The vacancy at Ely was filled with a most imaginative appointment – Michael Howard had applied for the post in 1949, and Sidney clearly felt that now he was leaving, Michael should have his ambition at last fulfilled. Howard did not want the post of Director of Music at the King's School, so that was offered to me, a post which I gladly accepted. Instead of the traditional Organist's residence 'The Old Sacristy' Michael was offered 'No. 2 The Almonry' which I thought a much more interesting house. He arrived in September 1953, and on my marriage to Mary in November – another November 14th! – that year he offered us the larger part of the house for a very reasonable rent. No. 2 implies that there was a No. 1, though that larger part of the house was occupied by a Canon and was still known as 'The Almonry'. Previously the whole house had been occupied by Canon Watson, the Cathedral Treasurer, who was unmarried and resided there with only one other occupant, his housekeeper.

Michael Howard was a brilliant musician, with an especial interest in early music – in those days a somewhat rarefied sphere of activity. He founded the Renaissance Singers after the War, and this ensemble was frequently heard on the BBC Radio Third Programme. His knowledge of the plainchant and early polyphonic repertoire was a strong element in his favour with the generally austere tastes of the Dean and Chapter at Ely, and it was anticipated that he would impart a distinctive character to the choral services. Certainly, from my point of view, he was an excellent foil to the more generalised taste of Sidney Campbell, and when I first heard him accompany plainchant on the 16' Gedact on the Swell (an octave higher of course!) it was at once clear that a distinctive musical intelligence was at work. It was completely modal, continuous, and no change of registration was needed.

Howard was trained at the RAM under G.D. Cunningham and also studied for a time with Marcel Dupré in Paris – "If you didn't know the music you were studying from memory, he took the view that you didn't know it!". His playing was meticulous, and yet he was not greatly concerned with recital work during his five years at Ely – possibly because he was not really at ease with the Arthur Harrison organ of 1908 – admittedly not at its best by the 1950s. Soon after his arrival he decided to experiment with the Choir division, moving pipes around to obtain a Nazard and a Tierce, whilst also asking the tuner to obtain an Unda Maris by retuning the Dulciana against the Gedact, and the Salicional against the Open Diapason to provide a Fiffaro. This somewhat radical approach was not a little disconcerting to someone of my experience – as a student at Canterbury and then in the Ely tradition with Sidney, who revelled in the Harrison sound. Nevertheless, those changes by Michael were the starting point for the rebuild of 1975, when I was able to realise my tonal ideals with the ready and sympathetic help and advice of Cecil (Sam) Clutton.

Howard's work with the Choir was of the highest order, and his distinctive approach to the repertoire and its interpretation was quite inspirational. His tonal palette tended to the forceful and dramatic, with perhaps some influence of George Malcolm's approach at Westminster Cathedral. His care over diction, both for sheer clarity and colour was often quite striking, but I do well remember that this care stemmed from a comment by Dean Hankey on one occasion to the effect that he didn't think the words were sufficiently clear! One of his additions to the repertoire stands out – 'Woefully arrayed' by Cornyshe. This intensely dramatic anthem is still hardly to be heard elsewhere even today, and Michael's interpretation (as opposed to a simple presentation) is an abiding memory.

Michael's interest in early music led to his recourse to the growing number of the scholars of the period, and as well as the Cornyshe many other works by such Ely composers as Tye, Amner and Barcrofte were transcribed and introduced into the repertoire. The original version of the Tudor Preces with the sung through Gloria, not yet included in the first E.H. Fellowes edition, were also made available for use at Ely. In contrast to all of this he was also one of the first Directors to perform Duruflé's Requiem in this country, and his love of plainchant must have drawn him to this unusual piece. The Renaissance Singers with the Ely Choristers gave two memorable performances of this work with myself at the organ – at the Royal Academy of Music and at the King's Lynn Festival. Opinions about the merit of the work differed greatly in those early days. I remember Bruno Turner saying rather dismissively "Why does Michael want to do this piece?" For purists used to doing plainchant and polyphony of the 15th–16th centuries in bold interpretations Durufle's sensuous harmonic language, derived as it was from that of Debussy and Ravel, came as something of a culture shock. I still have mixed feelings about the piece and given the choice would always opt for Fauré's wonderful simplicity of approach.

Howard could be somewhat irritating to work for – phoning from London at short notice to ask me to take a chorister rehearsal or even a Service. And if he objected to any aspect of my accompaniments he made it quite clear to all those present. In those circumstances you needed both broad shoulders and a thick skin! I had to develop both and thereby secured the armour which proved essential in my dealings with all sorts and conditions of men in later life. He could also be infuriatingly casual, as when he asked George Guest to play a Saturday afternoon recital without making any arrangements for the necessary hospitality, which Mary and I then gladly provided. After rehearsing during the morning, and then wandering about the College looking for Michael, George found his way to our rooms just in time to enjoy an omelette with us for lunch. But one readily forgave most such inconveniences, preferring rather to concentrate on the original genius of the man.

Both Michael and I shared a love of the French tradition in all the arts, so when in 1956 he mentioned that he was intending to visit Paris during the Easter holiday it was a strong incentive to want to meet him there. My wife Mary had given birth to our son Colin in the previous February and felt that she could not accompany me on the trip so I decided instead to ask Raymond (Paddy) Bailey. Paddy was a tenor along with Roy Stubbings on the Cantoris side. Roy, as a member of the Cambridgeshire Regiment, had been captured by the Japanese at the Fall of Singapore and forced to work on the infamous Burma railway. When at last back home he was always reluctant to talk about this, and never showed the slightest antipathy to the Japanese people thereafter. (I recall a typical instance of Howard's wit when we were walking round The College after the weekly Friday night rehearsal – "Choir Practices must be a doddle after that experience!")

But back to my trip to Paris with Paddy. The cheap flights were always timed for the late evening, so to save money we decided not to book a hotel as we were due to arrive in the early hours of the following morning. I remember we took a cab to the Arc de Triomphe and then began to stroll down the Champs Elysee. A first visit to Paris was always an exciting experience – then much more so than now. Paris was still regarded as the artistic capital of the world – Picasso was still as productive as ever, though more to be seen in Provence at this juncture, and Messiaen, at the height of his renown as a composer was still to be found playing the organ at La Trinité, Dupré at Saint Suplice, Duruflé at Sainte-Etienne du Mont and Langlais at Cesar Franck's church of Sainte-Clotilde. The city seemed to tingle with its exciting history and artistic personalities. We found a bar still open for business, though the only customers were two girls. Drinks seemed to be called for, so in we went and ordered two bières. After only a brief interval the girls naturally gravitated in our direction and some conversation ensued – their English being better than our French – only to be expected, I suppose. Paddy led the way in these exchanges while I listened benevolently. Eventually one of the young ladies decided to awaken my interest and turned to Paddy saying "Your friend – he is so big!" We eventually found our way to Les Halles – then still the Central Market and tingling with life – and smells. One of these lead us to a restaurant and a marvellous onion soup – I've never tasted a better breakfast – and then we found our hotel.

Later that week we met up with Howard for a couple of meals and also, wanting to savour the more sensuous aspects of Parisian life, decided to visit the renowned Folies-Bergère. We had found ourselves some aisle seats quite near to the stage in order to fully savour the fleshly delights on offer, but nevertheless were somewhat disconcerted when, after the interval, we were both hauled on to the stage by a group of the lovelies. My memory of what then transpired is somewhat indistinct, but we were required to take part in some games and contests and eventually returned to our seats each with a prize – mine was a tin of biscuits (I think) but I forget what Paddy was given. Other more respectable pursuits in which we indulged included a hugely enjoyable concert at the Theatre Champs Elysee conducted by Paul Paray – Berlioz Symphonie Fantastique before the interval – and 'bleeding chunks' of Wagner afterwards, ending with 'The Ride of the Valkries'. I was reminded of Wagner's eventual adoration by the French, after his initial disaster with 'Tanhauser' and the Jockey Club! A visit to the Opera though – 'Faust' – merely confirmed one's worst prejudices gained from the history books – it was slovenly in the extreme. Berlioz's problems with the musical Establishment, well documented in the textbooks, came vividly to life.

Michael's approach to the repertoire was quite idiosyncratic – he fitted in perfectly with Dean Hankey's stance – severe and austere. For a musician who had made a great name for his interpretations of the Renaissance repertoire with his Singers – perfect for the BBC Third Programme of those far-off days! – Ely in Hankey's time was the right environment. The Canticles in C and B flat and 'Beati quorum via' were the only Stanford pieces we did, but he strongly favoured Vaughan Williams – the Te Deums in G and F and 'O clap your hands together'. He rejoiced in the tough and angular polyphony of Blow and Purcell and also the verse anthems and services of Boyce with their Handelian operatic approach.

Howard's tenure at Ely lasted within a couple of weeks of five years, and in the final weeks of the Summer Term 1958 he had arranged to make a recording of an LP for the Argo Record Company – 'Music for the Feast of Christmas' – with the Cathedral Choristers, the Men of the Renaissance Singers, and some of the Lay Clerks. The agreed repertoire was all from the 15th–16th centuries – with one exception. A few days before the date of the recording sessions Michael informed me that the chosen repertoire had left space for another piece of approximately three minutes' length. "Would you care to play Messiaen's 'Les Anges'?" he asked. "I don't know it," was my response. "Well, perhaps you could learn it!" was his rejoinder and he left it at that. I did learn it, and though perhaps not immediately obvious, it was the just the right piece to be heard at that point in the recording. We did not know it then, but this was to be Michael's swansong and within a couple of weeks he was gone. My old Service sheets record that I was calling on Gerald Hendrie to act as Assistant Organist from Wednesday, 16th July and the Chorister's final Service of the Term was on Sunday 27th, when the anthem was a somewhat rare large scale Purcell verse anthem for solo treble – 'My song shall be alway of the loving-kindness of the Lord' – Michael's final chosen repertoire of his tenure at Ely. Howard's departure was abrupt and is dealt with succinctly in his memoir 'Thine adversaries roar'. After ten days I was offered the post – perhaps my recent Durham Doctorate helped, together with the probably wished for continuity of the traditions of the Campbell-Howard years.

Our second child, Rachel, was born on July 11th – a friend observed on the news of my appointment, "Things are going very well for you!" I had to agree. Unlike my B.Mus. examinations I passed both those of the Doctorate on one attempt. For the Second examination I chose to compose an orchestral symphony in four movements. I had become greatly attracted by the performances of Roussel's Third and Fourth Symphonies on a recently issued LP and these works – succinct, pointedly rhythmic and attractively dissonant, were, I decided, just what I needed as a model – French again, of course! I re-used part of the second movement for the Larghetto in my 'Five Pieces' for organ (1961).

As I write these words the news comes through of Michael's death at the age of 79, and I have been consulted about his obituary. I'm glad about this – but wonder what the finished piece will convey. His life was a rather incomplete one in spite of all his great achievements as a choral conductor – he could certainly 'Make choir sing!' as the Northern adage puts it, and he could play the organ supremely well, as his recording of the Three Chorals of Cesar Franck on the two-manual (!) Cavaille-Coll organ in Farnborough Abbey amply demonstrates. Yet the life was to a large extent unfulfilled – I remember a telephone conversation in which we touched on his time at Ely – I think that we were exchanging birthday greetings, his being only a few days before mine, when he uttered the sad valedictory comment "...and I threw it all away." There were too few compositions, though he possessed a distinctive voice, and nothing was at that time published – once again this has to be put down to his lack of will and persistence. He certainly wasn't a 'business-like musician' as I remember hearing Sidney Campbell urging the Canterbury students to become!

In my last year at the Cathedral Michael came to stay with us, and play an organ concert. My pedal piano, on loan from the RAM, was now in the sitting room and I mentioned that I thought that it had been left to the Academy by C.H. Trevor. Michael went to the instrument to try it, and I expected to hear a desultory improvisation. Instead he played the Bach Fantasia in G minor faultlessly and beautifully from memory. After he had sat down again we talked about the RAM, and for the first time I decided to mention that I had left school at the age of 14, and had not attended either a music college or a university course. He pondered this news for a brief moment and then said, "Blimey!" I considered this to be a reasonable reaction, and we left it at that. In one way though, that incident does sum up the difference between us. I considered him to be a much more naturally gifted musician than I was – certainly in the realm of performance, yet we are told that he suffered throughout his career from a diffidence following from the fact that he did not gain a university degree. Yet I obtained two degrees during my years as Assistant at Ely with a much less secure educational basis than he possessed. Very strange indeed. He admitted to a drink problem – frequently endemic in London artistic circles, then as now, but there was a deeper psychological problem – of that I'm sure.

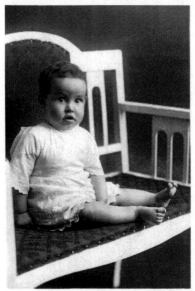

'Why am I here?' In cot 1926

M. B. M. TRIO,
INSTRUMENTALISTS.

B. WILLS.   SID GIBBS.   A. WILLS.
10, GILBERT STREET,
COVENTRY.

My Parents and MBM card: B. Wills - uncle, S. Gibbs - Father

St.John-the-Baptist Church, Coventry
By kind permission of the Rector and Churchwardens
www.St.John-the-Baptist.co.uk

St.Paul's Church, Warwick - Organist 1941-43
Warwickshire county record office C00/48/2

St.Albans Church, Leamington Spa - Organist 1943-46
Credit: Warwickshire County Record Office ref:PH352/111/176

St.Mary's Collegiate Church, Warwick - Ass.Organist 1946-48
With kind permission from the Vicar and churchwardens

Canterbury Cathedral - No.17 The Precincts(SECM) 1948-1949
By kind permission of Peter Giles

'How rise thy towers, serene and bright'

Paintings of Ely Cathedral By John Titterton (Mary's Grandfather)

The Harrison Organ at Ely Cathedral (1908)

Mary - Pupil; Arthur - Teacher 1949

Marriage - Dinner at Waldorf Hotel London. 1953

No 2, The Almonry (drawing by Owen Rees, 2nd Verger)

Colin and Rachel

King's School Orchestra at rehearsal in Porta

The Royal Academy of Music

Credit : Courtesy of The Royal Academy of Music

The Duke's Hall, Royal Academy of Music
Courtesy of The Royal Academy of Music

At the organ console, Ely Cathedral 1986

Choristers in the Lady Chapel with myself,
James Tilly (Housemaster) and Peter North (Assistant Housemaster) c. 1985.

Receiving OBE in 1990

Rome, 1990

Rehearsal of Guitar Concerto - Lethbridge - 1996

At the study in Paradise House 2006 - 'Still here!'

Chapter 4

Diversion: A City set on a Hill
('A certain idea of Ely')

'Ely' – a marvellous place to live and work. And from 1958 onwards work included a strong emphasis on composition. A simple and basic name – only three letters, and it could not be more simple or direct in its meaning. "The place of many eels" according to the Venerable Bede, writing in the 8th century. The eel – a very slippery creature, a rather unattractive image perhaps; but it is its natural habitat – the watery Fens – that so exercises the imagination and gives the place its enduring appeal. That and the fact that it is 'The City of Ely' – a Cathedral City since 1974 with, of course, a Diocese and a Bishop. This seems extraordinary to many people – brought up to an image of a city as a great manufacturing financial or business centre. It owes its existence to the hill on which it sits so naturally, and yet so surprisingly, in the surrounding flat countryside. The biblical reference to the Kingdom as a 'City set on a Hill' at once comes to mind, and if on a bright and sunny morning I walk from the river area up through the Park towards the Cathedral, without fail the words from the hymn 'City of God' spring to mind – 'How rise thy towers, serene and bright, To meet the dawning day!' Whatever my initial mood, that scene never fails to lift my spirits!

But the first time I saw Ely it was in rather different circumstances which I have already mentioned earlier. The vastness of the building, with the unaccompanied singing from the Lady Chapel, was a revelation which I have frequently recalled when singing 'The Carol of King Canute' which I composed in 1967 to be sung on Christmas Eve at the Blessing of the Crib at the West End of the Cathedral. The Liber Eliensis tells how Canute was visiting Ely on the Feast of the Purification, and approaching the Minster by boat was captivated by the sound of the Monks' choir in the distance. "Row nearer, my men, that we may hear these good monks sing!" Dean Charles Stubbs, in his book *In a Minster Garden* (1901) quotes this verse and then extends it into a carol with the addition of six further verses. Of the seven verses, I chose five for my Carol. Many years later, in 1981, I quoted from the Carol in 'The Vikings', the first movement of my Symphonic Suite 'The Fenlands' for Organ and Brass Band. This movement also uses the 'Fate' motive from Wagner's cycle of operas 'The Ring of the Nibelung'. Canute was a Viking who eventually became a Christian, and did much to pacify and convert his followers; the two motives fight it out, and naturally the 'Canute' theme triumphs! 'The Vikings' is the first of four movements which make up the Symphonic Suite.

In 1981 the Cambridge Brass Band commissioned me to write a work for Band and Organ which could be premiered at a concert in the Cathedral in November of that year. I readily agreed, as a composition for Brass Band would be a new venture for me. The initial idea came from Andrew Malcolm, who had been a Tenor Lay Clerk in the Cathedral Choir and now played Tenor Horn in the Band. I think that they had expected just a one movement piece, but my interest was aroused by the project, and I decided to write a work in several movements, and of symphonic proportions. I decided upon ideas of varying character – a movement dealing with the tumultuous early history of Ely; a Nature picture – Wicken Fen, the most characteristic terrain of the Fen country still preserved; a character study – Oliver Cromwell, Ely's most important figure in the crucial political developments in the 17th century; and finally a March: 'City of Ely' – celebrating my affection for the town and cathedral, and also paying tribute to the Cambridge Band, and the music associated with the Brass Band movement. The work was recorded by the Hyperion Record Company in 1982 in Long Play format and transferred to CD in 1988. James Day, the *Cambridge News* music critic, was present at this recording session and wrote enthusiastically about the programme and the recording, concluding his account: "With the 'Fenlands Suite' – the first work ever specially composed for organ solo and brass band – on one side; and some stirring marches (Pomp and Circumstances numbers one and four, and Walton's 'Crown Imperial', 'Nimrod' and 'Touch her soft lips' from Walton's 'Henry V' music) on the other, this record should be a great credit to Cambridge's fine band and Ely's distinguished organist-composer."

I transcribed three movements for solo organ in 1994, and gave the first performance of this version at St Michael's Church, Cornhill in February, 1995. The omitted movement is 'Wicken Fen' – the scoring here for delicate percussion and muted brass, in light, tenuous textures, did not lend itself very readily to organ sonorities. The structure of this movement is palindromic – an idea which arose naturally out of a visit to the site. After walking some way into the Fen I decided to turn around to view the scene, and discovered that the prospect was unchanged, from whatever point of view one looked. This similarity, irrespective of the position of the looker, suggested that the musical material could be used to parallel the visual experience, so that at the mid-way point of this movement the music is reversed, ending as it began.

The premiere performance of the Suite (10th October 1981) was recorded by the BBC and broadcast more than once later. James Day was emboldened to write to the *Cambridge Evening News* (2.11.81) thus:

"I have just been listening to a most exciting broadcast of Dr Arthur Wills' impressive and powerful 'Fenland Suite', with the composer at the organ of Ely Cathedral accompanied by the Cambridge Co-operative Band who commissioned the piece. It occurred to me that the band might perform this work with the composer as soloist as a superb climax to a kind of musical 'tour of Britain' at next year's Cambridge Festival, the other items being Elgar's 'Severn Suite', Holst's 'Moorside Suite', Arthur Butterworth's 'Northern Sketches' and Harrison Birtwhistle's 'Grimethorpe Aria'. Here is a substantial programme of colourful and varied music demonstrating great musical skill, admirably suited to King's and surely giving the hordes of foreign tourists a remarkable insight into what 'the Land without music' can achieve, all with a distinctly local emphasis. How about it, Festival Committee?"

This letter had some eventual response in 1983, as below:

Cecil Clutton wrote of a later broadcast of 'The Fenlands' from his home in the Isle of Man – "Just to say how enormously I enjoyed the Suite. I wonder why no one previously has realised that strings simply won't go with organ. In your Suite, for the first time, one heard an organ complementing a band and not fighting against it. And highly enjoyable, too, as music." (24.5.83).

There was a follow-up to the success of 'The Fenlands' when in 1983 the Cambridge Band commissioned a second work for Band and Organ. It was premiered in King's College Chapel on 1st October, 1983 with myself as soloist. This was my programme note:

Overture: 'A Muse of Fire'

When David Read asked me to write a work for tonight's concert he suggested that it should have a celebratory nature, possibly expressed by the character of a fanfare and march. The work was required to open the concert, so an Overture of a jubilant quality suggested itself and as I had included a march of a traditional style as the finale of my symphonic suite 'The Fenlands' I decided to expand this idea into a rather lengthier and more intricate piece than the typical band march, allowing of a more subtle development of its three principal ideas. Despite its quiet opening the work is predominantly buoyant and heroic in character, and the opening speech of Shakespeare's play *Henry V* suggested the title. It is a great experience for the band to play in King's College Chapel, and to have Harry Mortimer with them to mark the occasion. This year I am celebrating my twenty-fifth anniversary as Director of Music at Ely Cathedral; 'A Muse of Fire' may be considered as an attempt to evoke and give expression to some of these feelings.

These comments, taken from a report by James Day, appeared in the *Cambridge Evening News* (3.10.83):

"It was an evening of firsts all round – probably the first time that the great fan-vault of King's has resounded to the majestic strains of a fine brass band. Additionally the first time that an audience had heard Dr Wills' stirring new Overture: 'A Muse of Fire' composed specially for the occasion. The main soloist was James Watson, the principal trumpet of the Royal Opera House Orchestra, who showed that he could both sustain the melodic flow of a first-class cornet player, in Denis Wright's lively Elagarian concerto, or produce the brilliance of a baroque trumpet sound, as in the Purcell Sonata that he performed with Dr Wills. Dr Wills himself, forsaking his usual haunt of Ely Cathedral for King's, contributed not only his own new composition, but also his Variations on 'Amazing Grace' and a well integrated part in 'Jesu, Joy of Man's Desiring'."

A much shorter work inspired by the City is 'Ely', a miniature for two-part treble voices and piano, and dedicated to Raymond (Paddy) Bailey. The text itself was the inspiration for the piece, which was composed in 1984, and first performed by the Choristers at a summer concert in the King's School Hayward Theatre the following year. The words, by John Jennings, are very evocative:

Ely, Dream City of my childhood days,
Would I were standing now where I could see your
  stately towers,
Through summer morning haze nobly outlined;
Clothed in the majesty of golden sunlight glistening on
  the dew.
Fair guardian of the lush green-reeded fen,
The hours I spent by thee were all too few,
And continents divide me now from then.
But gulfs of dreary time and dusty space
That tinge my fondest memories with pain,
Can never from my mind thy form efface
Nor dim the fervent hope that once again O Fenland
  City,
I may soon behold the rising sun turning thy towers to
  gold,
Ely, Dream City.

John Jennings' fascination with Ely began in 1938, when he became an organ pupil of Dr Marmaduke Conway at the age of seventeen, travelling from his home in Swaffham, Norfolk for the lessons. During the Second World War he served as a Medical Officer, first at the RAF Hospital, Ely, and then from late 1940 in the Western Desert – the 'dusty space' referred to, no doubt. After the War he eventually qualified in medicine at Edinburgh, later specialising in Eye Surgery.

The minimal musical tradition at the King's School quickly developed from its 'virginal' beginnings, as was to be expected with the introduction of Scholarship Cathedral Choristers and Sidney Campbell's lively Directorship during his four years in Ely. When I took over as Director in 1954 there was already sufficient talent in the school for a Choral Society to be established, and over the years the repertoire developed from our first effort – J.S. Bach's St Luke Passion – to Bach Cantatas and the Requiems of Mozart, Fauré and Duruflé in addition to such things as Kodaly's Missa Brevis and the Poulenc Gloria. The Headmaster William Brown told me at the start of this enterprise, "I shall be happy if one boy in each year develops a love of music." Well, we quickly exceeded that hope beyond all his expectations. These works were staple fare for the end of the Lent Term and there was always an availability of highly accomplished soloists from the Cambridge College Choirs. For Britten's 'Rejoice in the Lamb' I was able to secure Robert Tear from King's – a marvellous performance. There was also a Summer Concert when more secular works could be tackled – Purcell's 'Dido and Aeneas' being a notable instance. Especially notable was an occasion when the same composer's 'Welcome to all the pleasures' was to be performed, and the engaged counter-tenor soloist from St John's College had to cancel with just one day's notice. James Bowman had been a characterful soloist when a chorister and was now in the senior school leading the altos. "James," I told him, "this is your opportunity!" The outstanding movement of this cantata is the counter-tenor solo on a ground bass 'Here the Deities attend' and James performed this with an outstanding flair and potency. James was less adept at theory, yet I remember that he managed a passable Grade Five! Singers are typically like that of course, but his true and ultimate vocation was clearly manifest in that memorable Summer Concert.

Naturally, some ex-choristers and others did display an interest in the academic study of music and one of my pleasures as Director was to introduce them to the delights of Harmony and Counterpoint as required for the Oxford and Cambridge O and A level syllabus. There was no Music Library so one had to be started from scratch. One of my first choices to be included was Music in Western Civilization by Paul Henry Lang. I was amused when one boy came to me in high dudgeon because Lang had opined that Widor's Organ Symphonies were of relatively little value. He had learned to relish movements from these Symphonies when hearing them played as voluntaries in the School Services in the Cathedral.

This was his first lesson in actually beginning to think about music, as opposed to simply listening to it – or even just hearing it!

Ex-Choristers whose daily fare had been based on the Tudor period relished having to complete Morley's Two-part Canzonets with their consummate economy of material. Indeed, so successful were the eventual examination results that I was summoned to the Examination Board in London to explain my methods. It's quite simple, I explained – they know this idiom 'in their bones' because they perform it several times a week, and the same is true of all the other idioms they are asked to demonstrate. There simply is no musical education to compete with this system – when one Chorister won a scholarship to Christ's Hospital in the early seventies I received an urgent request from the Director of Music – 'Please send us some more choristers!' In his first week at his new school the boy had demonstrated his ability to sing from memory any plainchant Office Hymn requested. Now I understand that even 'Oxbridge' University entrants have no such conception of these matters. The various Examination Boards have to compete for their candidates and so the Boards with the less demanding requirements put the others out of business. (I discovered this when I began work for the Cambridge Syndicate for several years.) This is 'dumbing-down' indeed, no matter what the apologists say. The consequence of this 'dumbing down' approach can readily be seen now in the remedial instruction necessarily and now routinely given to First Year students. But I'm sure that now it is possible to obtain a degree in 'Jazz Studies' – or any other test that you might devise so long as it did not reveal any weakness of actual ability. I am reminded that Charles Ives remarked that "Jazz is just a way of wearing your hat!" Or, as he might have said, "The air you breathe!" Why examine it – except to increase the 'throughput' of candidates?

There was a School Inspection one Lent term in the mid-fifties and the Music Department got off to a good start when I was asked to allow the Inspector to sit in on my Choristers' Practice on the Monday morning. (I was always left in charge on that day. Michael Howard would go to London after Sunday Evensong to rehearse his Renaissance Singers in the early part of the week; Tuesday was the Plain Day with a Said Service, and Michael would return on Wednesday in time for the Chorister's Practice.) The Inspector was immensely impressed and came to Evensong, commenting afterwards on the searing expressive impact of the dissonances in Boyce's 'Turn thee unto me, O Lord'. He gave a very good report on the School music and, this useful contact having been made, I later invited him to adjudicate the Senior School House Music Competitions which began about the same time as the Choral Society concerts.

Some years later, after I had succeeded Howard as Organist, I was somewhat embarrassed by his suggestion that I might care to join the Schools Inspectorate Staff. I also remember being asked to lecture at a Teacher's Course at Saffron Walden, and I then somewhat reluctantly agreed to attend an interview at the Inspectorate's Headquarters in Curzon Street, Mayfair. It was an idiotic idea and I shouldn't have gone – I was not that interested in school teaching anyway – let alone inspecting it – it was simply an adjunct to the cathedral work at Ely. Doubtless the salary would have been much better than that of a cathedral organist (I had no pensionable contract even until 1970!) – but what does it profit a man if he loses his own soul?

My school duties also included responsibility for congregational singing with a weekly rehearsal. On the Great Festivals there would be a school Eucharist, and in 1960 the Chaplain, the Revd Christopher Campling asked me to write a setting for unison voices in which the whole School could join. The Missa Brevis is a Unison setting of extreme compression, and makes an impression of strength and

55

virility from the outset with a Kyrie Eleison of unusual forcefulness, earning it the name in some circles of the 'crash bang' Service! But it did prove popular at RSCM Chorister Courses – an early indication that children did like my music, unlike many of their seniors in the Choirs!

The Revd David Walser succeeded Campling as Chaplain, and the era of the sixties introduced the concept of Responsorial Psalmody for congregational use and schools were quick to take this up. It is an attractive formula, with a chorus refrain, and verses which give an opportunity to alternate high and low voices. David did a version of Psalm 98 – 'Sing a New Song to the Lord' which proved to be popular generally, and then treated Psalm 130 – 'From the depths of my distress' in the same way – on the whole this was less popular – people do prefer to be cheerful! The School Chaplain was also a Minor Canon of the Cathedral, with the responsibility of singing the Services in the absence of the Precentor. Normally this was an unproblematic matter of simply singing the Preces and Responses. In the case of Men's Voices Services the question of cantoring the plainchant Psalms and Canticles in alternation with the Choir sometimes proved problematic. This could be a sustained test of vocal technique and style and often resulted in some uneasiness. David's ability in this respect sometimes gave cause for my concern – on one occasion I decided to 'rush in' – telling David that I had asked one of the Lay Clerks to cantor the Psalms that day. David wasn't having any of it, and when the Psalms began got in by a short head before the Lay Clerk. The Psalms that day included the words 'We are they who ought to speak, who is Lord over us?' David was a dear man and I decided to leave things as they were!

Another stimulus to composition at the School was the development of a Brass Ensemble under the leadership of Miles Amherst, who also occasionally sang alto in the Cathedral Choir. For the Speech Day Service in 1964 I composed a setting of Psalm 150 for the Chapel Choir (which also included the Cathedral Choristers for this Service) which drew on the Brass Ensemble and Cymbals. The organ part was toccata-like in its figuration but not particularly difficult in the original key of A minor. However, this key took the treble voices up into the stratosphere with several top A's. When I submitted it to Novello's they said 'yes', with the proviso that I transposed it down a whole tone – 'to make it more accessible for the average Choir'. This the key change accomplished, but with the disadvantage that the organ part now lies far less easily under the fingers (in my opinion, though all my Assistants played it with the greatest of ease!).

Another interesting challenge in 1961 was a School production of Dorothy L. Sayer's *The Zeal of Thy House* for which I was asked to provide the music. Rather than use Gerald Knight's piece, in which I had sung for the Canterbury Festival of 1949 (and liked), I thought that it would be an interesting challenge to do something different. At the conclusion of the performances one of the Theological College students suggested, "You should make a Mass out of that music." I took up his suggestion and the Missa Passionis Christi was the result.

Two settings of the Eucharist frame my career as Director of Music at Ely Cathedral. I was appointed in 1958 and in the Autumn of that year I began work on my Missa Eliensis, a setting in English of the Prayer Book text which was used in the Cathedral on weekdays and on Sundays. It was published in 1960 and first sung in the Cathedral in 1961, first on Quinquagesima Sunday and again on Easter Day. It was noted that while the piece fitted readily into the Darke in F tradition, the organ part was more independent of the vocal lines, and a certain 'French' influence in the textures and harmonies was commented upon. This trait was to be confirmed in many subsequent pieces; but after all I did spend many of my waking hours in a Norman Cathedral where we frequently sang the music of Henry Purcell, much of it patently influenced by French models.

At that time the required strict adherence to the Prayer Book meant that we were not allowed to use Latin for settings of the Communion Service and of course the Gloria in Excelsis Deo was placed at the end of the Service. For my retirement year of 1990 I composed the Missa Sanctae Etheldredae which offers a somewhat stark contrast to the idiom of the early sixties, although that era supposedly initiated (or confirmed) many departures from hitherto accepted standards of artistic 'good taste' in church music.

With the adoption of new Service books in the seventies a much greater freedom in the use of music became possible. The Eucharist was now the main Service with Mattins either omitted, placed second in the order of Services, or vestigial elements included in the Eucharist – at some length! Rite A offered minimal richness of either words or music, but the use of Latin for the Ordinary texts offered an escape route. 'In Latin Rite A is Okay!' seemed a strange outcome in a topsy-turvy ecclesiastical merry-go-round. But so it was that pre-Reformation settings by Byrd and Tye could now be used as intended, as indeed could be Masses in the Continental tradition from Josquin to Poulenc. The association of the Latin text with so many great compositions from Plainchant to Stravinsky certainly released the imagination, especially in rhythmic and harmonic invention. The Missa Sancti Etheldredae is based upon a plainchant Sequence melody of unknown origin, sung between the Epistle and Gospel to the following text: "Now our hymn to God upraising, Sing we of a Queen's amazing lowliness of mind today." (Etc.)

In addition to the Mass I have composed three organ works based on this plainchant melody:

Symphonia Eliensis (1975 – for the opening recital on the rebuilt organ), Etheldreda Rag (1984 – though a first piano version pre-dates it by around five years), and Scherzo-Fantasy 'The Ely Imps' (suggested by a reference in Dean Charles Stubbs' *Ely Cathedral Handbook* of 1906. Stubbs always wrote most imaginatively about Ely – the romance of the place affected him as it always did me. Here is his reference in Chapter Three to The Choir:

On the south side at the junction of the labels of the first and second arches of the choir is the curious grotesque known as 'the Ely Imps', concerning which the following lines have been written:

Ely imps you see,
Pickaback imps in glee,
With the wings of a bat
And the grin of a cat,
Making mock at you and me,
Sing nonny ho, nonny he,
Oh what fools these poor mortals be!

Etheldreda Rag was first composed around 1979 as an entertainment piece for piano very much in the Scott Joplin idiom. The Dean and Chapter always hosted a post-Christmas party at the beginning of the Lent Term, usually timed for the Epiphany weekend, and after dinner we were expected to 'sing for our supper'. Having often played a Joplin Rag on these occasions I decided to put the plainchant and 'birth of jazz' idiom somewhat incongruously together. It has since been well received as an organ concert encore.

The Symphonia Eliensis has seven sections corresponding to these areas of the Cathedral: (1) Galilee Porch (2) Catherine's Chapel (3) Lady Chapel (4) Nave (5) North Transept (6) South Transept (7) Octagon. The movements may be played in any order, just as there is more than one access to the building.

A cathedral organist's role is a very historic one, deriving from that of the Precentor in the monastic foundations before the Reformation. At Ely there is a considerable history of the organists composing for the liturgy, the most notable being Christopher Tye, Rober Whyte, John Amner and Basil Harwood. My first piece was a Sanctus, Benedictus, and

Agnus Dei in English for Men's Voices (ATB). The Kyries and Gloria were sung to Merbecke. When I became Organist in 1958 I added these two movements and the setting was published by Novello. (There is a noticeable difference of harmonic language involved – possibly identifiable as being that of Charles Wood and Vaughan Williams.) At that time we were not permitted to use Latin Masses, so it was by no means easy to find suitable repertoire. Missa Eliensis followed, and here the influence of French music becomes noticeable for the first time – Maurice Duruflé is the main influence, a recording of his Requiem became available around this time, and his inimitable idiom, which unites Plainchant with the harmonic idiom of Debussy and Ravel is fresh and quite enchanting. It's not at all surprising that this development occurred – modal elements can be found in the music of Faure, and much more so in the works of Debussy and Ravel. Saint Etheldreda was never far from my thoughts while I was in office at the cathedral, and in 1985 I wrote Now Etheldreda Shines upon our Days – a setting of the magical words of the Venerable Bede to be found in his History of the English Church and People. The following year the Choir sang it with great effect in London at St Paul's Cathedral – the astonishing acoustics enhanced an already notable occasion – the Annual Festival of the Sons of the Clergy with Archbishop Robert Runcie in attendance.

For well over ten years Novello were welcoming to virtually everything I offered them – in fact I recall only one piece – a Trio Sonata for Organ – which they turned down; Basil Ramsey opining that "It was just too difficult for the average player." On the other hand I was sometimes approached to make a contribution to an album; The Colours of the Organ (1959) included my contribution for the Strings, and Fanfares and Processionals (1960) a Fanfare for Colin and Rachel, our children – born in 1956 and 1958 respectively.

Looking at the year 1959 – my first complete year as Director – there were three organ pieces: Postlude, Elevation for the Strings, and Introduction and Allegro. This last was dedicated to my wife Mary, whom I had married in 1953. All three demonstrate a pervasive French influence – mainly Vierne and Messiaen, my favourites from a general leaning to the French tradition. Why should this be? Firstly, I think it's the colour, both harmonic and sonoral – both rich and intriguing – a trait which is observable in French organ music from the 16th century onwards. The instrument and the music are closely wedded, whereas in other traditions, lengthy structures and an emphasis on counterpoint and development of the material – these things interest the mind in a quite different way, and are more easily realisable on almost any organ.

The Postlude is mainly influenced by the Finals of Vierne's Six Symphonies, but both themes are heard in canon and then in combination. Compared with much English organ music of that period my use of the instrument favours the use of the left-hand part in the treble clef, and a general use of the upper compass of the manuals. The Introduction and Allegro uses a harmonic language closer to that of Messiaen and also is more rhythmically varied than any previous piece of mine – it was composed as a kind of reposte to Messiaen's Dieu parmi nous from his La Nativité and both were included at the beginning and end of my contribution to EMI's Great Cathedral Organ series in 1966. The Elevation is also reminiscent of the early Messiaen – which means that in the 1950s I was drawing on his 1930's manner. But at that time few English organists knew or played any Messiaen of any period. But – before any of the organ pieces I have so far mentioned – there was a Rhapsody (very influenced by the Vaughan Williams idiom) and an Elegy.

The first was given its premiere in the cathedral by Sidney Campbell in the summer of 1953 at a concert in which the Alexandra Choir also took part, and the other, a year or two later, was written as an exercise in my studies for the Durham D.Mus. degree. One Canadian critic has expressed the opinion that this is my finest organ work! I sent the Rhapsody to Novello, but it was rejected – not surprising I suppose, seeing that I was an unknown Sub-Organist at a provincial cathedral. Nevertheless, my naughty streak impelled me to use it as the last movement of my Eucharistic Suite, which was composed in 1960 and was readily accepted for publication under the title 'Sortie'. No problem then – I was a Cathedral Organist, and no doubt my compositional technique had matured somewhat. The Elegy was slightly revised in 1961 when it was accepted by Novello, and I dedicated it to the memory of Dr Marmaduke Conway who had died that year. It was influenced to some degree by the music of Mahler – I was introduced to his character and music by the book about him written by his wife Alma and published in England in 1946. I remember seeing the book in a Birmingham bookshop and buying it there and then. Interesting – the proximity of Mahler and Vaughan Williams in my early musical influences – the latter described the former as 'a tolerable imitation of a composer'! I shall never know what he might have thought about my music. One other work dates from1959 – an Evening Service for Men for Three Voices. This uses open sonorities based mainly on fourths and fifths with some use of diatonic dissonance. It provoked ribald comment from Lay Clerks at other cathedrals, suggesting that it was really meant to be in four parts, but that one part book had been lost!

On my appointment as Organist beginning officially at the start of the Autumn Term 1958, it was not possible to appoint an Assistant, so for that Term I had to rely on outside help. Gerald Hendrie was already known to me through his friendship with Miles Amherst – 'My friend Gerald Hendrie' was a standard joke in the Staff Room at the King's School, and I already knew him as a distinguished academic as well as an excellent organist. Based in Cambridge at Selwyn

College he was readily available for important Services, and otherwise the Choir was used to singing 'to the organ' from the many occasions when I was left in charge during the previous five years. Gerald certainly relished this involvement in cathedral music, and for some time nourished hopes of a career 'surrounded by wonderful architecture' as he put it. My first appointee from January 1959 was Christopher Scarfe, who had recently graduated from Oxford – most keen and enthusiastic, and he held the position until the summer of 1961 when he was enticed away to Dunstable Priory, a move which I believe he came to regret eventually. (On the occasion of the Royal Maundy Service held in Ely in 1987 I found myself sitting next to the Duke of Edinburgh on a settee in the Bishop's House and he, as an opening gambit enquired "What do you consider to be your most important task as a Cathedral Organist?" My immediate response was "Appoint a brilliant Assistant." He roared his head off at this answer, but he certainly took the point.)

Scarfe's successor was Michael Dudman, an Australian who at this time was in Europe and studying with André Marchal in Paris. He was recommended to me by Sir William Mckie of Westminster Abbey, who had recently heard Dudman play a recital in the Abbey. As a fellow Australian he was especially interested in helping Michael to secure an interesting Assistantship in this country and was aware of the vacancy at Ely. Michael was an outstanding success both as an accompanist and as a virtuoso soloist. After three years he wanted to move on and succeeded Martin How at Grimsby Parish Church, where there is a choir school foundation. When hopes of a cathedral appointment appeared increasingly remote he returned to Australia to become Director of Music at Newcastle Cathedral, NSW. He was an enthusiastic exponent of my music, recording my Variations on a Carol of 1965 and introducing Missa Eliensis to the Cathedral repertoire.

I renewed our acquaintance on two occasions when I visited Australia, and he enjoyed recalling 'those very memorable days' with evident pleasure. On his becoming Dean of the Faculty of Music at Newcastle University he established an annual Keyboard Festival and in 1992 he invited me to give the Keynote Address at the Opening Concert, and commissioned two substantial works which were premiered at the Festival – a Choral Concerto: 'The Gods of Music' which includes a substantial part for organ solo, and 'Eternity's Sunrise' – Three poems by William Blake for Contralto and Organ. As has been already mentioned, Michael had developed heart problems in his later years (some were of the opinion that these were not helped by problems of temperament), and sadly died at the age of 50 in 1994 while in hospital for a check-up.

1964 was a climactic point in my career. The Summer Term was dominated by the Enthronement of Bishop Edward Roberts. For this I composed The Praises of the Trinity – a traditional text for this Service and one peculiar to Ely. It is sung at the outset of the Service after the Bishop-elect has banged on the door in the Galilee Porch seeking entrance, and has been admitted. Acoustically, this position under the West Tower is ideal for unaccompanied singing, and incidentally is one of the best places to listen to the singing in the Choir, the West wall acting as a superb sound reflector. Every word of the Psalms can be heard – supposing them to have been clearly articulated in the first place of course. This Summer Term also marked the end of my post as Director of Music at the King's School – a position I had held since 1953. The position of a cathedral organist (at least in those far-off days) was/is not well paid, yet requires availability for early morning choir practices, and again in the late afternoon. While this fitted in easily with the school timetable I was now yearning for academic work at a rather more interesting level. I was prepared to oversee the O and A level examination work, but otherwise my interests were turning away from school work towards teaching in one of the London institutions – and eventually in the handily situated University of Cambridge.

I was already doing some Evening Class work in the Music Department of the Cambridge Technical College, now recently elevated to Anglia Polytechnic University, in its limited scope quite interesting as my first experience of post-school-age teaching, but in fact the standard of the work was below that of the Oxford and Cambridge Examination Board syllabus I was using at the King's School, so the London Colleges now beckoned as the best way forward.

Domestically, No 2 The Almonry had proved to be a most interesting and beautiful house in which to reside. By the late sixties we had taken over all three floors of the house, with its pillared undercroft and spiral staircase in a tower. But cathedral appointments, from the Dean downwards are necessarily 'tied-cottages' and must be quitted on termination of the employment. Mary and I decided that we should look well ahead and so we bought a house in Cambridge to let furnished. This had many advantages, as if needed, we could move there without legal delays. It also meant that we could furnish it with our post-war furniture and then look for the antiques which the Almonry rooms so obviously needed if we were to enable them to look their best. This we gradually did to my great satisfaction, as funds allowed.

Chapter 5

Put away Childish Things
Work and experiences at the RAM and Cambridge
(1964–74)

The Principal at the RAM was Sir Thomas Armstrong whom I had encountered at Christ Church Cathedral, Oxford on one of my many cathedral expeditions in the 1940s. He had a sister who was married to the Vicar of Little Downham in the Isle (as it was then known) a mere couple of miles down the road from Ely. He would often call in at the cathedral and stay for the Sunday Eucharist – and now he knew that I was indeed the 'full organist'! Having decided that I needed to move on from school teaching I decided to offer my services to the Academy either as a Harmony Professor (as the Department was then known) or in the Organ Faculty. There being no vacancy in the latter department, Harmony it had to be, and I considered rightly so, as my Durham degrees and my strong interest in composition amply covered this area. I was only prepared to offer one day in each week to the Academy, and that on the cathedral 'Plain Day' when there was neither Sung Evensong or Choir Practice. This meant of course that I would no longer have a free day off work, but this did not at all concern me, as a life in music was what I had always wanted – and had never regarded as 'work' in the usually accepted sense. Furthermore it was work in London – and although busy I would now be in contact with some of the finest musicians in the land and could experience vicariously what I had not known apart from that one year in Canterbury – the life of a student as well as a Professor!

Tuesday (Plain Day at the Cathedral) was my Academy day and I taught from 10.00 a.m. to 6.00 p.m. – fourteen students, with an hour for lunch. I was used to leaving my house at around 8.15 in order to get to the Practice Room for the Chorister's Practice each morning; to get to the Academy I had to leave some 30 minutes earlier for the fifteen-minute walk down the hill to the railway station and so be in time for an 8.00 a.m. train to Liverpool Street. That journey took around an hour and a half, followed by a fifteen minute tube train to Baker Street; and from there on to the Marylebone Road, past Madame Taussaud's and the Planetarium, was but a five minute walk to the Academy in its dreamy location adjacent to the Regent's Park.

I was allotted a room in the Annexe, usefully placed for ready access to the Library, where most of the harmony teaching took place. Immediately one had a sense of history – and the dust adhering to that sensation! Michael Howard had been a student at the Academy and he made it very clear that he regarded it as a very old-fashioned institution. So his observations definitely coloured my first impressions of the place.

After my first day, spent mainly in registering my allotted students, I made tentative enquiries about a Syllabus only to be told that there wasn't one – "Each Professor teaches how he wishes – just use some previous examination papers." This highly individualistic approach could be regarded as a strength of course, but it was just a trifle disconcerting to one who had not been a student at the Academy, as most of the other Staff had been. Nevertheless, the excitement I had fully expected to feel was present and palpable that first week. Of my first fourteen students, two stand out in my memory – Desmond Hunter from Belfast, a very brilliant organist and scholar, and Oliver Brockway (Horn) – an old Etonian, who went on to enjoy a distinguished orchestral career.

Though the teaching was clearly going to prove as enjoyable as I had envisaged, the contacts with the rest of the teaching staff were to prove even more stimulating, and eventually marked a definite move in my compositional interests from purely organ and cathedral composition to a much more varied vocal and instrumental approach. At this early stage, contacts with staff members were limited to the lunch-hour in the Professors' Dining Room. Amongst the younger Professors, Paul Patterson immediately attracted my attention – firstly on his personality, and then on his position as the Contemporary Music organiser, and even more because of his considerable interest in the organ. There was an age gap of almost twenty years between us but the rapport was immediate and productive. Paul had begun his studies as a trombonist at the Academy, but in the course of his studies composition became his chief interest, and he became the first Manson Fellow in contemporary music at the Academy, including an electronic workshop.

Paul at that time had enjoyed a close relationship with the English Sinfonia based in Nottingham, and had composed four pieces for that orchestra. He introduced me to his organ music and I was immediately interested in his approach to organ textures – influenced more by his experience as a wind player and his more secular pieces I thought. But Paul was of more practical value than just a personality. His contact with the Sinfonia and the Nottingham scene generally was instrumental in obtaining a first performance of my Organ Concerto for Strings and Timpani at the Nottingham Festival in 1970 at a concert in Southwell Minster, in which I also played the Poulenc Concerto scored for the same forces. The organ console in the Nave at the Minster was obviously the one to use for liaison with the English Sinfonia Orchestra and conductor Neville Dilkes, but it was in a very poor condition from the viewpoint of stop control and this led to one very sticky ensemble point in the Poulenc. Nevertheless the concert was a considerable advance in my career both as composer and soloist, and was repeated in Ely at the opening concert of the re-built organ in 1976 with the addition of a

Handel Concerto. On this occasion the orchestra was the City of London Sinfonia and should have been directed by Richard Hickox. He was unwell on the day and Neville Dilkes substituted at very short notice, and this time there were no problems of liaison – our experience five years previously had alerted us to all possible problems, and on this occasion I was playing an organ of my own design in immaculate condition, even though I was situated in an organ loft in the Choir and the orchestra was placed in the centre of the Octagon!

Probably the most glowing review of the Concerto in performance to date was from Morley Pooley of a concert in Bath Abbey on 9th October 1974, conducted by the Abbey organist Dudley Holroyd:

"As a rule 'modern' works give me the horrors, but this one had so much to offer, was so adventurous, so dynamic and often both shattering and shocking to the nervous system, but always gripping, that it deserves to be heard time and time again. The timpani has a field day, but the whole work is brilliantly conceived, full of clever invention, ghostly and with so many well contrived contrasts that one's interest is always held." In this concert I also played Handel's Concerto in B flat, Op. 9 No. 3.

Against this – welcome enthusiasm! – needs to be set the reaction of James Day to the second performance of the Concerto on 5th August, 1971 in King's College, Cambridge, when it was paired with Kenneth Leighton's Organ Concerto, composed about the same time as mine. Writing in the *Cambridge Evening News* he commented, "effectively written for the soloist, and cleanly laid out for the orchestra, [one always reads this kind of opening with dread!] it created a favourable impression though one felt that the composer had not quite managed to fuse all the various styles that he admires into a truly personal idiom." Enough – stop there! – one wanted to say. But no – "The result was rather as if a pupil of Shostakovich had decided to write a four-movement organ concerto on Lisztian lines, with plenty of resourceful metamorphosis of themes, but occasionally – particularly in the coda to the last movement – giving the sensation that the themes were being modified rather than truly developed."

My concerto (in three movements by the way – whatever Shostakovich's pupil might have done) was followed by the Leighton work, fully mature – with many major works behind him at this stage, and no necessity to startle or impress. (Maybe my maturity in large scale concertante work was to be reached ten years later with the Symphonic Suite: 'The Fenlands' – James Day thoroughly approved of this piece.) Both concertos were brilliantly played by Robert Munns, with David Willcocks conducting the London Chamber Soloists in this Cambridge Festival Concert. I was sorry not to be there to either play or listen, being already booked for a holiday/recital tour with my family – concerts in Stoke Hartland, Exeter Cathedral, Torquay and Truro Cathedral – this last recital was recorded by the BBC. Gerald Knight was directing the RSCM Summer School at Truro, with Roy Massey as Organist. One piece of mine was on the Service list – I think it was the Communion Service with a unison part for a congregation, commissioned by Gerald for publication by the RSCM.

The Southwell concert was rated a considerable success by the local critic Richard Maylan who reviewed the Concerto in these terms: "A new organ concerto had its premiere at a Festival concert last night. The composer, Arthur Wills, of Ely Cathedral, played it with the English Sinfonia Orchestra under Neville Dilkes before a large audience in Southwell Minster. It is a vigorous, direct piece which wastes neither note nor time. It creates recognisable moods; for instance, the opening conjures up a slow procession, in the fast section which follows the soloist and orchestra first appear to argue over one idea, then exchange thoughts on the more romantic theme. Maybe the ideas do not grow logically, but they set each other off well. The slow movement, a set of variants builds up to a convincing climax from quiet beginnings. The finale has a touch of bravura and finishes with a fine flourish. Dr Wills' Concerto should receive plenty more hearings."

Now there was talk of my providing another work for the following year – an important piece for soloists, chorus and orchestra. Gregson Williams, the Festival organizer, was enthusiastic, and I had envisaged a non-liturgical symphonic Requiem in four movements with words by Dylan Thomas, John Donne and Shakespeare. As quite often happens, the financial backing for this concert was not forthcoming, but I went ahead with the piece which I dedicated to the memory of my parents. Having completed it I let it rest, feeling almost too emotionally involved to want to hear it in performance. In fact it was not given its first performance until ten years later at the Academy, when its emotional impact on myself (and others) was even more intense than I had anticipated. Even Paul Patterson was impressed by this not too innovative work, though he was always well ahead of his colleagues in his interest in the avant-garde, especially at that period of Penderecki and the Polish school. Certainly Paul's interests had a considerable impact on the development of my own style, very noticeably in such organ works as Tongues of Fire, Resurrection and Symphonia Eliensis – this last composed to demonstrate the tone colours of the rebuilt organ at Ely. But Paul was an exception, generally speaking, when compared with other Professors who were apt to be both dismissive and envious of the post-Vaughan Williams school. I heard one such comment, "Benjamin Britten has only to f--t for Boosey and Hawkes immediately agree to publish it – naughty!"

It will be apparent that from my first term at the Academy my expectations of fresh experiences and stimulating ideas had been indeed exceeded beyond my highest hopes. Many of the finest orchestral players of the day were on the staff and the information and gossip about the conductors and soloists of the day were indeed things to be treasured.Gareth Morris, the First Flute in the Philharmonia had played for Beecham, Furtwängler ('Spoke very little if at all'), Klemperer and Karajan ('Very cold!') and had many choice anecdotes to relate. But one lunchtime I was riveted to hear him declare "What a wonderful thing to be Organist of Ely Cathedral!" I asked him why he thought that? "But of course it's wonderful working in a building like that – and surrounded by such history! And you've stayed there," he went on, "I always think that its such a pity when Cathedral Organists change their posts." This viewpoint was quite an eye-opener for me, who just then was thinking that it was about time I thought of a move. Observations like this from outside the cathedral world were a salutary jolt to my thinking on such matters.

To return to more mundane affairs – Sir Thomas joined his staff for lunch on most days, and after a year or two he initiated a Roast Meat course which you carved for yourself – under his eagle eye I may say: a helping considered too generous was clearly felt in the atmosphere – he was a master at provoking the guilty conscience! He retired in 1968 and was succeeded by Professor Anthony Lewis from the University of Birmingham, a delightful man of great charm of manner. Armstrong was Principal at the Academy for just four years of my time there, and I always found him most approachable. The Church Anthem Book included one of his anthems – 'Christ, whose glory fills the skies' – a piece I often read through in my youth, but have never heard performed. I thought that it must be tremendous to compose a piece of that length and interest. On one of his visits to the Academy, long after his retirement, I met him entering the Duke's Hall as I was leaving. He greeted me with – "I wish I could compose as well as you." I couldn't think of anything to respond within that brief moment, but it was an encounter to be savoured.

The penultimate week of each term was designated as Review Week. I'm not convinced that every student considered it was so to be treated, but it was a heaven-sent opportunity for those Professors who wished to go on a week's examining for the Associated Board (perhaps not the 'association of the bored' as the notable serialist composer Elisabeth Lutyens derided it!). I decided to join their ranks as I knew that many cathedral organists did this routinely – Douglas Hopkins was a notable role model in this matter – and so I went through the training sessions required, and undertook my first tour in the Summer Term of 1966. (Those training sessions – rather different from today's I'm sure. The room was full of my instructor's smoke, and he assured me that I shouldn't take the business too seriously!)

My first tour was a delightfully relaxed week spent in the Norfolk coastal countryside, often not required to begin to examining before 10.00 a.m. and rarely going on after 5.00 p.m. The high point was a day's examining at Gresham's School in Holt, where Benjamin Britten had spent his teenage years. One marvellously sunny afternoon session in Sheringham finished at 4.30, and I spent a couple of hours sunbathing on the beach, before driving on to Cromer where I had arranged to stay in the main Hotel on the Promenade and there dined on Lobster-Thermidor for the first time in my culinary experience – quite excellent. Needless to say, the Board's timetabling arrangements nowadays are rather less relaxed, and that hotel in Cromer? – just don't ask!

Eventually I was asked whether I would care to be considered for examination tours overseas, but always declined with the rider that on my retirement from the cathedral I might well accept such offers. Though when I mentioned this to my colleagues at the Academy they all took the view – "Fine, but don't leave it too long – the Board is getting restive about having to pay for coffins back from Singapore and Hong Kong!" But I felt that my primary interest was the cathedral music, and that of course was in fact a far more stimulating occupation than examining, which to me was never more than a chore, however delightful the venue. Douglas Hopkins, though, took a different view; from Peterborough he was appointed to Canterbury on Gerald Knight's resignation to become Director of the (soon to be) Royal School of Church Music in its new venue at Addington Palace, Croydon. But to my surprise he didn't stay in that marvellous cathedral very long, and after a very few years resigned in order (as he told me) to be able to undertake more overseas examination work. What an extraordinary thing, I thought and he could see that, going on to pontificate – "No cathedral organist should stay longer than ten years in the job." This didn't convince me either, and I went on – ratching up a total of nine years as Assistant and thirty-two as Director of Music. But his resignation from Canterbury meant that Sidney Campbell could apply for and obtain that prestigious appointment – a career move which must have had much significance for him after those years as Sub-Warden of the College of St Nicholas in the Precincts. Once again I reflected on what a small world the musical profession is, and even more so, how comparatively tiny is each sector of this endeavour.

In that year of 1966 I celebrated my fortieth birthday – a dangerous age I was told – and so it proved to be. I bought a second-hand Jaguar car, with automatic transmission. At first all went well. In the Summer term of the following year I drove down in triumph to do a week's examining in Brighton, staying at the now infamous Grand Hotel and delighting in parking in that crescent at the front. Alas, Harold Wilson's Selective Employment Tax meant that you couldn't get your shoes cleaned – the management could no longer afford such staff duties. And then driving down to the Incorporated Society of Organists at Llandaff, to play a recital at short notice and substituting for an indisposed player – and hearing the whispering "Dr Wills drives a Jaguar!" Childish of course, but great fun – for a time. I eventually discovered that automatic transmission and Michelin X tyres together with a heavy frame could be tricky in icy weather conditions. Two ditch and tree encounters early on bright winter mornings in the Fens shocked and disillusioned me sufficiently to want to swap the Jaguar for something more practical – if less glamorous. But this was a heady time – I was elected on to the Council of the Royal College of Organists and, even more exciting, I was offered some teaching work in the University of Cambridge. I had already made a tentative approach to the Professor – Thurston Dart, but my interview with him was somewhat less than cordial and he elected to dwell on the perceived inadequacies of the Ely organ for the mainstream early repertoire – this of course was something Michael Howard had already made abundantly clear to me – rather than address the matters on my mind.

As I was already fully aware of all these matters I came away rather more than a little irritated by 'Bob's' attitude. This 'intellectual arrogance' of approach is not altogether unknown amongst academic folk generally, and the squirm it can induce is something you simply have to ignore and 'keep beneath your chin' – not that I experienced many instances of this kind of rudeness. From the two leading church musicians in Cambridge – David Willcocks and George Guest – I had already received nothing but kindness and assistance; regular invitations to play organ recitals in their respective chapels, together with some introduction to the social life of the University. These opportunities were to be relished, and the first of these occasions of 'solid joys and liquid pleasures' was at the invitation of George Guest, very soon after the acquisition of my first car. The regular recital series at St John's College was a twenty-five minute duration exercise before Evensong at 6.30 p.m. One stayed in the Loft for the Service – George playing as far as the Psalms and then going down to direct the choir – perhaps George was the first to do this? – while the Scholar accompanied. He returned after the anthem and took one off to the handily placed Hostelry opposite the College in Bridge Street – the 'Baron of Beef'. There he introduced me to the delights of 'Whiskey Macs' – it was late in the Michaelmas Term – and then whisked (literally) me back into Chapel to hear the closing hymn and voluntary. From there to the Combination Room for a dry sherry and then into Hall for Dinner. The wine flowed lavishly, but there was yet another delight in store – back to the Combination Room for port, fresh fruit and genial conversation. On this first occasion I had not been invited to stay overnight so I had to drive back to Ely at around 11.00 p.m. on a wintry and misty A10, molto adagio, with the driver's window wide open for fresh air – and visibility!

There was a legendary story of Sidney Campbell driving back to Ely from Cambridge, and being stopped by a policemen at Little Thetford for excessive speed – "I'm Dr Campbell and on my way to an urgent patient problem." "Sorry, Sir!" – and he went on his way rejoicing. Many years later I remembered this ploy when driving from Ely to Ipswich for a day's examining. It was early on a Saturday morning and the A14 dual carriageway was virtually deserted. My mind was no doubt busy with matters musical and I failed to see the Police Car chasing after me and eventually requesting the pleasure of my company. I offered my driving licence and was just toying with the idea of trying Sidney's successful diversion when the Inspector (no less) requested, "What kind of doctorate do you have, sir?" I got away with the advice to keep a more diligent look out of my rear window.

In addition to the organ recitals I also took the Ely Choir to King's Chapel for a Saturday post-Evensong concert in June 1959. This won favourable comments from both David Willcocks and Boris Ord, as well as from undergraduates who chose to regard the different approach in tone and style as an attempt at 'King's-bashing'! Needless to say, this was not my intention. The following year, through the good offices of Gerald Hendrie, the Choristers were invited to give a concert in Selwyn College Chapel on a Sunday Evening, and I included a recently composed motet for two-part trebles – Ave verum corpus. It was an Ely custom to celebrate Saint's Days with a Sung Eucharist at 8.00 a.m., normally sung by the Choristers, and I composed this and 'O quam gloriosum' for these services. They were published by Novello as a pair in one copy. 'Ave verum' has proved to be the most popular – it's not as hard as 'O quam' – and has been recorded by several choirs. Apart from compositions done as part of the academic work it was exceptionally rewarding to compose for the Cathedral Services, and to realise that one was working in the CapelMeister tradition of supplying music for an immediate purpose as did composers from the 13th century onwards. Not of course in the financial sense – no performance royalties in the liturgical usage! But one was composing music for a purpose which was both meaningful and satisfying. And the increasing number of organ pieces were intended either as useful voluntaries or recital pieces. I played a recital for the Cambridge Organist's Association in King's Chapel in that year also and concluded it with a recent Postlude – very much influenced by Vierne – both themes are treated in canon and then in combination. In the same concert I also played two movements from Messiaen's L'Ascension – music surprisingly new to both Simon Preston and Philip Ledger, who were in the audience.

So I did already have a presence in Cambridge in the early 1960s, but it was Harold Wilson's Labour Government of 1964 (as was the case in the absence of shoe-cleaners in the Brighton hotel) which really changed my life. In 1966 that Government decided to radically increase the number of university places available, and as a result David Willcocks contacted me to see whether I would be interested in doing some First Year Supervision work from the coming October. Once again it was the opportunity I had been waiting for; it was for three days each week from 10.00 a.m. to 3.00 p.m., allowing each student an hour in which to have his work assessed and discussed. Lunch could be taken in the Dining Hall or the Combination Room, with the added interest of new contacts to be made, and these not only musical of course. Most of the Dons preferred to pursue a lonely lunchtime, but I found myself frequently talking to one elderly man who was noticeably ignored by most of the others present. Eventually I discovered his identity – E.M. Forster.

The students allotted to me were a lively collection, including several of the choral scholars. As time went on several other Colleges requested my help – Caius, Corpus, St John's, and as my presence in Cambridge became more widely known I was asked to give organ lessons, and not only to music students.

One of these was David Salter of Pembroke College. He did his ARCO successfully, but has since pursued a very successful career in Law whilst retaining an active interest in church and organ music. I also supervised Finals work with both Stephen Cleobury of St John's and Richard Hickox from Queen's College. In all I taught in the University for eight years – by that time sufficient full-time appointments had been created to render my 'outsider' work unnecessary. The last years though had been full of interesting students.

George Caird from Peterhouse was a very stimulating person – already a virtuoso oboe performer and the organiser of 'The Pelican Trio' with the tenor Neil Mackie and the pianist John Blakely. He suggested that I should write a piece for them, and so came into being 'Three Poems of e.e. cummings' which reflected our mutual affection for Cummings' work. This was completed early in October 1973 and given its first performance by the Trio at a Selwyn College Music Society concert a month later. The other student of especial interest to me was Judith Weir – another oboist, and of course a rapidly developing composer. In that last year of 1974 I was invited to play a Saturday recital in

King's College Chapel on the Eve of Pentecost. I decided to compile a programme of music appropriate for this exciting Festival including some Bach and Messiaen, and composed my 'Tongues of Fire' especially for this occasion. Judith also offered to write a piece – Komm, Gott, Schöpfer, heiliger Geist (1974) which I was very glad to include, following it with Bach's Chorale Prelude on the same melody.

I have mentioned the social aspect of this work in Cambridge – the renowned annual May Balls for instance, but an even more delightful feature of my membership of the Caius Common Room was the occasional offer of some excellent wine at greatly reduced prices when the number of the same bottles was less than that required for any given Feast.

With the eventual ending of the Cambridge work in mind after eight very fulfilling years, I had explored the idea of extending my work at the RAM to two days – Wednesday and Thursday – in each week. This needed the agreement of the Ely Chapter as it meant that my Assistant would be in charge for the Thursday Evensong and the Choir Practices that day. This arrangement already was the custom in several cathedrals so this was readily agreed – the more so in that the seventies were a period of high inflation with which the cathedral salaries could not keep pace. The Academy had an overnight room available for this purpose and the Canteen opened in time for breakfast – a very useful amenity. This two-day teaching commitment began in September 1975.

The extraordinary talent I had met in Cambridge had not extinguished the interest of the RAM work for me – far from it. In 1970 two very different but equally interesting students had entered my class – Anne Marsden Thomas and William Waters. An organist and a guitarist! Could any two instruments be more different? By this time I was allotted several students who were 'on the B.Mus. Course' and Anne was one of these. This was a federal degree bestowed by London University with the participating Colleges of King's

London, Trinity College, Goldsmith's College, the RCM and the RAM. In addition to Music Techniques (as the Harmony lessons had now been renamed) I had also to deal with essay work requirements for the University course. After Cambridge of course this was no great change for me, and something I enjoyed. Anne was an excellent organist and a dedicated student. Amongst the reading assignments I gave her was some material dealing with the Early Fathers. She ever afterwards asserted that this study alone converted her to feminism. Eventually she also became a vegetarian, but I am not suggesting that this was also due to my influence – heaven forbid!

William Waters was a very different character, dedicated to his instrument and only marginally interested in his harmony exercises. A lesson looking through these did not take 30 minutes, which allowed of some interesting conversations about the guitar as a medium for music, and the guitar world generally. He knew of my work as a composer, so inevitably and eventually came the question – "Would you like to write a piece for me?" A significant request, because I agreed to it and thereby produced my first solo instrumental work other than for organ – a Sonata in three movements. The question arose – how do I learn about the possibilities of the instrument? The answer was fairly obvious – listen to the instrument, study some scores, but – "The most useful thing you can do is talk to my teacher Hector Quine, he edits for OUP."

I had already met Hector over lunch in the Professor's Dining Room, so I did all of this, Hector looked at my rough sketch, pointed out the technical impossibilities I had included, the Sonata was ready in 1972, dedicated to Bill Waters, and appeared in print published by OUP three years later. 1973 saw the composition of Pavane and Galliard published by Ricordi; after that I was asked by OUP to contribute to an Album of Guitar pieces (1974) for which I composed Homage to Ravel, and then the idea of a song cycle for James Bowman with guitar suggested itself – Three Elizabethan Love Songs – extended to four in 1980 and entitled Love's Torment – now also in a version with keyboard accompaniment.

In 1979 I was commissioned by Margaret Peckham to compose a three-movement song-cycle for contralto and guitar to words by Kathleen Raine – A Woman in Love. Margaret Peckham gave a recital of songs with the guitarist Reinhard Froese at the Notre Dame Church Festival in Guernsey the day before I played at the same venue, and this coincidence I'm sure resulted in the commission. This introduced me to the often problematic use of copyright words by a composer. Several of my composer friends at the Academy had alerted me about this matter, so I made quite sure from Kathleen that she agreed to this – which she did enthusiastically. (Today, I see from a *Daily Telegraph* Obituary that Kathleen died last Sunday, 6th July 2003 at the age of 95. My very small contact with her over copyright matters was well supported by what was said about her lack of interest in worldly matters. Would that the same might be said about me!)

Some writers and/or their agents require payment or a share of the royalties, or give a downright refusal. Yet others will send you their latest work for you to consider using it. You have to be prepared for all eventualities. But it was important for my composing career to move away from the pigeonhole of 'a church and organ composer'. The profession likes to know what you are and do, and prefers not to be confused by fresh breakthroughs. But even my Associated Board work was proving to be a stimulus to composition – in 1975 I was asked to submit some pieces for new Wind and Brass Instrument Syllabuses. Out of the eight I submitted in the Grades 4 to 6 brackets six were chosen – all with piano accompaniment of course: 'Aria' for Oboe, 'The Brontë Country' and 'Bucolics' for Bassoon, 'Dance Piece' for Clarinet, 'September Gold' for Horn and 'Pageant' for

Trumpet. Of these 'The Brontë Country' appears to have made the most impression in view of letters received from performers. The Brontë sisters have always exerted a fascination on me, to eventually reach full expression in my 'When the Spirit Comes' – Four Poems by Emily Brontë for Mezzo-Soprano and Piano. The Associated Board pieces were comparatively tiny works but important for me to have to think away from voices and the organ as the only medium for my creativity.

In that same year of 1975 Sonnet 'When our two souls', the wonderful poem by Elizabeth Barrett Browning, immediately caught my attention as a 'must be set' project. The 'two souls' suggested two solo parts that could entwine – a female singer obviously, and a wind instrument of the same tessitura and flexibility – the clarinet. It was given its first performance at the Academy on the 26th May, 1982 in a lunchtime concert by Carol Green (soprano), Martin Powell (clarinet) and Paul Turner (piano). Afterwards Carol commented, "It grabs your audience from the first bar!" Georgina Dobree was Martin Powell's teacher and she recommended its publication by Nova Music (Now Spartan Press Distribution). I obtained some advice on clarinet technique from Julie Butler who was a B.Mus student of mine from 1976–79. It always proves possible to learn something from one's students! The regular lunchtime concerts at the Academy were useful both to the performers, and to the composers of any new work their teachers suggested they should study. 1975 was an interesting year in my compositional career – only one piece of church music was written, and that suggested by the Dean of Ely. All else was inspired by the Academy environment – the biggest piece being Moods and Diversions for Guitar. Hector Quine suggested an Italian publisher for this large scale work – Edizioni Berben.

Undoubtedly the star student of this period though was Simon Rattle, who turned up at the age of 17 in the

Michaelmas Term 1971. He was in my class for two of his three years, going on to John Gardner for his third year. Composition was not one of his interests, but our discussions were always of the most stimulating kind. I remember seeing him in the Duke's Hall when one of Douglas Hopkins' organ students was playing my Concerto in rehearsal. It was a run-through, and Simon's succinct comment was, "It needs rehearsing!" In that one remark I think that he summed up his career as the success it was to be – that of a conductor who thoroughly rehearses.

The two-day commitment at the Academy from 1975 onwards was to enable the development of fresh interests as time went on, in addition to increasing my income of course. I was asked to take a class in keyboard harmony in the Michaelmas Term, but in the Lent Term this developed into an improvisation class for organists. It seemed strange to me that this historically important aspect of an organist's work should be left to the last few moments of the organ lesson, with the syllabus not requiring anything of particular interest or significant length. A very different matter from the situation in France where the Services historically required structured improvisation on the chant material in use. So that was a step forward for the Academy – it is pleasing to note that now, from its start from scratch by myself, the class is taken by a distinguished visitor from Paris.

I have mentioned my increasing involvement with the B.Mus Course student work; the Academic Tutor at this time was Dr Arthur Pritchard (also organist of St John's Wood Parish Church). At the age of almost 70 he was considering lightening his work load, and he mentioned to me that he would recommend me as his successor in the Academic Tutorship if I would be interested. Of course I was interested – after my Cambridge experiences this was the ideal position for me in the Academy hierarchy. The Principal, Anthony Lewis, was fully in agreement with this, and I took up this position in September 1978. Apart from the administration involved there was a weekly history lecture which was attended by students from the GRSM (Graduate of the Royal Schools of Music) Course led by David Robinson. Dr Pritchard also mentioned that he wanted to relinquish his Associated Board theory marking work, and also his A level marking for the Cambridge Syndicate – would I like to take this on? The answer of course was – "Yes". "You will have to watch your tax position!" he pointed out mischievously. The two-day stint also led to other interesting developments such as a suggestion from Paul Patterson that I might like to be involved in an EMI recording of some of his organ music on one side of an LP whilst on the other would be some choral pieces with Roy Wales conducting The London Chorale. Of course – just the kind of enterprise that would interest me! The organ pieces were recorded in Westminster Cathedral in one evening, the page-turner was one of the organ students from the RAM, and that was that – easily managed with two days in London. This recording was issued in 1977 and received generally favourable reviews.

One of the most ghastly and catastrophic periods of my career erupted just before Christmas in the following year of 1978. I slipped on a patch of oil outside a garage in Cambridge and broke my ankle. I managed to drive back to Ely in excruciating pain and consulted a surgeon who informed me that I would be out of action for about six weeks. I could be wheeled into my position in the Choir and stand to conduct, but the Procession to the Crib on Christmas Eve was quite out of the question, so that a Lay Clerk would have to direct the music under the West Tower. (Mary had offered to push me, but Dean Carey had said no – he thought the packed congregation would have laughed!)

The post of Principal at the Trinity College of Music had been advertised towards the end of the year as becoming vacant in 1979 and I decided to apply. Why? The only answer could be – simply because it was there, and I wanted to see what might be the outcome. I was asked to attend for interview on the 24th January at 3.15 p.m., and so I had to turn up with my damaged ankle still in plaster and myself on crutches! Not the most encouraging sight to behold for any interviewing panel. The appointment went to Meredith Davies, four years my senior – and he having been organist at both St Albans and Hereford Cathedrals and then New College, Oxford, with much subsequent wide experience as a conductor in the concert and opera world. Certainly the man for the job! But for me it was sufficient to have been interviewed, and a source of some relief that I was not offered the post – administration is not one of my main interests.

Further to these difficulties, I had two important recital commitments quite early in the New Year – on the 3rd and 16th February. The first of these was a recital for the Harlow Organ Club which was to include the first performance of my Missa Ad HOC a work commissioned by the Club with financial help from the Harlow Arts Council. The Club's Secretary, John Horton contributed the following programme note: "Dr Wills was commissioned by the club to write a work for this evening's recital, and when he decided on an ommunion Suite he asked our advice on what to call it. The title reflects the fact that it is for the Communion – a Mass; that it was written for a particular event – tonight; and that it was composed at the behest of the club, the acronym of whose initials is HOC." The music is in sections suitable for use as voluntaries before and after the Service and also as interludes at the Offertory and Communion – the link with the French Organ Mass tradition being quite clear. I played this concert with a certain amount of ankle discomfort through inadequate practice time, but given the circumstances it went acceptably well I thought. This concert was a reminder that I had played for the Dedication of the Harlow organ when new, in July 1967.

The event on the 16th was a most disastrous affair – the most embarrassing of my entire career. It was for a BBC recording of my Prelude and Fugue (Alkmaar) and the Elgar Sonata in G. It was normal for me to teach at the Academy on Wednesdays and Thursdays and drive back to Ely in the early evening. But the weather since the New Year had been extraordinarily cold, with much snow and ice, and so it was that I could not face the ordeal of a two-hour drive in the darkness with the bad visibility of falling snow and icy road conditions. So I stayed in London, and drove back the following morning, when the condition of the roads still made the normal journey time impossible. So that it was almost lunch-time when I arrived home, and there was no possibility of using the organ for practice purposes during the afternoon. I have always regarded the Elgar Sonata as one of the most difficult works in the repertoire, on both musical and technical grounds, and I approached the evening's recording session with much apprehension. The ankle problem had prevented the normal build-up of the necessary technical preparation and control, and I should have anticipated the problems that I now faced. The hubris and nemesis of the situation ran their inevitable course – my Prelude and Fugue went well enough, but the Finale of the Sonata didn't, and the recording was abandoned. I should have requested well ahead for a postponement of the recording, which I am sure would have been granted. My good conduct record of over twenty years of BBC work was taken into consideration, and I did one more solo (consolation!) recording for the Corporation. But BBC work with the Cambridge Brass Band and other ensembles, and a rare solo appearance on BBC TV, as well as an entire programme on my work for Anglia TV made some amends. But even in the early 1980s the frequency of BBC organ recitals was beginning to become less in evidence, and I had enjoyed a good run of some twenty years.

It is interesting to look back to my first broadcast as a solo organist on August 16, 1961. This was the programme:

Prelude and Fugue in A minor (S.543) – Bach
Elevation - Wills
Toccata for the Flutes – John Stanley
Prière et Berceuse – Guilmant
Toccata – Gigout

Toccata for the Flutes was requested by the producer in the edition by Harry Wall. Sidney Campbell wrote to congratulate me on a successful debut broadcast, but pointed out that the BBC should not have asked for the Stanley piece in the inflated Wall arrangement with its filled-out harmonies and added pedal part. Only some 40 years back, with the Early Music movement by then well under way, but still the organ world lagging behind at that point – anyone surprised?!

I remember Sidney Campbell broadcasting live just once during his four years at Ely. Michael Howard did none as a solo organist during his time, but several with the Choristers, and of course many with the Renaissance Singers, as was so for many years before and after Ely. So from almost nothing in organ broadcasts before at Ely, I did a sustained twenty-year period of frequent organ broadcasts, in addition to some with the choir being also involved.

It should be abundantly clear now, that just as I had anticipated, the work at the Academy was becoming a significant area of my life well beyond merely the interest of teaching at undergraduate level. Of the professors of vital interest to me, apart from Paul Patterson and Hector Quine, no one quite riveted me so much as Eric Fenby. His book *Delius As I Knew Him* published in 1936 had been of extraordinary interest to me – here was an account of how one of the leading composers of my boyhood had composed – with Fenby's help – against the most difficult of circumstances. I could write a book 'Lunch-time encounters of my life in Cambridge and London' with E.M. Forster and Eric Fenby in mind! Eric didn't join us in the Dining Room, but could usually be found in the Coffee Room. Not shy exactly, but certainly the unassuming character I had met and loved in his book on Delius.

In 1974 I was asked to compose an anthem for an Organists' Convention in Newcastle. I chose the wonderful poem 'Prayer' by George Herbert, and decided to dedicate it to Eric. He was pleased and commented that he thought I had 'got to the essence' of that superb poem. Whilst talking about that remarkable man, to my surprise he phoned me one evening in the early eighties to say that he was working with Yehudi Menuhin on the series of books dealing with instruments – the prestigious *Yehudi Menhuin Music Guide Series* – would I be prepared to undertake the book on the organ? Yehudi had already asked one of his collaboraters to do this, but nothing had transpired and they were now looking for someone else. Of course I agreed – in 1975 I had been able to have the Ely Organ rebuilt, and I felt that this book would a very good way of considering the present position of the organ as a musical instrument in the light of that experience. And I also wished to include material dealing with improvisation in a fairly full way which I had already sketched out in 1973. So I went ahead, having signed the usual contract with Macdonalds. A book of around 250 pages was envisaged, including organ specifications and music examples, so a considerable amount of work was entailed. Eric Fenby was delighted with my acceptance of the contract. So, after I had worked for about a year on the project I was more than a little surprised when Macdonalds contacted me to say that the *Series of Music Guides* was to be terminated as it stood, and therefore my contribution would not be required. Of course I immediately phoned Eric, and he was extremely embarrassed by this 'bolt from the blue'. "Leave it with me!" he said.

Macdonalds was of course part of the Robert Maxwell publishing empire BPCC plc – not that this had given me any particular cause for concern at that point. After a week or so Eric was able to tell me that Yehudi had taken Maxwell to lunch and explained the extreme embarrassment this decision had caused for himself, Eric and me, and it was agreed there and then that my book would be published as the final contribution to a distinguished but sadly incomplete series. (I already knew that one of my luncheon companions at the Academy was working(?) behind schedule on the trumpet volume.) My volume was published in English and Italian in 1984. The reviews were generally approving, and my own 'word of mouth' was that the Academy students found it extremely helpful in their preparation for the LRAM Diploma. Eric Fenby was much relieved at this outcome, though by then he had resigned his Academy teaching post in order to concentrate upon the definitive publications of the Delius Society. In 1993 the Menuhin series was taken over by Kahn & Averill (who have now added several of the missing instruments to the series) and I produced a second revised version for that publisher.

An organ work from this period has a specific Academy link – 'The Song of Songs' – Six Pieces for manuals only (1974). These were originally dedicated to female pupils of mine, but on their later computer-set publication I decided to omit their names. Anne Marsden Thomas found them 'rather harsh' but asked me to write a two-part carol for a choir she was directing at that time and I did a setting of 'There is no Rose of such virtue' which was published by Basil Ramsey on his departure from Novello Ltd in the mid-seventies. Basil's setting up on his own leads nicely to a consideration of the general publishing scene as it developed after the 1960s. For the fifteen years or so following on my appointment as Organist at Ely, I offered almost every choral and organ composition on completion to Novello, and virtually everything was accepted. This was a time of great progress in the English organ scene – in the early 1950s the Festival Hall had received its organ designed by Ralph Downes, with a focus on its usefulness for the complete repertoire – Baroque and the Romantic French School, and as a result the organ as a concert instrument occupied a prominence for many years during which, as Ralph liked to say, organ concerts became 'the talk of the town'. Boosey and Hawkes were not particularly involved in this evolving organ world, but as a consequence of my friendship with Martin Hall, who was on the staff at Boosey's, they accepted a Sonata (1963) the Organ Concerto (1970) and the Trio Sonata (1971). Oxford University Press also beckoned, taking the 'Alkmaar' Prelude and Fugue (1971) and then commissioning 'Bells' for an album of pieces for manuals. My friendship with Paul Patterson was also a continuing influence on my composition, and his publisher Weinberger took (appropriately enough) two of my most adventurous organ pieces – 'Tongues of Fire' and 'Resurrection' as well as an anthem for the RSCM Albert Hall Festival in 1977 – 'The Light Invisible'. This period was a high point in English organ composition – and its ready acceptance by publishers – and high points necessarily have both an ascent and descent.

The publishers filled their warehouses with music of inevitable slow sales, their accountants told them to stop doing it – and great was the fall-out thereof. At the outset of this new world publishers would put the works out of print and then let the composer have the copyright back to place it with another publisher – if this proved to be possible. Sometimes they lived to regret doing this – as time went on the publication of compilations of anthems and services, for Trebles or Men's voices, became popular and the original owners of the copyright would ask the composer permission to do this, only to find that the piece in question had already been placed elsewhere and was no longer available. But then technological progress via the computer enabled single copies to be printed to order, Novellos being a pioneer in this respect, and this is now the norm unless publishers can guarantee large orders – from the USA for example.

There was one very significant development going on during the 1950s and 1960s in the field of Church music and that was the gradual emergence of the Royal School of Church Music as a leading player through the development of their publishing department under the Directorship of Gerald Knight. For the Royal Albert Hall Festival of 1965 he commissioned me to compose an anthem and I chose the text from Psalm 134 – 'Behold now, praise the Lord'. This would be sung by a choir of several thousand in a vast space, so nothing too rhythmically complex was required, at least in the voice parts. But I decided to enliven the organ part with reiterated mildly dissonant quaver chords, and some syncopation. Douglas Hopkins told me that it was known as 'the Stravinsky anthem'! It proved too much for one of the less experienced choirs and I received a torn-up copy without comment through the post. Ah well, it was bound to happen! On the other hand, Gerald told me that it had been a great success with the choirs, and I received an enthusiastic letter from a boy chorister who was later to be among my first batch of King's students at Cambridge. Gerald felt that he ought to modify my tempo marking for that great auditorium and under his baton it plodded somewhat, needing a rather greater electric charge. I listened to it sitting on the platform next to Malcolm Williamson, the Master of the Queen's Music, and wishing that I was conducting. But I never comment on the way other people perform my music – one is only too glad to have the thing done at all. Lionel Dakers followed Knight as Director, and made even more determined efforts to develop the Publications department. But after some initial success, it became clear that the tide was changing, and clergy were looking for a simpler and more popular product with which to engage and attract their less numerous congregations.

One other useful player in the field of publications was emerging towards the end of the seventies – Barry Brunton. After I had failed to interest Ramsay Silver, of Banks Music Publications, in my transcription of Mussorgsky's Pictures at an Exhibition – "too long for us," he objected, I phoned

Barry to see if he would be prepared to do it in his usual reproduction of the composer's MS format, and the answer was in the affirmative. Barry then took several other pieces, including secular works so far unpublished such as songs and song-cycles, and the Sonata 1984 for piano.

So began an almost twenty-year association with Oecumuse and Barry Brunton Music Publisher. Several previous and as yet unpublished works were taken by Barry, as were new pieces commissioned from various sources. In his early years Barry would only produce photo-copies of the composers' manuscripts – a method of some personal interest, but not always conducive to the performer's ease and accuracy! But in the mid-nineties the advent of the computer led to the availability of several programmes which enabled composers (although necessitating a steep learning curve!) to set their pieces either for self-publication, or for a publisher to use for some agreed recompense on their part.

This new art of computer-setting is a discipline very exacting in its demands on the detailed precision of the finished object, which does not always fit easily with the compositional imagination and temperament. Nevertheless, it will not readily be supplanted by any other technology, and in the case of the ease of production of several versions of the same work it cannot be equalled in its usefulness. An obvious example of this is to be found in the case of my Symphonic Suite: 'The Fenlands'. Commissioned for the standard British Brass Band instrumentation the Hyperion recording made it well known worldwide, leading to requests for it to be available in versions for concert band and other smaller ensembles – these were especially desirable in the USA.

Finally, in 1990, the year of my retirement from the Cathedral, Barry took the somewhat hazardous step of moving his operation to Ely and opening the Arthur Wills Music Shop. Though demonstrating a touching faith in my compositional future, this was obviously unsustainable as a main commercial enterprise, and was necessarily underpinned by a more profitable stationary division. It 'ceased trading' in October 2003, and as Barry had previously decided to close his catalogue of five thousand pieces to new works after the year 2000 the future of his business was already beginning to look somewhat less than secure.

In 1978 Elizabeth and Raymond Chenault (Organists and Choral-directors from All Saints Church in Atlanta) had asked me for a duet for their growing repertoire of such unusual pieces. I wrote for them Toccata for Two – and they premiered this work at Washington Cathedral on September 30th 1979. This was my programme note included in the CD of Duets they recorded for Gothic Label in 1990:

My first idea for this commission was a set of variations on the plainchant 'Dies Irae'. Then I decided to write a purely abstract piece in which the musical material and its development would be the sole concern of the composer, performers and the audience. The title chosen, apart from its pleasantly alliterative sound, merely designates the music as a keyboard and pedal piece for duetists. In this sense the music is about the exploitation of the resources of a large modern organ and the technique of two virtuoso performers. Nevertheless, on reflection, the initial idea of the dance of humanity, as pictured in the apocalyptic works of such painters as Breugel and Bosch, may well have exerted a below-the-surface influence on the music, and this in turn may help the listener to enjoy the violent eruptions in both rhythm and sonority which are such an important feature of the music.

A review by Levin Houston in 1983 – The Free Lance-Star, Fredericksburg, Virginia – includes the following comments: "An impression I received on the earlier occasion (the premiere in 1979) is strengthened: this complexly rhythmic work makes the organ sound like a full symphony orchestra.

Much more than in the other duo-numbers, each player sounds like one of the orchestral groups in an orchestra, and, generally, the players can be clearly separated. Despite the number's occasional dissonance and complex rhythmic plan, the unfamiliar listener has more to grasp hold of than is usual in extended works for the organ, either as a solo, or duo instrument." The following year, two of my Improvisation Organ Class students at the RAM – Jeremy Allen and Alan Childs – included it in a concert they gave in Ely Cathedral.

Without a doubt the first performance of my 'An English Requiem' at the Academy on March 5th 1981 was arguably the most important event in the whole of my composing career – certainly the most moving for me.

My mother died in 1971 and I then felt the need to compose a work which would adequately express my feelings about the loss of both parents; my father's demise in 1950 was at first emotionally enshrined in a very early organ work – Elegy (1955) – the second to be composed after the Rhapsody. This was a deeply felt piece, but once I had envisaged a large-scale non-liturgical work dedicated to both of my parents and readily found the 'right' texts, I knew that the Elegy could be diverted to an Ely character – the former cathedral organist Dr Marmaduke Conway who had recently died and that was published firstly by Novello in 1961.

I planned 'An English Requiem' as a choral symphony in four movements. Brahms' 'A German Requiem' was an obvious model for a non-liturgical Requiem, but he chose Biblical texts rather than liturgical, whereas I wanted to use poems of great depth that would express my personal thoughts on this most emotional issue. A choral-symphony in the traditional four movements was what I envisaged, with orchestra, chorus and baritone and soprano soloists. The orchestration was perhaps influenced by the large-scale composition which had preceded it – the organ concerto with strings and timps. For the Requiem I included also a harp and two pianos. The choice of texts was quickly decided; two poems by Dylan Thomas – 'Do not go gentle into that good night' and his 'And Death shall have no dominion' frame, Donne's 'Death be not proud', and Shakespeare's 'Fear no more the heat o' the sun' as the expressive core of the work. With texts of this superlative quality the music practically wrote itself – but the first performance was delayed until some ten years later. There were two reasons for this; one was that following my organ concerto's first performance at the Nottingham Festival in 1971, where it was well received, there was a possibility that the Requiem might also be premiered there, but this was not to be. The second reason was that the work on completion had such an emotional hold on me that I could not readily contemplate hearing it. It wasn't broadcast by the BBC, or (as yet) recorded, as was the case later with my 'Fenlands' Suite, but it was performed before an audience of students and professors who could be expected to be quite unforgiving in their reaction to a Professor's composition if they thought it was a 'duff' piece. The piece was ten years old and I suppose I must have mentioned its existence to Noel Cox, who conducted the RAM Choral concerts. He asked to see a score, and then said that he would do it if I would provide the vocal scores and orchestral parts. It was an ideal venue for the premiere of the work, as it didn't depend upon a paying audience to finance the enterprise, and the rehearsal time available was quite adequate. But because of its intensely personal character, and also the fact that it was the first time I had experienced the work in any realisation in its full sonority, I was already emotionally tense and 'on edge'. The first half of the concert began with Alessandro Scarlatti's 'Dixit Dominus' and this was followed by John Ireland's 'Concertino Pastorale for string orchestra'.

After the Interval Noel Cox informed the audience of the untimely death of Gordon Greene, a greatly esteemed piano Professor at the Academy, on the previous evening. "We are all very sad," he said, "And we wish to dedicate this performance to his memory." A few technical imperfections did not mar a riveting performance from all concerned, which shook me to the core, and even then I was unprepared for the storm of applause which greeted the close of the work. Mary and I were seated in the gallery, and I naturally thought I should hurry downstairs and into the Hall to get to the platform before the applause began to lessen. No need – the audience reception exceeded all my expectations, and the thunderous 'feet on floor' was even more shaking.

The work is scored for soprano and baritone soloists and chorus, string orchestra, timpani, harp and piano duet and organ. This was the programme note I provided:

An English Requiem was composed in 1971 and is dedicated to the memory of my parents. It is closely related to the symphonic song-cycle conceptions of Mahler, and the four movements are designed as follows:

1. Allegro moderato. 'Do not go gentle into that good night' (Dylan Thomas). This is mainly for the baritone soloist, with the chorus work confined to two repeated phrases of a refrain character.

2. Allegro ritmico. 'Death, be not proud' (John Donne). There is no solo writing in this, the scherzo movement of the symphony.

3. Molto adagio. 'Fear no more the heat o' the sun' (William Shakespeare). This is mainly for chorus, with the baritone soloist reiterating the phrase 'Fear no more' at the close of each verse. The soprano soloist is introduced in the coda at the words 'And renowned be thy grave', which serves to prepare for the important role this voice is to play in the finale.

4. Allegro. 'And death shall have no dominion' (Dylan Thomas) Soprano solo and chorus. This movement is strongly rooted around a C pedal but in the last few bars it slips down a semitone on to a B major chord, recalling the tonality of the first movement. The idea of this is not to

establish any resemblance to a classical tonal scheme but rather to link up with the first movement in a way suggestive of a circular view of life and death; the recurring and vacillating attitudes to death we all share; grief at the loss of loved ones; a desire to cling to life; hope for immortality; acceptance and some measure of consolation; final assurance in the face of physical dissolution. The poems I have used bring out these ideas in their thought and imagery gloriously well and there are many correspondences between them which only fully revealed themselves to me after I had composed the music.

I had several letters from professors (never an audience inclined to excessive enthusiasm!) commenting on the performance: "I was very impressed with it, it came over as a strong work. I am sure that it will get many performances in the future." (Paul Patterson); "I must write to say how wonderful the evening was yesterday. Your Requiem is a marvellous work, and I found the performance deeply moving – a real experience." (Marjorie Thomas); "What a marvellous experience you gave us last night with your 'English Requiem'. I was absolutely thrilled and deeply moved by it. Its musical imagery is most compelling and its beauty quite magical." (Margater Hubicki); John Gardner was equally enthusiastic – "You scored something of a triumph last Thursday in the Duke's Hall. We were riveted by the elemental power of your music and enchanted by its moment of tender reflectiveness." He went on to disagree with my reference to Mahler's symphonic song-cycles, saying 'It has nothing to do with the symphonic structures of Mahler' – but I said 'symphonic song-cycles' – not symphonic structures. But as a fellow composer on the staff of the Academy I was greatly touched by his words of appreciation. One other letter was especially appreciated by me; the soprano soloist, Elizabeth Anne Stuart, wrote – "I felt very honoured in being able to take part in the first of what will be many performances of your work. I found it both a moving and invaluable experience, and look forward to hearing or participating in many more performances!" Sir Anthony Lewis offered to approach Novellos about its publication, saying – "It certainly should go the round of the Festivals." Novello did agree to take the work, but only on hire. One problem with the piece is that the accompaniment is so orchestrally conceived that it cannot be convincingly realised on either organ or piano. It would make its point without any vocal participation, and perhaps it should be made available as another 'Sinfonia da Requiem'!

Harrison Oxley was present at that first performance, and sufficiently impressed to programme it with his St Edmundsbury Choral Society later that year in the Cathedral, Bury St Edmunds, together with music by Elgar, Vaughan Williams and Parry. David Robinson programmed the Requiem with his Harrow Philharmonic Choir in March 1983, together with Handel's 'Zadok the Priest' and Haydn's 'Nelson Mass'.

Peter Moorse with his London Cantata Choir did a performance to honour my 60th birthday in St Margaret's Church, Westminster on 30th June 1987 and excerpts from the rehearsal were later featured in an Anglia TV programme about my life and work. The other work featured was Purcell's 'My heart is inditing'. I attended a performance by the Finchley Choral Society in March 1989 conducted by Michael Hamm, in a programme which also included the 'Serenade for Strings' by Tchaikovsky and Schubert's 'Mass in G'.

In the meantime Sir Anthony Lewis had retired in 1982 and David Lumsden was appointed Principal in his place. Possibly to some extent because of the success of the Requiem the previous year, I was asked whether I would be prepared to apply in order to be the Academy's internal candidate for this prestigious position. Just as in the case of Trinity College a few years earlier I knew that it was not what I wanted, but it was flattering to be asked, and I attended for interview at a hotel within walking distance of the Academy. David Lumsden was a distinguished Principal of the Royal Scottish Academy of Music and Drama in Glasgow, and his appointment to the RAM was a virtual foregone conclusion – and a considerable relief to me!

Commissions of many kind continued to come my way, and looking back at this point it is interesting to see that over the years commissions account for much of my compositional activities. Peter Smith, Director of Music at Bishop Stopford's School, Enfield, asked me for a piece based on their School Hymn 'Marienlyst' so I produced a Toccata-Finale on that melody, which work I premiered in a recital at the School on 1st May 1984. The following year David Robinson from the RAM, asked me for a piece suitable to be played at a dedication Service of a new Tuba stop on the organ of St George's Church, Headstone, Harrow on 2nd June 1985. For this occasion I produced 'Praise Him In The Sound Of The Trumpet' (Or Tuba, Or Whatever) and for that I had the 1940s 'Big Band' sound of Glenn Miller and 'That Old Black Magic' in mind.

My 60th birthday year of 1986 was observed with several events, both local and national. In the September issue of *Musical Times* Michael Musgrave contributed a substantial three-page article – Arthur Wills at 60 – which was both thorough and perceptive, coming as it did from a noted scholar and writer. Concerts of music by Professors at the Academy performed by students were always encouraging events, and the one in my 60th birthday year was of especial note. On Friday 14th March a programme at the RAM included a performance of my 'Sonata for Piano' (1984) by Adrian Sutcliffe. This work was repeated by Adrian at a more significant event in 1988, at the British Music Information Centre at Stratford Place in Central London. This concert was entirely devoted to my music, but again performed by RAM students and Professors. The programme began with 'Love's Torment' (Four Elizabethen Love Songs) performed by Andrew Watts (Countertenor) and Fiona Richardson (Guitar), followed by Adrian Sutcliffe playing the 'Piano Sonata' (1984). After the Interval we heard the solo Trumpet piece 'Joie de Vivre' played by Traugott Forschner, and the concert concluded with 'The Dark Lady' (Eight Sonnets by William Shakespeare) sung by Mark Wildman (Baritone) with Ian Ledingham (Piano). As an unsolicited encore I rounded off the concert with the piano version of 'Etheldreda Rag'. Then in May 1992, my last year at the Academy there was a Concert of Chamber Music with Guitar which included several of my works: two movements from the 'Concerto Lirico' played by Mark Ashford, Gina Goldsmith, Daniel Kirsch and Anthony Phillips, followed by the 'Suite Africana' played by Fabio Zanon, and 'A Woman in Love' with Marianne Anderson and Julian Cowie. Finally, a group of organists from the RAM played a concert of my organ music in the St Marylebone Church. Two performances have stayed in my mind – Huw Williams played my 'Sonata' and Colm Carey 'Tongues of Fire'.

But undoubtedly the most interesting event of my final few years at both the Cathedral and Academy was a feature on my life and music in the *Folio series of Arts* programmes televised by Anglia Television Ltd based in Norwich. I had been impressed by several of these films, and it did seem to be an excellent way to further interest in my work both in Ely and London, so it was very gratifying when the producers agreed to go ahead with this project. The programme was eventually televised at its usual time of 22.30 on 14th January 1988. The planning for this project began in January 1987, and the idea was to cover as many aspects of my activities as possible in both Ely and London. One composition I wanted to highlight was the 'Piano Sonata' (1984) which Adrian Sutcliffe had premiered at the RAM. He had teaching connections with the William Ellis School in Highgate, and suggested that we could do a session on the operatic treatment of the Orwell book, and its relationship to the Sonata, which would interest the boys who had already studied the novel in some detail. This we did, and Adrian also expressed his willingness to take part in the Anglia TV project.

The week beginning 16th March was concerned with the work of Olivier Messiaen at the RAM, and he adjudicated the annual competition performance prize for organists, held at St Pancras Church on the 19th. I was introduced to the great man, and both of us were somewhat nonplussed by the experience; he was diminutive in stature and I am built on a somewhat larger scale – I thought that he looked as though he had been asked to shake hands with the devil incarnate! Anglia TV were visiting the RAM in the afternoon to look over a couple of rooms for the Folio programme, and I was needed to be on hand to advise and book availability for the filming day on the 26th. This included my B.Mus. lecture (on chromatic harmony this week) and Fiona Richardson in a performance of The Year of the Tiger for guitar, and Adrian Sutcliffe playing excerpts from the Piano Sonata (1984). I commented on their performances and they returned the compliment with their view of my music! Further preparation for the programme took place on 2nd April when the use of The Old Sacristy sitting room (where I talked in general about my career) and the music room in The Almonry (where I improvised on the piano, and talked in some detail about the process of composition) was under consideration. On the 9th I recorded organ pieces for Anglia TV – Etheldreda Rag (scenes from the Town) and Tongues of Fire (organ playing, and talk about the organ and the music) with scenes from the casework and the Cathedral interior. One of the most important features of the Folio programme was a performance of my 'An English Requiem' to be given at St Margaret's Church, Westminster at 7.30 p.m. on June 30th in honour of my 60th birthday. For obvious reasons this public performance could not be filmed, so it was agreed that the rehearsal should take place in St John's Wood Church in the morning with myself present, and then after lunch attending at King's College for an M.Mus. meeting, I was able to attend the performance in the evening. This rehearsal for the concert was given the most filming time necessary for its prominent role in the whole programme. It necessitated some tension between Peter Moorse, in his anxiety over the rehearsal time available, and the Anglia crew in getting the shots they needed for the film – a situation not easily resolved! But finally an acceptable resolution was reached. The scherzo-like second movement 'Death, be not proud' was used at the outset of the programme, and the penultimate movement 'Fear no more the heat o' the sun' made a most moving and fitting end to the film.

The following morning after that concert I needed an early start as I was booked to play an organ concert at Bryanston School that evening. When I look through my diaries I am frequently astonished at the hectic lifestyle I chose to pursue. I suppose that it was all so greatly enjoyable that I hardly noticed at the time.

There was an extended sequence with the Choristers in the Practice Room rehearsing 'Caedmon', my Cantata about the boy who thought that he couldn't sing, and three movements from the Symphonic Suite: 'The Fenlands' – 'The Vikings', 'Wicken Fen', and the 'March – 'City of Ely', using the Hyperion recording with appropriate pictorial images in each case.

I was well satisfied with the resulting end-product, as was Michael Edwards, the Folio producer, who made this comment: "We were especially pleased that you were able to pinpoint so many elements for inclusion. Television audiences are a fickle and restless lot, and expect to be ushered about from one thing to another at an alarming rate. For them to be left wanting more is what one hopes the reaction will be."

A week later on July 8th, I played 'The Fenlands' Suite with the Brighouse and Rastrick Band in Peterborough Cathedral. This had to be done on an electronic organ as the Peterborough organ is high pitched, and cannot be used with wind instruments. (The Ely organ was slightly flat in pitch, but this was corrected in the 1975 rebuild.) In this concert I also played Sibelius' 'Finlandia' with the band – an exciting experience. And the week after that something quite new – an American TV Christmas programme with Jesse Norman and the American Boy Choir, trained by James Litton. Our Choristers were invited to be part of this programme, as was I as the Organist with the orchestra and adult professional Choir, but it was more a matter of the cathedral being used as a background rather than our own programme. Of course the temperature was baking, but it had to look like Christmas had come early in the Cathedral. But Jesse was charming with the Choristers, and though the programme was swathed in sentimentality one felt 'better here than somewhere else'.

The Ely Choristers were featured in a *Blue Peter* programme in December 1989. The Advent Procession music was an important aspect, as well as a Chorister rehearsal. As always, the producer wanted me to find an excuse for a Choirmasterly tantrum with one of the boys. It frequently happens without effort in the normal run of things, but it's something I find very difficult to simulate. (These days it's probably illegal anyway.)

Chapter 6

Choirs and Places (Problems and rewards)

Dean Hankey retired in 1969 and this was clearly the end of an era for Ely. The Chapter that had welcomed him in 1951 had of course long disappeared, but he was still the only Dean I had worked for; yet during his long reign I had known three Bishops, and was to know two more – just! Ely was unusual in having its Bishop's Throne on the right-hand side of the Presbytery which of course meant that the Dean's stall was on the left hand side. So the Choir Decani stalls (of the Dean) and Cantoris stalls (of the Precentor) necessarily reflected this positioning. The very structure of cathedral music reflects this architectural and liturgical feature, though in modern times only in the antiphonal singing of the Psalms. The music of Tye, Tallis and their successors, in settings of the Canticles especially, demonstrates this antiphonal singing, and also proves that there must have been two altos on each side with the frequent use of five-part textures in alternation. Provincial cathedrals often have provision for only three Lay Clerks on each side, certainly in the weekday services, and this means that in five-part settings the use of altos from both sides loses the true contrast of antiphony.

Anthony (and Joanna) Trollope's books based on cathedral life largely concern themselves with the political aspects of cathedral activities, as does Hugh Walpole's *The Cathedral*. Naturally the cathedral organist is in a very advantageous position to observe much of this power-play, and it adds considerably to the interest of such an occupation. I was not expected to attend the monthly Chapter Meeting during most of Hankey's time, and there was no weekly Staff

Meeting until the late seventies. In those early years only one mildly amusing spat interested me. It concerned the presence (or not) of a Sanctus bell in the Sanctuary. I'm not sure who wanted the bell and who didn't, but its presence and regular removal created some little diversion. But the Cambridge Divinity Faculty was giving much thought to theological developments, and Bishop John Robinson's polemic 'Honest to God' was now in print. I was rarely present for the Mattins sermon, but was informed by a Lay Clerk that on one Sunday Canon Bernard Pawley had inveighed against the book's de-mytholising stance and had been followed the week later by Canon Geoffrey Lampe (the Ely Professor of Divinity at Cambridge) who had thoroughly welcomed it. None of this is in the least surprising of course – Christianity has been dogged by dispute and division from its earliest times, and this is certainly also the case today and would be surprising if it was not always thus.

Christopher Stead, who followed Canon Lampe as the Ely Professor summed up Dean Hankey's stance thus: "Hankey was a rigorous Anglo-Catholic who had no qualms in imposing the observances he valued. His aim was a dignified act of worship in the medieval tradition; those who liked it were welcome, but otherwise there was little attempt to attract a congregation from the city."

Once Bishop Roberts had settled in he clearly felt the need for fresh thinking about the role of the cathedral and made several appointments to the Chapter which he thought would aid this process. A notable example was Peter Moore who had been Vicar of Pershore Abbey, and was to be followed there by Christopher Campling. I had known Peter since Canterbury days – he was a Minor Canon of the Cathedral, he taught in the Choir School and also occasionally lectured we College students. One of his remarks has stayed in my mind to the effect that by the end of the century England could easily have become an atheistic country – this prediction in 1949! Peter's effect on Ely was quite electrifying, as I had anticipated, and was no doubt what Bishop Roberts had hoped for.

Dean Hankey was approaching 80 and his regime was to be followed by many changes. Some I regretted; after all my first years at Ely were concerned with the 1662 Prayer Book and its usage with Sunday Mattins followed by the Eucharist as primarily an exercise for the Chapter and Choir – monastic rather than parochial. The Cathedral had no Parish to minister to – this was of course the function of St Mary's Parish Church, just a short walk away from the West Door across Palace Green. But from 1566 a Parish of Holy Trinity was established in the Lady Chapel, supplanting an earlier Holy Cross Parish Church on the north side of the nave, and this usage lasted until 1938. Certainly the accelerating decline of church attendance after 1945 could not have persuaded the then Chapter of the need for a more congregational style of worship, in an agricultural community still blessed with a great number of churches.

From 1970, with the introduction of the new Series A and B Service Books, Ely gradually changed its ethos from a quasi-monastic haven of plainchant and polyphony to a widely embracing parochial-style institution with a congregation of 'habitual worshippers' leading some commentators to equate this with 'habitual criminals' – of course they jested! In an entrepreneurial spirit Peter Moore introduced a new version of the Psalter which the latest scholarship claimed to be more accurate than Coverdale's version. Hankey demurred mildly, but he was on the point of retirement and the Chapter prevailed. It lasted for some while, but the Prayer Book version was eventually reinstated – in the course of time forceful beauty will always oust pedantry – 'Even at the Waters of Meribah' – Bah! But Peter did introduce the idea of 'Welcome to Ely Cathedral' for concerts and special events and this outreach has proved very beneficial.

The last Sunday Mattins and Eucharist was sung on Christmas Day 1968. The following Sunday saw the introduction of The Liturgy with its vestigial remnant of Mattins – psalmody in an opening procession, an Old Testament Lesson and a Canticle, in this case the Te Deum. I had been involved in much discussion with the Chapter about the loss of the sung Mattins psalmody and also the retention of the Mattins canticle repertoire – and also the length of the sermon; it will be ten minutes Peter Moore informed me. It was – for a time, but of course I realised that it wouldn't be left at that length for very long. The end of an era – yes, but in some ways a victory for Hankey's Anglo-Catholic tradition. From this time onwards the main Sunday morning service would be a celebration of the Eucharist – nationwide. With a ten-minute sermon we got it into an hour – nowadays, with numerous pauses and twenty-minute length sermons, one and a half hours is the norm – sometimes a truly enervating experience!

Hankey left the Cathedral in mid-November 1969 – truly the end of an era. He passed on to me (for £20) a most elegant settee acquired during his time in charge of the English Church in Mentone. It was a 19th century copy of the Louis XIV period and still graces our sitting room. He also sold me a useful corner cupboard for £3, and on my retirement from the cathedral I sold it on to my successor for a somewhat larger sum. Hankey and I had maintained an excellent relationship – I recall only one contretemps, when my Voluntary after a Sunday Evensong held up a family christening I had not previously been told about. It was the Liszt Fantasia and Fugue on B.A.C.H. and I was not prepared to truncate this on a Verger's request, even though originating from the Dean. A meeting the following morning (best suit!) cleared this up reasonably satisfactorily. I must confess to one deception though – in the early sixties the organ blowing system was becoming both extremely noisy and unreliable. As ever the Chapter was short of money, but eventually they agreed to fund Cuthbert Harrison's very reasonable quotation. Cuthbert and I got on very well, and I was emboldened to ask him, while the organ was out of action, whether he could liven up the reeds on the Great, Pedal and Solo organs. He replied that he couldn't provide open shallots, but that he was prepared to re-voice them at no extra cost. The organ when reinstated was quite startling in its fiery tutti, and somewhat louder in overall effect than before. Dean Hankey commented on this, but I merely pointed out that the organ was now getting more wind from the renovated bellows! He appeared satisfied with this and that was the end of it.

Compositions associated with Hankey's last years included 'The Carol of King Canute' to be sung under the West Tower at the Christmas Eve Carol Procession, which sets words by Dean Stubbs from the beginning of the 20th century, and plays a significant role in 'The Vikings' from the Symphonic Suite for Brass Band and Organ 'The Fenlands'. For organ solo I composed the five movement Christmas Meditations – something of an homage to Messiaen. It was pleasing to receive a commission from St Mary's, Warwick – a Te Deum for unison voices; and for the Ely Choristers I composed a set of Evening Canticles. Following on from Michael Dudman in 1964 my Assistants were firstly Anthony Greening and then Roger Judd. Tony was a most gifted musician, but somewhat unstable at times, and Roger went on to St Michael's, Tenbury. Tony produced a useful booklet on the Organists of Ely and, more importantly, significant editions of the music of John Amner (Organist of Ely 1610–1641). An interesting local organ student at this time was Gerald Gifford from Cottenham. He was blessed with a very fluent technique and after becoming an articled pupil for a year became my Assistant from 1973 to 1978, becoming also Director of Music at the King's School for much of this time. One problem was becoming more pressing at this time and for many years after – the number of Choristers affordable by the Chapter. At the beginning of the change to the provision of boys holding scholarships to the King's School in 1949, when Sidney Campbell and I arrived at the Cathedral, their number was sustained at twenty. But soon after Michael Howard's arrival their number was reduced to eighteen because of inflationary pressures on the fees charged by the School throughout the 1960s and 1970s. This was an ominous situation and over the next ten years or so the problems worsened until we were down to fourteen boys on full chorister scholarships. Then it was that we attempted to keep up the numbers with boys already in the School who could demonstrate some singing ability, and for this they received a free instrumental lesson. It was a long time before matters improved, but the services were still well provided for musically during this perilous period.

On Saturday the 9th May, 1970 the Venerable Michael Carey was installed as Dean. The music sung included the anthem by Christopher Tye 'O come ye servants of the Lord', Parry's 'I was glad', and the Canticles setting which Amner dedicated to his Dean – 'Caesar's Service'. This last was an interesting choice, as just about this time Gerald Knight had commissioned me to write a Communion Service for Congregation, Choir and Organ, which soon became known in the Cathedral as 'Carey's Service!' Gerald had asked for this piece in response to clergy requests for settings with an opportunity for the congregation to join in. This was not applicable to the Ely situation except when the King's School Boarders attended the Sunday morning Eucharist at the beginning and end of each term. In fact they never did sing along with the Choir, and I suppose it was unreasonable to expect them to do so. Michael Carey was a friendly and supportive Dean, but strong in his belief that the Ely services could not return to the monastic ethos of the previous era. He could get quite heated over some matters under discussion, as Paddy Bailey reported to me after a number of Lay Clerks had asked for a reversion to the former Sunday liturgical arrangements as used in Dean Hankey's time. As Michael Carey had been appointed precisely to change that regime I could have advised them that they were wasting their time in trying to negotiate its return. He was a spiritual man, not at all austere in Hankey's mode, and as he explained to me – 'really a country parson with a care for people'. Yet he revelled in Ely's history, generally managing to skate over the desecrations of the two Cromwell's – 16th century Thomas and 17th century Oliver – with the emollient comment – "It's what men do when they get angry!" This history was high on his agenda with the year 1973 marking the thirteen hundredth anniversary of the foundation of the religious house on this site by Saint Etheldreda in 673 – a mixed community of monks and nuns.

For the Annual Diocesan Choirs Service I composed 'Let all men everywhere rejoice' with words specially written by the Precentor Raymond Gilbert. This was structured as a palindrome with the first and last verse sung by all the choirs and the congregation, two and four by the Cathedral Choir and the Diocesan Choirs, and three by the Cathedral Choir alone. In addition to the organ it was scored for obligato brass and percussion. This same year saw the composition of 'The Child for Today' a sequence of Five Carols with an introduction and coda for organ solo. The Precentor Raymond Gilbert also wrote texts for two of these carols, both in an astringent vein which looked at the start of the 'consumer Christmas' and its attendant disastrous influence in a suitably mocking fashion.

Dean Carey had a great love for Choral Evensong and when taking visitors on a tour of the cathedral, and so arriving at the Choir he would say, "And this is the Workshop of the Cathedral!" An excellent way of describing it, but thinking of the daily Evensong I much prefer the way it was done in the Hankey/Carey era rather than in today's style. There was no overt welcome to visitors, it was done as an Office in which visitors were obviously welcome, but not needed. It began with the Preces and went on to the Psalms for the Day (all of them) and the Clergy and Congregation stood throughout. After the first Lesson – no irritating pause – the Ely speciality was the Office Hymn sung to plainchant, and immediately followed hot-foot by the Magnificat. Dean Carey inspired (the best word for his participation) the composition of my Evening Canticles on Plainsong Tones.

The celebrations for the Thirteen Hundredth Anniversary of the Cathedral Foundation by St Etheldreda in 673 occasioned some tensions in the preparations thereof. My relationship with Peter Moore had cooled somewhat over the passage of time since his arrival, and the idea of a commission for a work from Benjamin Britten had been discussed – no problem with that obviously. But Britten declined this commission being, as he pointed out, much too involved at this time with his new operatic project 'Death in Venice'. It so happened that the Choir had been asked to give a short concert of music by Christopher Tye in one of the venues in a 'church crawl' (as they were known) which would be recorded by the BBC Overseas Service. This was a programme item in the 1971 Aldeburgh Festival to take place on June 25th, and it was an early afternoon performance. Obviously we all wondered whether Britten would attend this event. I was somewhat apprehensive, as I had not attended any Festival in Aldeburgh at any time – mainly because it always coincided with a very busy time in the Cathedral Calendar – St Etheldreda on the 23rd, John the Baptist on the 24th and Petertide Ordination on the following Sunday, as well as my London commitments. Shortly before the concert Britten did appear, accompanied by Peter Pears. He didn't seem entirely at ease I thought, but he greeted me amicably enough and we had a brief discussion about Peter Moore's idea of a commission from him. He ruled it out at once on the grounds of his involvement in his new opera – "You should do it!" he said. And I do think that he meant that, but equally

I was sure that I would not get the commission. Peter Moore was great friends with Alan Wicks, who was much involved with Alan Ridout, the then composer in residence at Canterbury Cathedral – Ridout got the commission!

Richard Butt always produced and recorded as many of the Aldeburgh Festival Concerts as were desired for the BBC coverage of this prestigious event, and I soon realised that this was one of the artistic highlights of his year. He would talk freely of the 'behind the scenes' atmosphere, and was illuminating on the perhaps surprising sensitivities of the two leading personalities. One instance has stayed in my mind – quite late in life Britten became very involved with the Cantatas of J.S. Bach, perhaps not surprisingly, given the dramatic intensity of Bach's solo writing in these works, both sacred and secular. Butt was recording one of these performances (or perhaps merely balancing a run-through prior to the concert) and on emerging from the recording van ventured the comment – "That recitative!" Consternation from Pears and Britten when they took this as a critical comment on their performance, rather than on Bach's overwhelming mastery of dramatic word-setting and the impact of their interpretation. But easily misunderstood – recordings of all kinds are an unnerving experience, however much you steel yourself – but I suppose that it helps to avoid a routine performance.

Dean Carey retired at the end of the Summer Term in 1982, after firmly establishing the new Sunday Eucharist order of Service, and we awaited the announcement of his successor with some apprehension. His successor Allan Shaw was Installed on December 4th after a comparatively brief interregnum of only four months. He had been Canon Precentor at Hereford Cathedral with a considerable interest in all the Arts, so that boded well from my point of view. Before his Installation he heard a BBC Evensong broadcast of Choral Evensong from Ely, and wrote me a congratulatory note on that. But it became evident in the course of 1983 that not all was well with his relations with the Ely Chapter, although I found him to be very sympathetic, supportive – and the only Dean in my experience to attend the occasional Choristers' morning rehearsal – make what you like of that! But undoubtedly, the highlight of that year for me is succinctly summed up in this excerpt from *The Friends of Ely Cathedral Year Book*:

'To witness Dr Arthur Wills rendered speechless is a rare privilege, and one not to be missed. It was not missed by more than 150 people on the evening of Saturday 25 June, St Etheldreda's Day, when they gathered in the Crush Hall of the King's School at Ely to help him celebrate the 25th Anniversary of his appointment as Director of Music at Ely Cathedral. The only person who knew nothing about the celebration was Dr Wills himself. His wife, Mary, had said she was taking him out to dinner with family and friends – after the Choristers had made a small presentation. When the party appeared around the corner by the Cathedral South Entrance, spotters in the Dining Hall called for silence. It was broken by an enormous cheer when Arthur and his party entered the Crush Hall. His jaw dropped for, oh, at least a couple of seconds, before he recovered his composure and joined in the fun. Then Mike Banyard announced the reason for all the secrecy. "Arthur Wills, Director of Music at Ely Cathedral for twenty-five years TODAY – THIS IS YOUR LIFE." There followed tributes from around the world, the climax of the evening almost brought the house down – Psalm 178, a parody of Psalm 78, written and conducted by Ordinand Bill Barnett to music selected and specially written for the occasion by Tony Ransome. Whilst it is far too long to reprint here in full, the Gloria gives a hint of the spirit of the piece: Glory be to Arthur, and to the Choir, and to the Dean and Chapter. As he was in the beginning, he is, and probably ever shall be. Wills without end, Amen.'

Such an occasion is humbling to the nth degree, but apparently I managed to say a few words which made some kind of sense and appropriateness to this quite remarkable event. Just a little time later I had occasion to write to Bishop Peter Walker, and in his response he alluded to my words thus:

"And thank you, while I have the chance to say this, for the splendidly personal, (and serious, which was what was so good about it, if I may say so) speech which you made on that special occasion a fortnight ago. It was in fact altogether a memorable evening."

Sadly, Dean Shaw, for a variety of reasons, decided to retire at the end of this year. The Prime Minister's Ecclesiastical Secretary, whose business it was to deal with Church appointments, came down to Ely to discuss with the Chapter and other significant people in the life of the Cathedral, the finding of the right man to succeed Dean Shaw. For the first time in my work at Ely Cathedral I was asked for my views on this subject, and at the conclusion of our discussion I was somewhat startled to be asked "Do you know anyone suitable you could suggest?" It so happened that a short time before I had been chatting with Christopher Campling, Minor Canon at Ely in the late 1950s who was at that time Archdeacon of Droitwich. He had – quite light-heartedly I thought – said, "Do you know of anywhere looking for a Dean, Arthur!?" I didn't, just laughed it off, and promptly forgot about it. But faced with a request for a possible name by this representative of the Prime Minister – there it was. Sometime later I was more than a little intrigued to read an announcement of Christopher's appointment to be Dean – of Ripon Cathedral! Ely though still languished waiting for an announcement. Then it came as a truly marvellous choice – William J. Patterson, Archdeacon of Wisbech and Vicar of Wisbech St Mary.

The three Deans I worked with for longer than a year or so all found it required of them to launch and lead a substantial Appeal. Dean Hankey restored the Octagon – the most original and striking feature of the building. Dean Carey had to deal with the West Tower and the Organ restorations, and Dean Patterson was responsible for beginning the complete restoration of the whole building, a mammoth task eventually largely completed in triumph by Dean Michael Higgins.

Bill Patterson was the last Dean I worked with, and he had been a student at the Ely Theological College in the early 1950s. So he of course knew the Hankey tradition very well, and to a large extent managed the considerable feat of uniting the best of that with the most useful possibilities of the new liturgies. He greatly regretted the excesses of the Second Vatican Council and its effect on the Catholic Church, especially in France – his spirited wife Elisabeth was French, and they would normally use that language domestically. He was greatly helped by Canon Dennis Green, who had worked with the two previous Deans, and was now Treasurer. Both men saw that beyond any Appeal outcome the finances of the Cathedral needed to be put on something more than a 'hand-to-mouth' basis. Ely thus became the first cathedral to charge admission to its visitors – not for Services, or individual desire for private prayer (that was always available in the St Catherine's Chapel, near the West Door of the Cathedral).

The improvement in income made an increase in the value of Chorister scholarships possible and the standard of entries for the Voice Trials greatly improved the boys' efficiency, while the provision of work in the cathedral Chapter Office for some of the Lay Clerks performed much the same function for the men's section of the Choir. One outcome of the Appeal launch was a new anthem composition noticed in the *Cambridge Evening News* as follows: (Friday, January 8, 1988). After mention of my featuring in an Anglia TV *Folio* series programme the writer continues: "Not all Dr Wills's works have had TV airings. Platform 10 at Liverpool Street Station was the venue for the premiere of 'The Spiritual Railway' a work composed, performed and published within 12 days in aid of the Ely Cathedral Restoration Appeal. The words of the work are taken from a tombstone in the South Porch of the cathedral which the composer had always wished to set to music, and for which Liverpool Street Station provided the perfect backdrop."

The last of the Lay Clerks I knew from 1949 onwards had retired by the end of the 1960s and these were gradually replaced by a rather different breed of comparatively youngish men. Many were still in their twenties and could readily obtain work in local schools as music teachers; obviously their efficiency as musicians, both vocally and in perception and sight-reading was of enormous benefit to the professionalism of the choral results which now became much more readily obtainable. In 1973 Chandos offered to record a programme to be entitled 'Choral Favourites' – clearly intended to be of some popular appeal and with the use of some arrangements by Humphris. These included Bizet's Agnus Dei and Brother James' Air – both admittedly extremely effective. This LP proved to be very appealing, with great staying power – frequently used by Richard Baker in a Sunday evening popular series of 'sacred' recordings programmes. Many items on it were transferred to two CDs, involving also contributions from the Choirs of Westminster Abbey and Worcester Cathedral. Ely's participation included Mendelssohn's 'Hear my prayer' with its even more fetching second part with treble solo – 'O for the wings of a dove'. (When I arrived at a church in Philadelphia USA to prepare for an organ concert, I was greeted by the organist with this LP, offering it to be autographed!) I was also glad to be able to include my 'The Carol of King Canute' – an Ely-specific piece, ten years later to be included in the first movement – 'The Vikings' – of my Symphonic Suite: 'The Fenlands'. In its turn ten years later this Suite was to feature in an LP of

Music for Brass Band and organ on Ted Perry's recently established Hyperion label.

The quality of the fresh (in every sense of the word!) Lay Clerks brought with it some rather less attractive features, notably a post-sixties distinct lack of deference to their elders and betters! One had to learn to live with this – after all they had all attended Teacher Training Colleges which did not exactly encourage 'toeing the line' as a respectable way of life. Silly institutions! Girlfriends were frequently in evidence at Services and elsewhere – some more decorative than others of course, and a tendency to occasional pranks. When the copies of Howard in D Evening Canticles mysteriously disappeared I immediately thought of the usual suspects, but mature thought perhaps put a Cleric in the frame – Michael's somewhat astringent idiom did not always go down well with either the Lay Clerks or the Chapter, whereas I relished it, and wanted to keep his name on the Music lists. Then nearing fifty, I was not the most tolerant of choirmasters, but nevertheless realised that some adjustment of attitude needed to be made. There were a few incidents that amused me – during the Lesson readings at Evensong I sat next to the Altos in the Lay Clerks stalls. During one Second Lesson the sentence occurred 'Does your Teacher pay the tax?' – "Doesn't he just!" came from my neighbour who was a teacher typically trying to get on the housing ladder in the early seventies.

This was also a time when my output of compositions, in response to commissions (and also 'inner need' of course), was reaching a new intensity – in 1974, probably my most productive year of all in sheer numbers, I produced fourteen quite substantial works. At this time of course I was heavily involved in the Cathedral, the RAM and University teaching at Cambridge. Not a great deal of time available for socialising with the Lay Clerks! This is the tally of compositions:

1. 'A Rite' – A Eucharist for Congregational use. (Commission from USA Seminary of the Southwest) (fagus-music.com)

2. 'Prayer' – A setting of the wonderful poem by George Herbert, commissioned for the 1974 Organist' Annual Congress at Newcastle-on-Tyne. (Novello)

3. 'Homage to Ravel' for an Album of music for Guitar commissioned by OUP.

4. 'Tongues of Fire for Organ' (Weinberger) Composed for a recital in King's College, Cambridge on the Eve of Pentecost. I also premiered a new piece by Judith Weir (a First Year pupil of mine at King's College).

5. 'I sing of a Maiden' for sopranos and organ. (OUP) Commissioned by the Diocesan Mother's Union for a Festival Service in Ely Cathedral.

6. 'The Song of Songs' Six Pieces for Organ Manuals based on verses from the Book of that name. (fagus-music.com)

7. 'Homage to John Stanley' for Organ Manuals. (fagus-music.com) A commission from Timothy Lees of Wolverhampton for a modern equivalent to the English 18th century Voluntary. Three movements.

8. Scherzetto for Organ – A contribution to an album dedicated to the Duchess of Kent – a Patron of the Royal College of Organists. (Cramer)

9. Three Poems by e.e. cummings for Tenor, Oboe and Piano. Commissioned by the Pelican Trio. (fagus-music.com)

10. Sarabande Sacrae for Organ (Cramer) Dedicated to Lesley Darlington, an organ student of mine.

11. 'Welcome Yule!' (OUP) In addition to organ accompaniment there are brass parts on hire. (This piece was suggested by an RAM student Clive Conway-Gwilliam, who organised players from the Academy for its first performance

in the Cathedral in a concert of music for choir and brass. It was done twice at the beginning and end of the concert, which also included music by Praetorius, G. Gabrieli and Purcell.)

12. 'There was a Boy bedded in bracken' Carol for Men's voices. (fagus-music.com) Commissioned by William Barnett.

13. Variations on 'Amazing Grace' for organ (Novello) and included in the same volume –

14. Toccata

This was quite a tally for a very busy year in all other respects – but needs must!

The improved standard of the Lay Clerks led to more interesting recordings, with some emphasis on 'verses' (solo sections for each voice pitch) in the repertoire from the 17th and 18th centuries. The recording company Saga had acquired the Rights to my Vierne: Symphony Three recording and in connection with Saga I got to know Ted Perry who, from the mid-seventies onwards, was to play an increasingly important role in my recording career over the next ten years. Ted welcomed suggestions for new recording ventures so that when I suggested an LP of Anthems and Voluntaries by William Boyce (at that time hardly represented on record) he was eager to take up this idea. Of Boyce's Ten Voluntaries I played I, II, IV and X which provide a well contrasted ideas of his range of invention. I also included my favourite four of his Verse Anthems: O where shall wisdom be found – I have surely built Thee an house – Turn thee unto me, O Lord and By the waters of Babylon. The Choir at that time was well furnished with lively Treble soloists, and I was able to include the brothers Andrew and Richard Wigley; Mark Turner and Ross Thain. Equally lively were the Lay Clerk soloists, which included the Altos Anthony Ransome and John Aitcheson; Colin

Flanagan – Tenor and Kenneth Burgess – Bass. Gerald Gifford was the accompanist. (Saga 5440 1976 but eventually transferred to another label.) Critical response was generally approving, and two years later I decided to couple Purcell and Blow in a similar LP venture: Anthems and Voluntaries by Henry Purcell and John Blow.

By this time Ted Perry had set up a new company with John Shuttleworth – Meridian – and as was always to be the case in his career, was looking for new repertoire. The organ, as rebuilt with its 5-rank Cornet on the Great manual, was well equipped for such pieces as Purcell's Voluntary for double organ, and this featured along with Blow's Voluntary in A and also his Echo Voluntary in G. Two years later we find Trebles Ross Thain and Richard Wigley still going strong, aided now by Kim Clark; additional soloists among the Lay Clerks included the Alto Steff Scott, the Tenor Adrian Goss, and the Bass Christopher Gove. The accompanist was Stephen Le Prevost, who also features on all my following choral recordings. As was the case with the Boyce record, this repertoire held a great appeal for me and included anthems for the Coronation of James II in 1692: Purcell's 'I was glad when they said unto me' and Blow's 'Let Thy hand be strengthened'. Two of Purcell's most magnificent pieces completed the first side of the recording – 'Jehovah quam multi sunt hostes' and his 'Benedicite'. Even in this company Blow shone with 'O pray for the peace of Jerusalem' – of which performance one critic remarked – 'admirably sung by the treble soloist (Ross Thain) – a paradigm of the Anglican ethos. Recommended to lovers of English church music in its great days.' The Evening Service in G well exploited all eight soloists, whilst the intense drama of Salvator mundi was evoked to my complete satisfaction. 'English church music in its great days.' I'm glad that the Anglican ethos came across so unmistakably – yes, because how can one convey in words the sheer breathtaking satisfaction of a Cathedral Evensong with such a repertoire, sung with an intense commitment in wonderful surroundings? (Meridian E77013 1978 – some organ items transferred to CDE 84305.)

The 'great days' referred to must be the 16th and 17th century with fewer and less 'great' pieces in the succeeding centuries. William Boyce and Maurice Greene certainly in the 18th century and it is a great regret on my part that I never managed to programme on record Greene's 'Lord, let me know mine end'. Today (19.03.2004) I read these words by the Arts Columnist of the *Daily Telegraph*: "People who work in the arts aren't in it for the money – it's lousy. They are fired by inspiration, dedication and a passion for, well, beauty. Crush that idealism and the esprit de corps that fuels it..." He was referring to opera companies, but could have been equally referring to Cathedral Choirs and their Directors. Let us consider the male voice tradition as an integral element in the 'sound' of this music, and there is a natural and inevitable progression from the treble section to the alto, tenor and bass sections, both in the logical continuity of the physical, mental and spiritual development of the species. Political correctness has no place in artistic effort, and its cost is both financial and artistic. Girls can usually sing more easily than boys, (though less effectively than boys in the polyphonic repertoire) but the very effort involved in the training and development of the boy's voice is of the essence in the 'all-through sound' eventually produced. In the Parish Church Choirs, the boys have gradually left it to the girls, now there are many choirs without any children at all. What does that bode for the future?

After 'the great days' of the 16th/18th century, one certainly had to choose more carefully, but for the next Choir recording, entitled 'Service high and anthems clear', I looked for some of the best pieces of the 19th and early 20th centuries, to include Samuel Wesley and his son Samuel Sebastian; Attwood, Stainer, Parry, Stanford, and Charles Wood. In this territory critical opinion varies considerably, but I looked for some of the most widely accepted pieces in the repertoire. In fact, the opening number Samuel Wesley's Exultate Deo is not to be found in every repertoire, but I loved it from the first time I heard it under Gerald Knight in Canterbury Cathedral, way back in my student year 1948/49. After doubling the voices throughout, the piece ends with an exultant organ solo coda, obviously meant to sum up the whole musical argument. Otherwise the anthem could be sung unaccompanied. To my surprise, Gerald opted for the worse possible procedure; after an unaccompanied performance he had the organ enter just for the coda – a high risk strategy as the lengthy vocal writing could not be guaranteed to stay in tune, and more often than not didn't. But it's a wonderful piece of musical argument, fully worthy of 'the great days' tradition and a great opener for the original LP. By now Ted Perry and John Shuttleworth had reached a parting of the ways, and this LP was one of the first to be issued on Ted's new Hyperion label (1980). Later it enjoyed an even longer life on Helios CDH88006 (1988). There was some excellent solo work from the Trebles Dicken Stainer (S.S. Wesley's Blessed be the God and Father), Simon Ellis, and also the Baritone Kenneth Burgess (Stanford in G Evening Canticles).

After these rather carefully focussed recording programmes I decided that the next LP should try to take the widest possible historical 'look' at the English Cathedral repertoire, this time for John Shuttleworth and his Meridian label (1984). Hence 'Music of Six Centuries' a truly fascinating programme beginning with the 15th century anonymous Carol 'Eya, Martyr Stephane'. This truly gripping Carol in a two-voice texture – Alto and Tenor – was also the inspiration for my Mass commissioned by St Stephen's Church, Bournemouth in 2002 – Missa Sancti Stephani. The soloists were Anthony Barthorpe (alto) and Peter North (tenor). Next we have an alternim (plainchant alternating with polyphony) treatment of the Office hymn for

Compline during the Lenten season by Robert Whyte, organist of Ely 1562 to 1566 – Christe, qui lux es et dies. The 17th century composer Hinde is not known apart from his anthem 'O sing unto the Lord a new song'. A verse anthem (alternating sections for solo voices and chorus) with accompaniment for either viols or organ, it is sung here in lively fashion by Benjamin Stainer and William Morgan (trebles) and Anthony Barthorpe (alto) Peter North (tenor) and Paul Smith (bass). Benjamin Stainer is heard again in Sir John Stainer's 'Lead, kindly light'. Ben was the youngest of three Great-great-grandsons who all graced the Ely Choir, and led to the inclusion of rather more of the great Sir John's music in the repertoire than had recently been the case. Other composers featured on this recording included John Travers, both Wesleys, Charles Wood and C.V. Stanford (his 'Evening Canticles in C' this time). This LP was later transferred to CD format. Then in 1986 Priory Records recorded an LP record of some of my choral and organ music, and also a Christmas music LP which once again featured some of my work.

Apart from any intrinsic artistic merit any such recordings may possess, at the very least they are an historical and immediate record of the composers, choirs and organists who worked in these great ecclesiastical institutions. What would we not give for such revelations as Monteverdi at San Marco, Venice; or J.S. Bach at Leipzig – or Purcell at Westminster Abbey? Looking through the lists of choir members at once brings back memories of far-off days, with both problems and rewards, – in my case of forty-one years in office, as either Assistant or Director. Those boys who matured into characterful soloists – and those who didn't. All though contributed mightily according to their lights, and whatever their achievements found the experience ultimately rewarding. 'Not at the time!' they will remember – 'More fun to kick a ball about!' And perhaps I should have found more leisure time to socialise with the Lay Clerks, and thereby possibly avoiding at least some problems. Nothing here for regret though – now let's look at almost the last of these commercial recordings: 'Music for a Royal Year in Ely Cathedral' (LP Alpha label). Side One contained 'Music from the Distribution of the Royal Maundy by Her Majesty The Queen'. As usual the Choir of the Chapel Royal was also present for this occasion, with their Choirmaster Richard Popplewell. I knew Richard well through our membership of the Council of the Royal College of Organists, so there were no problems in working together on this occasion. I composed a setting of Psalm 23 for the Service, with a prominent part for a treble solo, as if the Psalmist was remembering his childhood days as a shepherdboy. Then of course some items are obligatory for this great occasion, including Handel's 'Zadok the Priest' and Hilton's 'Lord, for thy tender mercies' sake', as well as certain hymns.

As was to be expected all went well for this highly rehearsed and somewhat tense occasion. Referring to the broadcast Service I received a letter from Mr G.A.E. (St Leonards-on-Sea) referring in glowing terms to the performance of the solo chorister in my setting of Psalm 23: "You will have gathered that what impressed me in no uncertain way was the quite astonishingly effective singing of the young man who took both the demanding treble solo and the unfriendly acoustic entirely in his stride, and came across in a most vivid and compelling way. This seemed to me a performance of exceptional robustness and certainty, and, in my view, his achievement, in one so young, and in such demanding, intimidating circumstances was beyond praise." I'm sure that this verdict was entirely merited, but occasional listeners are probably not aware that these performances are worked for on a daily basis – whether or not it is a great occasion, or simply the damp February Tuesday Evensong, with only the Chapter and Choir – and God? – in an act of worship which needs to be 'right' to be undertaken at all. And of course soloistic abilities in a choir of some eighteen boys aged between eight and thirteen will vary from year to year, but the training and the goal is always there – and the more compelling simply because of its essentially transient nature.

Things were not quite so secure for the Royal occasion recorded on Side Two, though the problems were nothing to do with the Choir, who were on their usual good form. This was a visit by Her Royal Highness The Princess of Wales to open the Festival of Flowers being presented by the East of England Area Association of the National Association of Flower Arrangement Societies, which was to culminate with Evensong in the Lady Chapel – a glorious building with even more resonant bloom than King's College, Cambridge. Another high tension occasion? – yes, but rather more memorable for the unintentional drama played out against its pre-Service music than for the well rehearsed procedure of the Service itself. The Canticles were those of Henry Purcell in G minor and for the Anthem the same composer's 'Rejoice in the Lord alway'. This Verse anthem was composed with accompaniment for strings, and so it seemed reasonable to use these resources to provide music before and after the Service. With the choice of Service music in mind I turned naturally enough to the great Chacony in G minor by Purcell in the edition by Benjamin Britten. In the sixties I had heard Britten conduct this piece in the Cambridge Guildhall, and that performance had left a lasting impression. On this Royal occasion the Lady Chapel was full to capacity, and its somewhat over-generous acoustics somewhat muted. I had asked the congregation to be as quiet as possible so that the recording would not be marred by 'noises off', especially in the Chacony, as the respectful hush before a Service of former times was now more likely 'to be honoured in the breach than the observance'.

So I began the Chacony. After a couple of pages I was approached by a Verger, who whispered that the Canon-in-Residence who was escorting Her Royal Highness had finished the tour of the Flowers, and was now ready for the Princess to enter the Chapel. "No, I can't do that," I whispered in reply – "I can't stop a piece in the middle, and anyway, it's being recorded." So she retreated into the vestibule to give the Canon this intelligence. After another page or so she returned to inform me that the Canon was now not prepared to wait any longer. "Sorry," I said, "but I'm almost through." After the Service was over I was told that the Canon had then told the Verger, "Go and tell him that if he doesn't stop now, he's fired!" "I can't do that!" was her response, and Her Royal Highness entered to the strains of the hymn 'Praise to the Lord, the Almighty' and took her seat immediately behind mine, lowering her eyelids in that characteristic fashion. But after all that, the Chacony was omitted from the recording, possibly whether from the noise of the footsteps of the Verger, or our conversations, or simply through lack of time, I'm not entirely sure. Fortunately the out-going voluntary was included – a tremendous performance of Mozart's Church Sonata in C K.336 by Stephen Le Prevost and the String Band (Alpha ACA 572).

That contretemps at the start of the Service was a classic example of the problems that can arise between the clergy and the musicians – problems that are much more acute and damaging to my colleagues in these latter days, when I no longer am required to take 'holy orders!' But it is truly wonderful to live and work in the architectural and acoustical ambience of a Cathedral such as Ely.

On another Royal occasion in 1973, celebrating thirteen hundred years of the Foundation by Queen Etheldreda in 673, Her Majesty the Queen was present at a great Service of Thanksgiving and many of us were lined up afterwards to be presented to her Majesty. Demonstrating as usual her interest in some detailed aspect of the occasion, she enquired of me 'How is it that there is so little reverberation in such a large building?' I might have mentioned the absorbent woodwork of the Nave Roof, the Octagon and the Choir Stalls, but rather than deal with such technical matters I simply replied "It's due to you Ma'am that we have such a large congregation today, which absorbs the resonance. Normally there is a considerable reverberation!"

One of my favourite Biblical passages comes from The Prophet Ezekiel – Chapter 7. 'And he said unto me, Son of man, can these bones live? And I answered, O Lord God, thou knowest.' And often, looking around the Cathedral or the Lady Chapel, for 'bones' I instead easily substitute 'stones'. With music, either in a Service or a concert, these stones can and do live, and we all hear and recognise its vital life. After all, the central space under the crossing of a monastic church or Cathedral was always named 'The Choir' – even if after the dissolution of the Monasteries that sacred space was moved around somewhat – the place of daily worship through music – the 'workshop' as Dean Carey liked to describe it to the visitors he was guiding. And from the 20th century onwards these sounds can indeed live – for ever? – with our ever increasing technology in images and sounds?

And then, from the eighties onwards, came the new phenomenon of the Choir Tour. Visits from the Choir to Churches in the Diocese had begun in the seventies, usually on a one or two each term basis, Friday being the generally favoured evening and such visits being very well received, whether in centres such as Cambridge, or in the depths of the Fens. Occasionally we were invited further afield, as in December 1975 when we visited two churches in Leicestershire at the invitation of the County Music Advisor. It was the Christmas season, and the Choristers had just a few days previously recorded Britten's 'A Ceremony of Carols', together with some Carols by John Rutter and accompanied by the harpist Osian Ellis, for the BBC. We were able to include this work in our tour with a very accomplished harpist from the Royal College of Music. A week later we broadcast Choral Evensong for the BBC which included the first performance of the Magnificat from my Fauxbourdon Service – composed at the suggestion of Dean Carey for this broadcast to connect the more easily with the plainchant Advent Antiphon: O Clavis David. The Nunc Dimittis was by Tye and the anthem by Gibbons – Hosanna to the Son of David.

The twinning of Continental towns with their English counterparts naturally led to visits by Council Officials; these often being accompanied with whatever local cultural assets might be displayed in order to enhance the visit, music being an especially welcome vehicle for this purpose. Ely was twinned with Kempen in Germany and we visited that town immediately after Easter, 1981. Our hosts were full of kindness and generous hospitality – we were a large group, as the Ely Band was also in the party. We were asked to record a generous number of pieces from the programme and they produced an excellent LP from that selection. The Propsteikirche was full for our concert, and I quote from two reviews: "It certainly has nothing to do with sentimentality and doesn't just concern the wonderful music of John Blow, the teacher of the great Henry Purcell, that one feels deeply touched, when a young English boy, who probably has not heard much about the horrors of the world, sings 'O pray for the peace of Jerusalem' dressed in the robes of the choristers of the Anglican Church – news transcending thousands of years. The spirit, whichever it may be, which led the Ely Cathedral Choir on its first trip out of England to its twinned town Kempen, could not have found better expression." And this – received with some derision by our choristers!: "The English singers were performing under a certain handicap because, like it or not, they had to stand comparison with the world-famous St John's College Choir from Cambridge who had enchanted the Kempeners before Christmas. Well, the 'little brother' passed the test brilliantly. Not quite drilled to such perfection and the voices understandably not of the unique standard of the Cambridge Choir, the thirty singers were however, more relaxed and easy with the same accuracy of intonation and with absolute flawlessness of dynamics."

Given the inevitable comparison with the Cambridge Choirs highlighted here, it is worth considering the comparative financial state of Ely Cathedral at this period of the early eighties. From twenty boys on full scholarships in 1949 when Sidney Campbell and I arrived, that number was reduced to eighteen during Michael Howard's tenure in office, and progressively down to sixteen and then fourteen during my long reign of thirty-two years; only beginning to recover from 1985 onwards. And of course the value of the proportion of the scholarships offered varied according to the Chapter resources from two-thirds to a half in value.

This is the point at which the appointment of Michael Tavinor as Precentor needs to be recognised. I happened to meet a previous Precentor of Peterborough Cathedral and mentioned that Michael was to be our next Precentor – "They will love him!" came his excited approbation. I mentioned this to Dean Patterson on one of our coach trips to a Parish Church concert – "Good!" – he said, but I think that he had already made up his mind on that point! Michael was an ARCO (he told me that I was one of the panel of Examiners!) and had a degree in music (M.Mus.) from the University of Durham. A man of commanding personality and remarkable energy, it was clear to me that he would be a Precentor to be reckoned with. (Dean Carey held the view that the Precentor's status rendered him as always in danger of being crushed between the Chapter and the Organist!) Michael came to the Cathedral in June, 1985 and immediately established himself as a man of charm and charisma. In 1986 Shrove Tuesday pancake parties for the choristers were instituted and, in September, a surprise party to mark my sixtieth birthday – these were but two occasions on which he took immense trouble and imagination to both surprise and entertain the Cathedral fraternity. My sixtieth birthday party was a supreme instance of both Michael's imagination, and the amount of time and trouble he would devote to getting an occasion 'just right'. Mary and I knew that there was to be a party, but I at least knew little about it. After drinks and a welcome to all (who knew what was going to happen) Michael announced that there was to be a presentation of the robes worn by a Doctor of Music of Durham University, but that first I had to demonstrate my worthiness to receive such an adornment by undergoing a viva voce. I think there were six questions, which I managed to answer reasonably satisfactorily except for the last, which gave me some pause. It was a bass line at 16' pitch – I thought long and hard, but with just a little prompting I eventually realised that it was a phrase for the double basses from the orchestral symphony that I had composed for my D.Mus. degree almost thirty years earlier. Michael had taken the trouble to contact the University Library for access to this score – typical of the man! Having passed this test (just) the robe and cap was produced and I was helped into the robe by some of the larger choristers; but the cap had to be placed on my head by a first year chorister – Francis Ambrose, whose diminutive stature necessitated his climbing a pair of steps in order to reach my lofty cranium. All in all quite a spectacle! And all down to Michael Tavinor's generous imagination.

Dean Patterson's wife Elisabeth came from Normandy, and it was inevitable that the Choir would be invited to undertake a tour in that beautiful countryside, with its historic connections with the Conquest and Ely and the Fens – Abbot Simeon, a kinsman of William began the building of the Norman Church in 1080. The previous year Dean Patterson decided to raise the necessary funds by cycling from Ely to the Abbey of Bec in Normandy – incredible? But that was our Dean. Radio Cambridgeshire provided a phone-in link every afternoon at 2.00 p.m. as he meandered (his own words) through Chelmsford, Rochester, Newhaven, Dieppe and all points to the Seine. He did the distance in three days and collected £3000, and as he said then falling asleep in his stall after pedalling into the Cathedral on the June Feast of St Etheldreda!

We sailed to France on June 10th, 1986, returning on the 17th – the Summer Half-Term break in fact. The Dean said that the French had regarded our visit as a 'Norman Conquest'! There was time, and the coastal waters at hand for much recreation, and on a notable occasion the choristers conspired amongst themselves with the complicity of my wife, to carry me into the sea and there deposit my by no means light body. Another unusual feature was the burning heat in mid-June, leading to a decision to allow the Choristers to wear just a pair of pants under their cassocks for the evening concert. Well – after all, we were in France!

Dean Patterson recalls the event mentioned above thus: "The last morning was on the beach at Etretat. It was tropically warm. Arthur and I had, as the Irish say, drink taken. That venerable doyen of cathedral organists was recumbent on the shingle. A group of fiends accosted me – 'Can we chuck him in?' I gave the only possible answer – 'Ask Mrs Wills.' Like a true Ely girl she came straight to the point – 'Give me his wallet.' Psalm 104 says the rest – 'There go the ships, and there is that Leviathan'. It was a profoundly impressive sight."

Two years later, at the end of the Summer Term in 1988, a four-day visit to Guernsey proved most enjoyable – as a visit to any of the Channel Islands always is. A concert in the Notre Dame Church elicited some favourable comments from the music critic Christine Le Poidevin in a review headed: 'Four Centuries in the course of the evening.'

"A packed audience at Notre Dame heard the choir from Ely Cathedral give a concert of ancient and modern church music. Choirmaster Dr Arthur Wills is a distinguished composer, as those of us who have played his instrumental pieces set for the grades examinations will testify. [!] His cantata 'In Honour of Etheldreda', which brought the concert to a triumphant end, was in the latest tradition of English harmonic writing. The text concerned Ely's Foundress and was taken from the writings of Bede. The rise and fall of the beguiling discords cleverly evoked the whistling wind over the reedy East Anglian fens.'

And a remark from the Precentor Michael Tavinor sitting on the sea-wall has stayed in my mind, and I sometimes use it as if my own invention – 'Solemn High Tea!' Perhaps he also got it from someone else, but it always raises a smile – especially from Clerics.

June 1989 saw us in Antwerp via Ramsgate and Dunkirk – a truly wonderful venue in terms of its historical and artistic history. Dean Patterson commented – "The Cock-pit of Europe!" when I recalled the many battles fought over these flat-lands on our way to Ghent – a somewhat sobering thought. We broke the journey there for refreshment and a visit to the cathedral – very ornate in decoration and rich in powerful paintings. On arrival in Antwerp we had an hour's rehearsal to get the feel of the Cathedral and its generous acoustics. It was undergoing restoration so it was necessary to tread carefully in the usable two-thirds of the building, but one always manages after the initial 'Oh no!' It is a city of delights, both artistic and culinary. On the day of the concert Rubens' House was irresistible in the morning – as was shopping for some, but the afternoon was fully taken up with preparation for that evening's concert.

The programme included the anthem for Epiphany 'O God, who by the leading of a star' by John Bull, who was a former organist at Antwerp. The repertoire for this evening concert was constrained by the use of a chamber organ, but there is no shortage of masterpieces in the English Cathedral tradition for this accompaniment of voices! But the real thrill for me – and many others was the Sunday morning Mass with the Choir in the great West Gallery in front of the gorgeous Cavaille-Coll organ. We had chosen the Langlais

Missa Solennelle and it was one of the great liturgical experiences of my life to direct that setting with those resources. Stephen Le Prevost was in his element and his Postlude compelled the attention and applause of the congregation, most of whom had remained to listen. And then at the end of the day an opportunity to sing Evensong in St Boniface Anglican Church with Stanford in C and Basil Harwood's 'O how glorious is the kingdom'. Normally they expect a congregation of around twenty, but had printed one hundred and fifty service sheets. The attendance was nearer three hundred, and afterwards there was a delightful reception in the garden of the Church which served as a final expression of thanks from visitors and hosts. The next morning we began the journey back to Ely, via Bruges for lunch at 'The Holy Grail' restaurant.

There was a final memory for me some twelve years later, when I received an e-mail from the Cathedral Choirmaster informing me how much the Antwerp Cathedral Choir enjoyed singing my Missa Eliensis – hardly believable – a continental cathedral choir singing their Sunday Mass to a non-Catholic English setting! Whatever next!

A fitting climactic tour to conclude my time as Director of Music at Ely was the visit to Rome in 1990. We were there for five full days which included the Fourth Sunday in Lent – Mothering Sunday. Once again, Michael Tavinor had planned a most imaginative sequence of venues – he had spent a considerable time in Rome as part of his theological training, and therefore knew the Holy City very well. This was indeed a tour with a difference – cunningly paced and varied so as to build up to the Papal Audience in the morning of the final day, with a concert at the British Ambassador's residence in the evening, providing a finale quite different from anything we had experienced on any of our previous tours. From a musical point of view a tour of this kind, with six or seven venues, needs a choice of repertoire which will be sufficiently comprehensive to bear repetition and supply alternative items to suit different venues, and also provide enough variety to hold the performers' interest. If we count the Papal Audience as a concert (we sang four pieces) the itinerary was carefully structured to include four concerts and three services.

The concert occasions were not so very different from our twice-a-term visits to churches in the Diocese. The preparation is largely done beforehand, but there is always final polishing to be done, standing and seating to be arranged, fresh acoustical conditions to adjust to (mainly a matter of slowing or quickening the tempi) and a satisfactory balance with the organ to be achieved. Also the Assistant Organist has to try to find time to practise his solo interludes. Often the time allowed for proves inadequate, and a feeling of urgency, if not stress is frequently engendered. Sometimes this is not a bad thing, especially if the performers are feeling somewhat inert after a long coach drive!

The first service – a Sung Eucharist – at All Saints Anglican Church was just like being back in England, with my Missa Eliensis and Vaughan Williams' 'O taste and see how gracious the Lord is'. During the Communion we sang Bairstow's 'The Lamentations' which seemed even more poignant than usual. In the evening a totally different experience awaited us at Santa Maria Maggiore, where the Mass was said in Italian and we sang the Lassus Missa 'Bell' Amfitrit Altera together with a varied selection of motets for the Introit, Gradual, Offertory (Bruckner's Ave Maria was an obvious choice), Communion and Dismissal (my The Praises of the Trinity.) A very large congregation was unreserved in the enthusiasm of their appreciation.

There was little 'Monday morning feeling' the following day (apart from the horrendous early morning traffic) when we visited the Catacombs of San Callisto. This perhaps was the highlight of the trip in atmosphere and intensity of response. The musical contributions were just two hymns – quite sufficient to express the emotional charge of feeling. To see the grave of St Cecilia, Patron Saint of Music, was indeed most affecting. On our return to the surface, a request by a group of pilgrims from Moscow for us to sing to them (Wood's Oculi omnium) capped the experience for all concerned. In the afternoon to St Peter's Basilica for the 5.00 p.m. Mass. We sang Byrd's five-voice setting and his 'Tu es Petrus' for the Introit. As we had been led to expect, the arrangements for our reception and adequate rehearsal time were somewhat less than satisfactory. It was an undeniably fine experience to sing there, but I have to admit that I was plagued by some uneasy speculation about the musical facilities in heaven, if this was typical of St Peter's, Rome! After the Mass, one of the nuns at the Pensione where we were staying remarked, "The angels in heaven will have to look to their laurels after your singing!" Maybe she was also troubled by the same doubts as myself!

I needed a change from liturgical usage after that experience, so it was a stroke of genius on the Precentor's part to have arranged a trip to Tivoli and the Villa d'Este the following morning. I found this visit truly fascinating, not simply for the beauty of the place with its extraordinary arrangement of fountains and waterfalls, but even more for the opportunity to let my imagination rove freely over the past musical associations of the Villa. Especially one thinks of Liszt, who spent much time there due to the kindness of his friend Cardinal Hohenlohe. The finest of the pieces inspired by the Villa is undoubtedly 'Les Jeux d'Eaux a la Villa d'Este' – a work which anticipates the impressionism of Debussy and Ravel and is one of the most forward-looking in the whole of Liszt's output. He confessed to being spellbound by the wonderful arrangement of fountains at the Villa, and his tribute was to find a fitting response in Ravel's 'Jeux d'eau' of some thirty years later. 'Music of fountains and waterfalls' as Ravel described it.

One of the most memorable concerts of the tour took place that evening, at St Elena's Church. This was a change of venue with very short notice, allowing no time at all for rehearsal. Yet, as soon as the first notes of Amner's 'Come, let's rejoice' sounded, I knew that it was going to be extraordinary. The acoustics were marvellous, and the audience (most of them staying after a 6.00 p.m. Mass) vociferously enthusiastic. St Elena's is situated in one of the poorer areas of the city, as was made abundantly clear by the many posters and graffiti we saw en route – all in support of the Communist Party. But the response of the parishioners to our music was equally fervent, and we were left with an unforgettable impression of the most genuine appreciation. But the change from graffiti to the glitterati at the Ambassador's Reception the following evening found an audience as equally enthusiastic. I was surprised to experience the obvious impact our church music made in the opulent salon, all gilt and crystal, but we were also able to offer some appropriately lighter pieces given by some of the Lay Clerks (the Shades of Blue), and also Jeremy Filsell's brilliant piano solo version of Gershwin's 'Rhapsody in Blue'. All these were very well received. There were few solo opportunities in the repertoire we took to Rome, but on this occasion Francis Ambrose sang the opening of John Ireland's 'It is a thing most wonderful' with consummate security and poise.

Earlier that that day though we were privileged to sing at the weekly Wednesday Papal Audience at which several thousand people are routinely present. The Audience Hall looked pretty full to me, and the crowd was certainly the largest Ely Choir will have sung to live up to that point. Before the Audience began we sang Stanford's 'Justorum animae' (in Chorister-speak 'Just store'em anywhere'), my own 'The Praises of the Trinity' and Byrd's 'Tu es Petrus'. During the Audience we sang 'Come let's rejoice' when our group was announced. Apart from the waiting tension of having to begin the Amner anthem at just the right point, I found that there was no greater sense of nerves than during a daily Evensong at home. One simply concentrates on the music, forgets oneself and gets on with the work in hand. It's what I am always telling the Choristers to do and it's certainly the right advice. I wasn't looking, but the Precentor assured me that the Holy Father clapped us very appreciatively. In his walkabout he took the trouble to seek me out for a handshake and he knew my Christian name, which I took to signify his enjoyment of the Choir's work. But after that I was moved most deeply by the scenes of general spiritual enthusiasm engendered by the Pope's charismatic presence. True power resides in love and the relinquishment of power, was the thought I came away with. Later, I remembered that the Holy Father does not have to take choir rehearsals!

Chapter 7

Necessary to invent? – Music and Religion.

Previous chapters will have made it clear that from boyhood onwards my musical and religious experiences were based upon participation in the Services of the Anglican Church as either singer, organist or director. Further, the church Services that I particularly relished were of the High Church or AngloCatholic persuasion, with their emphasis on ceremonial in which the music was required to play an essential and closely ordered role, and in which the Clergy were required to be able to intone the Versicles and Responses, and also the Epistle and Gospel. At the great Services of Holy Week and Easter the Passion settings required some vocal ability and stamina to maintain the narrator's part, and the Easter Vigil was even more taxing upon the singer's ability to cope with its lengthy oration in the Exultet.

This intimate association of music and religion has not surprisingly persisted, and just as my knowledge and experience of music as an art has developed and changed, so has my knowledge and experience of religion. The close connection of the two phenomena in my experience and development has equally persisted and also radically changed. On the one hand, the beauty and force of former ecclesiastical language – that of Church Latin and the English of the 1662 Prayer Book – and the essential connection between that and the musical settings down the ages, make their usage essential for me in order to enjoy worship, whether as a performer or as a silent participant. On the other hand, the development of Christian thought down these two Millennia, from the writings of the Early Church Fathers to 'The Sea of Faith' musings of Don Cupitt, as well as my contemplation of other religious beliefs, have led to a personal exploratory journey leading to a conclusion perhaps best succinctly summed up in the words of St John's Gospel – 'God with us'. For me, God is not 'a God who hideth Himself', rather God is ever-present, and can be called upon at any time by anyone in any circumstances as an unfailing friend and guide in these ever-expanding universes. This conviction is both personal and, I am convinced, is absolutely universal in its application and efficacy, no matter whatever faith, church, or no adherence to any is the individual stance. Emily Brontë's great poem 'Last Lines' which concludes my song cycle of four Brontë poems 'When the Spirit comes' (1985) puts it incomparably:

(2) *O God within my breast*
   Almighty, ever present Deity!
   Life – that in me has rest,
   As I – undying Life – have power in thee!

and,

(4) *Though earth and man were gone,*
   And suns and universes ceased to be,
   And thou were left alone,
   Every existence would exist in thee.

But let us begin at the beginning of my 'necessity to invent' music. My earliest piece of 'worship music' (in today's jargon) was a setting of three texts from the Communion Service for Men's voices – Sanctus, Benedictus and Agnus Dei. This was a purely utilitarian exercise done to provide some relief from Merbecke's unison congregational setting. It was composed sometime during the early1950s, in Sidney Campbell's time, and regularly used thereafter. We were not permitted to use Latin settings for the Eucharist and so its use was continued throughout Michael Howard's tenure, but when I became Director in 1958 I added settings of the Kyrie eleison and Gloria in Excelsis Deo. The change of idiom between the early and late fifties is somewhat obvious – Charles Wood to Benjamin Britten perhaps? This was my first piece to be published, and it was readily accepted by Novello. To my delight it was quickly taken up by John Dykes-Bower at St Paul's Cathedral – "A feather in your cap, Arthur!" was Sidney Campbell's comment.

Much of my compositional activity was directed towards providing useful material for immediate use – hence Missa Eliensis and the Two Latin Motets for Treble voices. The Choristers sang an early weekday Eucharists on Festivals such as Saints' Days, and thus my choice of 'useful' texts – Ave verum corpus, and O quam gloriosum. In these circumstances one was always conscious of one's historic role as a useful workman, of whatever calibre, attempting to follow in the steps of the stone masons who lavished superb craftsmanship on work which would for ever be hidden from the eyes of mortal man – or heard by very few listeners. This comparison is far from precise of course – my motets were quickly published and could be heard in many services and concerts, and were eventually recorded, but nevertheless this outcome was not the immediate driving force behind their composition in 1960. However, one did think of J.S. Bach at work on a new cantata for St Thomas' Church at Leipzig on the previous Monday – and also remembered with a wry smile the New Yorker cartoon which pictured Bach at his desk immersed in his fresh inspiration, with Anna Magdalena bursting in at the door, and demanding "Johann – the garbage!"

I felt it an enormous privilege to be able to compose for the services in such a beautiful building and such a historic Ely choral tradition, going back to Christopher Tye at the Reformation. And such home-grown work then led to paid commissions such as the Two Anthems for Men's Voices asked for by St Margaret's Church, King's Lynn in 1965. I was allowed to choose my own texts for these anthems – a really crucial matter because unless a composer really loves the words he is setting to music, nothing good will come from it – except of course the fee. But even that is a 'thirty pieces of silver' if the music is poor because the text does not excite. Just as with the Latin motets I chose two very contrasted texts from the Psalms – 'By the waters of Babylon' and 'Their sound is gone out into all lands'.

A work well outside liturgical requirements is 'Caedmon' (1985) a Children's cantata for Treble/Soprano voices in unison and Piano with the text provided by James Tilly, a master in the Junior King's School. The practice of taking the Cathedral Choir out into the Diocese for an evening concert once a term gave an opportunity to include this piece, which provided a contrast to the Service repertoire normally used in these concerts. The text offers a good deal of fun about the 'Abbey on the Yorkshire coast' (Whitby), and its Abbess, St Hilda. Caedmon's ordeal begins on Midsummer Day – the Feast of St John Baptist, when after Vespers and their Festal Dinner the nuns decide to have a talent show as part of their 'knees-up' and all present are required to perform. The classic situation comedy begins when Caedmon, a cow-herd serf, runs away with an acute attack of stage-fright. He hides in his cow shed and eventually falls asleep. An angel then appears in a dream and tells him that he can and must sing. After initial refusals Caedmon discovers that he can indeed sing and so becomes the medieval portent of a contemporary 'pop-idol'! It readily falls into the 'Cinderella – Ugly Duckling' literature genre, and I found that audiences 'in the sticks of Cambridgeshire' found nothing irreverent in the piece and readily grasped the point of its 'fun and games' especially when performed by choristers. 'That must have been fun to write!' was a common reaction from the audiences. But when Paul Trepte did the piece in a concert in the King's School Theatre, with myself at the piano, at least one member of the audience objected to its 'irreverence' and apparent 'send-up' of monastic behaviour in the Middle Ages! Perhaps one shouldn't be either too surprised or worried at this reaction.

That same year of 1985 I composed 'Now Etheldreda Shines' – a setting of words by the Venerable Bede in his 'History of the English Church and People'. The Choir was invited to take part in the annual 'Service for the Sons of the Clergy' in St Paul's Cathedral that year, and this new work was an ideal contribution in every possible way for the Ely Choir to perform. It is of substantial length and exploits the reverberant acoustics of large buildings such as St Paul's, and its performance was well received. Bede's text centres on what was known of the life of the Foundress and first Abbess of the Ely monastery, but there was an interesting collision of conflicting views on Bede's account of the Life of Etheldreda between the fifties and the nineties of this century in my own experience. The earlier Chapter encouraged devotional attention to the two Feasts of the Saint. But towards the end of the century I found this devotional approach bitterly scorned by the right-on feminist wife of one Canon. Her derisory 'rendition' includes:

Queen not of hearts, nor of Clubs antenatal
Rapture, if careless, she knew could be fatal.
Sexual love had for her no delights –
Twelve years poor Egfrid sought conjugal rights.

At this point in time (2003) it might be pertinent to ask – is religion 'simply' a geographic and ancient cultural phenomenon in which its ethics are the main and enduring element of the appeal and hold it still exerts? In the case of Christianity, its message and especially its expression has been constantly revised down the ages, often on political grounds, and significantly in the interests of individual interpretations. In the case of Anglicanism one immediately thinks of the British Empire and 'The day thou gavest, Lord, is ended'. The 1928 Prayer Book Good Friday Third Collect included these two versions of this prayer: O MERCIFUL God, who hast made all men, and hatest nothing that thou hast made, nor wouldest the death of a sinner, but rather that he should be converted, and live: Have mercy upon all Jews, Turks, Infidels, and Hereticks, and take from them all ignorance, hardness of heart, and contempt of thy Word; and so fetch them home, blessed Lord, to thy flock, etc. (1662) and then this substantial alteration of tone: O MERCIFUL God, etc. Have mercy upon thine ancient people the Jews, and upon all who have not known thee, or who deny the faith of Christ crucified; etc. At the present time this Collect is often omitted entirely.

When one talks to members of the present day clergy they readily agree that 'religion' is at the ostensible root of most of the warring divisions creating havoc in the world today, and if the factions who exploit this care virtually nothing for the particular 'religion' they find so useful in support of their political objectives – so what?! Undoubtedly the many translations of the Bible into the vernacular since the Reformation have increasingly divided the Christian world, and these divisions have been further increased by Biblical Criticism Studies during the last two centuries. So we have an unfortunate and increasing gulf between what the Clergy are taught and believe, and what they are prepared to teach their congregations. This is not a situation that can be tolerated for ever. Surely the use and informed understanding of the Scriptures must be a priority of congregational enlightenment?

The incidents one can encounter when living in close proximity with the Clergy in a Cathedral Close are enough to make one squirm with embarrassment. Two of my experiences will serve to illustrate this. In the seventies I was invited over for 'drinks' at the house of the Canon Ely Professor of Divinity, where there were several overseas students at Cambridge present. One USA student could be heard remarking in a somewhat incredulous tone of voice "and they still believe in the Virgin Birth!" "Shh!" muttered his host hastily. And one feels distinctly uneasy on hearing one Dean explaining the damage to the stained glass and statues in the Lady Chapel to visitors as "what men do when they are angry". The hideous executions and wanton damage of the Reformation and the Civil War cannot not be glossed over so easily with yet another "Shh!".

Also the entire issue of accurate Biblical translations likewise cannot be permanently ignored. And the gulf between modern versions of the *Book of Common Prayer* and the dignity of the 1662 original are too blatant to be tolerated by a sensitive ear and need to be addressed. We will be told that 'religion' is not a matter to be confused with aesthetics, but at this stage of civilised development this issue cannot be avoided. Put bluntly, congregations are increasingly divided between those who need modern translations but do not wish to have their faith disturbed by history and Biblical criticism, and those who prefer the beauty of earlier renditions but are also eager to know what the scholars of the last two centuries have unearthed. But even with the most accepted of 'accurate' Scriptural translations there still remains 'interpretation' – whose 'interpretation'? The truth, allied to artistic beauty, does make you free. One other thing – the withering away of that 'triumphalism' expressed so blatantly in hymns such as 'God is working his purpose out' which I enjoyed so much as a child, is well satirised in a version once sung by Francis Jackson, equally enjoyed – 'God is walking his porpoise out'. Well, one gets the point!

A considerable work of 1985 was a commission from Leeds Parish Church for a substantial piece for the Leeds Festival of that year. For the text I chose the Benedicite, giving an important role to a solo treble. Increasing attention has been given to man-made changes to the ecology of the natural world in recent years, and I find that the Benedicite has been given greater prominence in the minds and liturgies of the Western Churches. In Ely we had frequently used this canticle as an alternative to the Te Deum during Lent, but only Purcell's setting and that of Francis Jackson seemed really worthy, so we were now able to use my piece in addition. And then Timothy Lees, from St James the Greater Church in Leicester, asked me for a setting of 'Bread of heaven, on thee we feed' for their choir – "With a treble solo of some prominence please." This was published by the RSCM, though Lionel Dakers asked me to truncate the treble solo, a request I should have ignored and later regretted not doing so, as did Tim.

Also published by the RSCM was The Sacrifice of God composed the following year. This sets words from Psalm 51 together with some verses from *The Ballad of Reading Gaol* by Oscar Wilde. It was provoked by the suicide of Pauline – a young niece, and it was a moving experience to hear it broadcast during Evensong from Westminster Abbey in August 1987 by an RSCM Summer Course Choir directed by Martin How, who has always been an enthusiast for much of my work. In addition to those two anthems 1986 produced two further significant works. That year saw the launch of an Appeal for the restoration of Ely Cathedral, the tidy sum of four million pounds being required, and one venture saw the Choir travelling to Liverpool Street Station in London and singing 'The Spiritual Railway' on the platform with a collection box! The text for this was found on a memorial slab near the South Door entrance to the Cathedral. It commemorates the death by accident of a railwayman on the track near Ely. Another important anthem composed in this year was 'The Lord is my Shepherd' composed in readiness for the Royal Maundy Service to be held in the Cathedral in 1987.

My retirement from Ely Cathedral in the year of 1990, was marked by a remarkable Saturday afternoon concert and Evensong. Several Assistants came back for the occasion as well as former Choristers, amongst whom was James Bowman. He contributed two items – Here the deities attend (words exactly right for the occasion!) from the Ode 'Welcome to all the Pleasures' by Purcell and gave the first performance of a new work I composed specially for the occasion – 'The Hound of Heaven' with words by Francis Thompson, both with Jeremy Filsell at the piano. The Purcell item was especially suitable for the occasion on two counts – the text, and the fact that it was James' initiation into the secular concert world while still at school (see Chapter 4). 'The Hound of Heaven' was also important for me on that occasion, its choice reflecting my continuing concern with the Spirit and spirituality on leaving the Cathedral and what was to come afterwards. My important involvement with the Guitar was marked by Fiona Richardson's performance of 'The Year of the Tiger'. The Cambridge Brass Band (alas, without David Read) with myself at the organ played two movements from 'The Fenlands' Suite – The Vikings and March: City of Ely. The Choir sang excerpts from Missa Eliensis. Alastair Stout had composed an organ piece for the occasion, which he played and at Evensong the Canticles were sung to 'Wills on Plainsong Tones' and the anthem was my 'O praise God in his holiness'.

The Eastern religions Buddhism and Hinduism have always played an important role in my thinking, and during the sixties I recorded an LP in the 'Great Cathedral Organ' series which made mention in the sleeve note of my interest in these matters. Canon Bernard Pawley happened to take note of this and remarked "We must have a yarn about this some time, Arthur." But he never took this any further, I know not why. Three pieces of mine are concerned with Eastern Philosophies – Buddha-Song for Bass/Baritone and Piano (traditional text); The Shining Sea for Tenor, SATB Chorus, Strings, Organ, Piano and Percussion; and Symphony Bhagavad Gita for Organ solo. Buddha-Song was commissioned by Michael Tavinor, while he was Vicar of

Tewkesbury Abbey, for the dedication in an Abbey Service of Four Touching Souls (Soles) a sculpture of four seated children which is situated near the main gate of the church on Abbey Street. My understanding of this sculpture is that it demonstrates the unity of religions rather than the separation of them. This is the text:

May I become a medicine for the sick, and their physician,
Their support until sickness come not again.
May I become an unfailing store for the wretched,
And be the first to supply them with their needs.

My own self and my pleasures, my righteousness past,
*   present and future,*
May I sacrifice without regard, in order to achieve the
*   welfare of beings.*

The Shining Sea is a four movement work with a duration of twenty-six minutes. It is dedicated to the memory of Michael Dudman, who died at the age of fifty and had been associated with me and my music since being my Assistant Organist in the sixties. The text is taken from the Eighth Book of The Light of Asia by Sir Edwin Arnold, based upon the life and teaching of Gautama, Founder of Buddhism. It concludes as follows:

The Dew is on the lotus! – Rise, Great Sun!
And lift my leaf and mix me with the wave
Om mani padme hum, the Sunrise comes!
The Dewdrop slips into the shining Sea!

The Symphony Bhagavad Gita for solo organ also has four movements, with a quote from the Gita after each movement. This is a quote from the end of the second movement – Adagietto:

When his soul is in peace he is in peace, and then his soul is
 in God.
In cold or in heat, in pleasure or pain, in glory or disgrace,
 he is ever in Him.

There is no question but that the combination of being a Cathedral Organist/composer is the most rewarding of all occupations for those with both abilities, and it is certainly the most historic in origin. The Opera Director/composer comes next in more recent times, with Monteverdi, Haydn, Wagner, Mahler and Richard Strauss all managing the juggling act with more or less success. In order to survive the claims of both occupations the performance side will keep you more or less solvent, whilst you write the music your choir will readily perform for you, however tricky, and you may demonstrate no apparent interest in the market. Good for your soul, if not for your pocket. This will sometimes prove a hindrance when dealing with publishers, who may well be eager to print your offerings, but then tend to flag if the public does not share their enthusiasm in sufficient numbers. The only advice one can give is – it all depends on you – work at it! And do what you must – whether the Devil drives or not, but more about this in the next chapter.

I have already mentioned the incomparable satisfaction of combining composition with performance, and the social interaction which results thereby. My last two compositions were Latin Masses, both commissioned. The first was for St Stephen's Church, Bournemouth as part of their Annual Festival held in May 2001. I was delighted to have this commission as it gave me the opportunity to write a Parody Mass – a setting based upon some pre-existent material – in this instance the 15th century carol 'Eya, martyr Stephane'. At the start of the Service the two-part carol was sung by men's voices with solo verses and the refrain full. The setting was not entirely straightforward from the Choir's point of view, but I had tried to judge the demands of the piece to their capability as I had known it from visits in the past. The organ part was an essential part of the texture and I knew that it was safe in the hands of Christopher Moore. Ian Harrison, the Choirmaster said, "We haven't got the Gloria up to speed I'm afraid." But I wasn't worried to hear this – in fact the Gloria was so composed that it would simply have to move at the indicated tempo for it to make sense to either the choir or the listeners, and that was indeed the case once the rehearsal got under way. I was simply thrilled at the results achieved in the time available. An additional bonus was the fact that Michael Tavinor had been invited to preach at this Mass, and he was able to include much interesting material about the history of the Parody technique to emphasise the point of the message in his sermon. And he was also present at my lecture in the afternoon on The Ely Tradition and was able to raise some pertinent points. But this was not the only small miracle of the weekend, which coincided with the Spring Bank Holiday. I had been in touch with Barry Ferguson, who was now Director of Music at St Paul's Church, Shaftesbury, about the possibility of his writing a brief note to mark my 75th Birthday in *The Organists' Review*. He gracefully declined to do this, but instead suggested Basil Ramsey, who did agree to do this.

Barry then suggested that as I was in Dorset for the Festival Weekend in Bournemouth I should agree to play a concert of my organ music in his Church on the afternoon of Bank Holiday Monday. This was a brilliant suggestion, with one unlooked for and very significant consequence. The programme (which I introduced as it went along) included nine pieces composed between 1955 and 1984. At the conclusion of the proceedings, as I was putting my music away and changing my playing shoes I was approached by a man who introduced himself as Robert Slogrove – a former Chorister with me at Ely, and producing a copy of my Missa Eliensis said "My choir sang this recently and it went down very well!" This was a promising gambit, and that meeting prompted Robert to suggest a Re-Union of Choristers and Lay Clerks to take place at Sherborne Abbey in 2002 as a celebration of my 75th Birthday. I did point out that it might appear a rather belated tribute, but Robert then countered this with, "It's still within your 75th Year!" which of course was true – just. He then put in motion all the plans and preparation needed for the Chorister Re-union held at Sherborne School and the Abbey for the weekend of July 19th–21st 2002. On Friday evening I played an organ concert in the magnificent Abbey which began with my Carillon on 'Orientis Partibus' and ended with my 'The Fenlands Suite' transcription. I used the chamber organ for some pieces by Handel and Haydn. Etheldreda Rag was the obvious encore! Then we all met up for supper at a nearby hotel. More people arrived for an al fresco lunch, and even more for Tea at the Old School Room in Sherborne School.

Then we went to the Abbey to prepare for Evensong. This was to be according to the Ely Use of the Dean Patrick Hankey period – 1951–1969, with E. De T. Longford as Precentor. The treble line was provided by the girls in Robert Slogrove's Choir with Former Choristers and Lay Clerks providing the rest. The Versicles and responses were sung to Smith of Durham, the Canticles to Wood in D, and the anthem was Parry's 'I was glad'. But for myself and many others the highlight of the service was the Office Hymn for Saturdays – 'O Trinity of blessed light' sung to plainchant. Nothing was announced and only the State prayers were used at the end. "How old-fashioned!" many would chortle – but does God follow the latest or any fashion? The Service was accompanied by my first Assistant Organist – Christopher Scarfe. The Dinner was held in The Old School Room, and in my speech of thanks to all who attended I began by quoting the Duke of Wellington's aside to his Officers when reviewing his troops before Waterloo – "I don't know what they will do to the enemy, but by God they frighten me!" It was an emotional occasion, with many of the auxiliary staff of the King's School present, and one long to be remembered, as was the Eucharist with Missa Eliensis the following day. But once again the occasion did illuminate the difficulty of bringing together the two traditions of Choristers – those of the five hundred years tradition of boys mainly drawn from the town and attending the Cathedral School, and those scholarship boys at the King's School, from the 1949 intake and being educated within a revived tradition going back even further to Edward the Confessor. All those present were from the King's School, and more particularly from the 1950's–1960's traditions who would have known me as Assistant and then Director of Music. A wonderful occasion then – but such events do serve to remind one somewhat forcibly of the passage of time which – 'like an ever rolling stream bears all its sons away' – and as Shakespeare puts it 'What's to come is still unsure…'

Chapter 8

The World, the Flesh, and the Devil.

My work at the Royal Academy of Music from 1964 greatly expanded my horizons in composition, but until 1969 all the texts I chose or were required to set were either liturgical or Biblical. In that year however William Barnett, one of the Cathedral Lay Clerks who also taught in a local school, asked me to set the Browning poem 'Boot and Saddle' for his class to sing. (Much later, and to my surprise, it has been taken up by a Male Voice Choir in St Louis, Missouri, leading eventually to further collaboration with that Choir). This choice of poet was an interesting portent of my later increasing fascination with Browning's work. An English Requiem, composed two years later is a much more important instance of non-liturgical text setting, but 1972 was even more of a radical diversion, inasmuch as it saw the commission of 'Sherwood' (words by Alfred Noyes) by Pamela Cook for her Cantamus Ensemble, and then my first piece for Guitar solo – the Sonata in three movements for William Waters – a guitar student in my Harmony Class, followed the following year by Pavane and Galliard, and then Homage to Ravel in 1974. This year proved to be my most prolific ever, notching up sixteen pieces. It also included 'The Song of Songs' – Six pieces for Organ (manuals only) and based upon surely the most erotic texts to be found in the Bible, or anywhere else for that matter. But the most important secular work of this year was undoubtedly Three poems by e.e. cummings for Tenor, Oboe and Piano and commissioned by George Caird for his Pelican Trio. (George Caird – Oboe, John Blakely – Piano, Neil Mackie – Tenor)

They broadcast it for the BBC and also included it in many public concerts – apparently always to great acclaim. At a concert arranged by Ripley Recitals Association N.H. noted – 'Possibly the most remarkable item was the setting of three poignant poems by e.e cummings made for the Trio by Arthur Wills. This cycle proved highly effective, beautifully written, and of real musical value. The combination of tenor, oboe and piano blended admirably into the poet's personal vision.' J.S.B. wrote "The trio ensemble concluded the concert with a setting of three of e.e. cummings' poems especially composed for it by Arthur Wills. To choose this as a finale was incredibly daring but somehow from these young men a strange ethereal beauty floated over the audience, which after a moment's silence burst into three successive rounds of applause. A remarkable tour de force to complete a memorable evening."

My growing predilection for erotic poetry was taken further the following year of 1975 with a set of Three Elizabethan Love Songs entitled Love's Torment for Counter-tenor and Guitar with poems by Samuel Daniel, Thomas Lodge, George Peele and dedicated to James Bowman. He premiered them with the guitarist Forbes Henderson at the Wigmore Hall in 1980, and later that year I added a fourth song to a text by Michael Drayton 'An evil spirit, your beauty, haunts me still,' which ends 'Sweet angel devil'! This is now published as the third song, completing a set of four. Without the London and Cambridge connections I very much doubt whether this flowering of interest in secular music would have blossomed so readily. In *The Times* Frank Dobbins commented – "a fascinating work of rare lyrical quality. Mr Bowman was again in fine voice here, warmly responding to the work of the composer who as organist and choirmaster at Ely Cathedral nurtured and encouraged his vocal development first as a treble then as a counter-tenor in the 1950s."

Also in this year of 1975 there was my biggest work for solo guitar 'Moods and Diversions', a twenty-minute piece commissioned by another of Hector's students and published by the Italian firm of Berben. I also contributed eight pieces for various wind instruments, commissioned with several other composers by the Associated Board of the Royal Schools of Music. And the final secular work of the year was a setting for Soprano, Clarinet and Piano of Elizabeth Barrett Browning's Sonnet from the Portuguese 'When our two souls stand up erect and strong'. I think that this piece might have been suggested by Georgina Dobrée a clarinet professor at the RAM, and it was a great experience to encounter these wonderful words.

The following year I was asked to write a piece for solo trumpet by another RAM student – Traugott Forschner which I entitled 'Joie de Vivre', taking inspiration from the Picasso painting so entitled. There was also a song – 'Dreams' which I neglected to publish, which was composed with the exceptionally beautiful voice of the baritone cathedral Lay Clerk Kenneth Burgess in mind. 1977 was exceptional in its total neglect of the secular music world, but 1978 saw a collaboration with Hector Quine on an instructional work called The Contemporary Guitarist. I suppose that this was something of a compliment to me as Hector was considered to be a leader in his field of guitar teaching, and it further ensured my growing reputation as a composer outside the confines of the Cathedral Close.

In the following year of 1979 further confirmation of my growing reputation in the secular music world came with a commission from 'out of the blue' (Germany in fact) for a three-movement song-cycle for mezzo-soprano and guitar – A Woman in Love. Margaret Peckham suggested three poems by Kathleen Raine, who when approached made no difficulty about copyright, nor did her publishers George Allen and Unwin – somewhat unusually in my experience. The titles of the three poems are: 1. Woman to lover 2.

Winged Eros 3. Amo Ergo Sum. Apart from the addition of a fourth song to Love's Torment it was 1982 before I ventured again into the secular sphere with New Year Music for Flute, Horn, Bassoon and Piano, which was asked for by a student group for a lunch-time Duke's Hall concert at the RAM. But the coming year of 1984 was a very different matter. Once I had read through Orwell's prophetic book I knew that I had to provide a musical setting, and a post-Christmas holiday in the Canary Islands in 1982 was an ideal respite and opportunity to get to work on a first sketch of the libretto. I worked throughout 1983, but copyright problems with the Orwell Estate made any agreement for a production of the opera unlikely, so I decided instead to compose a three-movement Sonata for Piano out of the opera material, in order that there would be a commemoration of that year 1984 in my musical response to Orwell's great book. The Sonata was premiered at the RAM by Adrian Sutcliffe and this most significant year for my composition was marked by two significant pieces for Guitar – The Year of the Tiger – my birthday year in the Chinese Calendar, and Suite Africana – a three-movement work sparked off by a visit to South Africa in that Summer to play organ concerts in Johanesburg, Durban, (with a Safari trip) Port Elizabeth, Grahamstown, and Capetown.

Two secular pieces (both commissioned) stand out in 1985. Peter Moorse had conducted a performance with his London Cantata Choir of my 'An English Requiem' in St Margaret's Church, Westminster and also performed it for Anglia TV, in a programme about me and my music, in St John's Church, St John's Wood. As a result of this collaboration he then asked me to write a short unaccompanied piece for this choir for a forthcoming concert at the Purcell Room. For text I went back to e.e.cummings – his 'sweet spring' which includes the memorable line 'and everybody never breathed so many kinds of yes yes yes yes'. And in the Autumn, Bryanston School asked me for a piece which their choir could sing at the opening of a new extension to the Music School. I had previously composed an anthem for the School – 'Think on these things' – which their choir sang in Salisbury Cathedral at an end of year Service, so I readily agreed to another commission. I chose a poem by Wilfrid Owen – Music – a really remarkable text that fuses music, war, and the erotic, in images strikingly memorable:

I have been urged by earnest violins
And drunk their mellow sorrows to the slake
Of all my sorrows and my thirsting sins.
My heart has beaten for a brave drum's sake.
Huge chords have wrought me mighty: I have hurled
Thuds of god's thunder, And with old winds pondered
Over the curse of this chaotic world,
With low lost winds that maundered as they wandered.

I have been gay with trivial fifes that laugh;
And songs more sweet than possible things are sweet;
And gongs, and oboes. Yet I guessed not half
Life's symphony till I had made hearts beat,
And touched Love's body into trembling cries,
And blown my love's lips into laughs and sighs.

Sir Neville Marriner opened the new building, and it was indeed an evening to savour. I had taken an afternoon out of a week of examining for the Associated Board at Winchester in order to be present, and so had to drive in the late November evening from Dorset back to Hampshire – tedious but well worth it!

But the following year saw me at work on even more devilish poems dealing with the pleasures of the flesh. I had long been fascinated with Dr A.L. Rowse's theories about the identity of the 'Dark Lady' of Shakespeare's Sonnets in his book *Shakespeare the Man* (Macmillan 1973). My choice of eight of the Sonnets encapsulates his thoughts into a viable length for a concert song cycle, and the dark baritone timbre seemed absolutely right for these passionate musings. The second – 'How oft, when thou, my music, music play'st' – demonstrates once again Shakespeare's passionate insight into the musician's mind and feelings. And even more intense is the devastating 'Th'expense of spirit in a waste of shame' – truly an analysis of a human predicament which is true for every age. And the play on names in 'If thy soul check thee that I come so near' – which gave me the title for this book – is morbidly comic! My fellow professors at the RAM told me that the Sonnets were impossibly difficult to set – but I found the task absolutely compelling – something not to be resisted.

The following year I was commissioned by the English Guitar Quartet – led by Roland Gallery – to write a substantial work for them. Perhaps influenced by the work of Alban Berg and Leos Janacek in their overtly programmatic String Quartets, in this Concerto Lirico I decided to continue to some degree the mood of the Sonnets but now in entirely instrumental terms. The individuality of the four instruments in the textures I created was commented upon by several reviewers. The world premiere of the Concerto was on the 9th November 1988 at the Colchester Institute School of Music. In *Guitar International* Martin Plackett commented – "The highlight of the evening was undoubtedly the new Arthur Wills composition, written for the EGQ. The Concerto Lirico, sponsored by the Eastern Arts Association, is a substantial and rewarding work with a tightly-knit three-movement structure, few composers have the skill, or enough understanding of the instrument, to create such a worthwhile and cohesive piece. The Finale was dominated by a strong, persistent movement. The energy and excitement of both composition and performance were constant even through the central, more percussive section, which featured several tambora and étouffe effects. Wills then magically changed direction with a haunting reference to the atmosphere and texture of the Arioso…"

The first London performance was on the 8th May 1989 in St John's Smith Square, London. Colin Cooper remarked in *Guitar* Magazine – "The first two movements are particularly impressive; the Allegro Furioso has an urgency conveyed by a sometimes displaced rhythm; Arietta Amoroso, the second movement, has passages of individual beauty, one of them using a requinto tremolo over a walking bass to achieve a remarkable effect."

And then in 1988 the boldest of all my guitar works – Concerto for Guitar and Organ, with the subtitle 'Of Innocence and Experience' – this title taken of course from William Blake. It was premiered at the Harrogate Festival of 1990 by Fiona Richardson and myself, and viciously reviewed by at least one critic – (see Chapter 10, page 264). Of course the guitar has to be amplified, as is always the case with orchestral concertos such as that by Rodrigo which we also included in the programme. The Concerto was preceded by the composition of 'Soft Guitarr' – that title being taken from the poem by Nicholas Brady – Wondrous Machine! in which the poet compares the relative merits of the guitar and organ thus:

In vain the Am'rous Flute and soft Guitarr,
Jointly labour to inspire
Wanton Heat and loose Desire;
Whilst thy chast Airs do gently move
Seraphic Flame and heav'nly Love.

The long planned opera '1984' was completely sketched out in the same year as the concerto, but 1989 saw only two short secular pieces, both with texts by John Betjeman – 'Lenten thoughts of a High Anglican' and 'Agricultural Caress' – both highly erotic poems – but with the inimitable wry treatment so characteristic of this author. Lenten thoughts together with 'A Subaltern's Love Song', 'Hunter Trials' and 'Investiture In Wales' was to be absorbed into Betjemania – Four poems for Tenor and Piano (1993). The year 1991 saw a version for guitar of Etheldreda Rag and also a new rag for piano – Peach Blossom Rag – much less technically demanding than the earlier work. But 1992 saw my first return to Browning with Rabbi Ben Ezra (Grow old along with me) since Boot and Saddle of 1969. Abt Vogler followed the next year. Both are marvellous poems, and I eventually coupled them in Dramatis Personae for baritone and piano (and then did a transcription for organ solo!) but the Browning poem I had been longing to set came with a commission for a piece to celebrate the 50th birthday of James Bowman from one of his admirers – Maxine Handy. James asked for a string quartet accompaniment, and this I agreed to use, but the poem I had already chosen – Scena: A Toccata of Galuppi's – is of course about keyboard music, and so it seems almost necessary that sometime in the future I must do a version for harpsichord/piano.

What is the difference between the sacred and the secular in music? I have done versions of my Etheldreda Rag for piano and organ – is there any essential difference in its reception here? The piece is still a take on the Scott Joplin idiom – which had its origin in the brothels of New Orleans, and played an important role in the birth of the Blues and the jazz style generally. In discussions with fellow musicians in the sixties, if one raised the question of the usage of dance music in the Classic and Romantic periods – the minuet, the waltz, the polka and so forth – it seemed that these were now accepted as models of well-behaved restraint, but that jazz still somehow vulgarised music and thereby lost all self restraint. But of course the Negro slaves in the USA were often both deeply religious, and yet quite uninhibited in the expression of their feelings. Debussy's Golliwog's CakeWalk – would that title even be allowed today? – released the rhythmical possibilities of music as this composer did in all other aspects, and composers such as Stravinsky were not slow to take the hint. The link between Jazz and the Baroque idiom has often been commented upon, and used brilliantly in George Malcom's 'Bach goes to Town'. The spirituals in 'A Child of our Time' are remarkably apt and Bachian in their placing in the drama. And when 'A Whiter Shade of Pale' first came to our attention the unmistakable allusion to the Adagio idiom of J.S. Bach was quite riveting, and even the 'vestal virgins' allusion seemed quite in place! The basso-continuo of the baroque is replaced by the piano and percussion of the jazz band, but both are linked by the art of improvisation. George Gershwin is a key figure in all of this, and still the most successful in the fusion of jazz idiom with the extended forms of concert music, together with Ravel's Piano Concertos and the Bolero and La Valse. Following Ravel there is Poulenc in his Organ Concerto, and there is certainly more scope for the use of jazz idioms in the organ music of the concert hall. However, what about music of the Flesh and the Devil in church services? The idea that the language used in Services must continue to evolve along increasingly popular lines certainly implies the same for the musical idioms in use. So far, the composers in this field have tended to the over-simplistic and banal. The popular 'Lord Jesus Christ, you have come to us' seems to me to be totally nauseous – 'combing its greasy locks' was one description I have been advised – and thought remarkably apt. The attention span required for popular music since the 1960s appears to be about three minutes, and its most chilling aspect, even if we ignore the paucity of invention, is the usually total absence of rests and dynamic variety – which must be as loud as current technology allows. In that it is still in its childhood, and at some stage will need to show signs of healthy growth and development in performers and listeners, Luther's concept of 'the best tunes' certainly seems to have gone to the Devil!

Chapter 9

Paths My Feet Have Trod

Rough paths my feet have trod,
Since first their time began;
Feed me, thou Bread of God;
Help me, thou Son of Man.
(J.S.B. Monsell)

The majority of my musical travels have been concert tours as a solo organist (I refused lengthy examination tour offers until I had retired from the Cathedral and the RAM), and the most frequent venue has been North America. This is not surprising as the great number of venues there also offer the largest total remuneration, although this does depend to some extent on the state of the USA economy – already in a somewhat parlous condition since the start of the New Millennium. My first such tour was in the Autumn of 1967 and included both Canada and the USA – my inexperience showed in an itinerary which sometimes led to insufficient time for practice. Nevertheless, it was a highly enjoyable experience and led to a strong desire for more such travels! They are rewarding in more than just monetary payment. Whatever the financial remuneration though, touring is a stimulating exercise for any performing artist and composer. It is a great opportunity to introduce new compositions and to make useful contacts amongst concert promoters and performers, as well as earning some useful income. Here I intend to give an insight into what touring as an organist is actually like, thereby perhaps dispelling any popular misconceptions.

The tour under consideration here (September/October 2002) was not decided upon until February of that year – at rather short notice you might think. It was my thirteenth tour and therefore already possibly problematic – especially on account of the terrorist attacks of the previous year. I am not in the least superstitious though and so began to make contacts, using the names and places from my previous trips which were stored in my files. Within a few weeks these had produced enough offers to enable me to go ahead with confidence. My last USA tour was in 1998 and I had a few e-mail contacts from that era, but also a large amount of correspondence dating back to my first tour in 1967 and subsequently. Chestertown Emmanuel Church in Maryland offered me my first date of 27th September and Dallas had already expressed a preference for the end of October – the 29th was eventually agreed. This established a timescale which was rather more extensive than I had originally envisaged, but it clearly required a timetable of sufficient dates to make the trip economically viable. Ideally, such a tour needed to make a logical journey without too much zigzagging around over previously covered territory. But this is rarely achieved, especially in a tour planned with so little time to negotiate venues and dates.

It began well with Chestertown (September 27) followed by Chevy Chase Presbyterian Church – in a suburb of Washington DC (29th). But now came the first diversion: the First Presbyterian Church of Bonita Springs (Florida) offered me October 3rd, and St Paul's Episcopal Church, Akron (Ohio) October 6th. Bonita Springs allowed me three days' practice time, Akron only two. I had played in Akron previously though (1983), it has a very large four-manual organ, and the choir had sung my Missa Eliensis on the Sunday morning of my afternoon concert, so that it was not unknown territory, as was Bonita. Sunny Florida always attracts though, and on this trip it beckoned irresistibly. The weather was firmly in the 90s at Bonita Springs and it was a considerable shock to take a twin-propeller plane to Akron from Charlotte, South Carolina. Akron was cold and rainy at the outset, though the weather improved steadily. I allowed myself an extra day in Akron in order to relax and be shown some of the surrounding countryside. Then on to San Francisco (always a marvellous place to visit) for two concerts – St Bede's Episcopal Church in suburban Menlo Park on Saturday, October 12th and the National Shrine of St Francis of Assisi – right in the hectic city centre where the Italian and Chinese areas noisily converge – a wonderful, vibrant atmosphere! But this concert the following day was in their series of Sunday afternoon events at 4.00 p.m. immediately after Sung Vespers, with the attendant problems of practice and transport requiring careful planning. But I was sure that it could be done, albeit in a slightly hair-raising fashion! The following day, Monday, I flew to San Diego, only an hour and a half journey, the venue here being St Paul's Episcopal Cathedral where I played on the Wednesday following. On Thursday I flew to Los Angeles for a concert on the following Sunday afternoon at the All Saints' Parish Church, Beverley Hills – this was advertised as 'Ely Inspirations: A Place and its Music'. On Monday I made the coast to coast (three time zone changes) flight to Savannah, Georgia – arriving at 22.30! Fortunately I had until the Friday to rest and prepare for the concert at Christ Church – just as well given the circumstances. The last two concerts were less favoured in the practice time available – Trinity Episcopal Church in Tulsa, Oklahoma on the Sunday, and the Church of the Incarnation at Dallas, Texas on the Tuesday. My return journey back home began on the following day, and I arrived at London Gatwick Airport at 7.30 on Thursday. Many people would consider this a somewhat stressful experience, but it does indicate the reality of being 'on the road' as a touring artist.

Having fixed the venues and dates, the important matter of the programme content requires attention. Much thought needs to be given to this, as the choice of music to be featured is second only to the performance skills and the personality of the performer from the audience point of view. Each of the pieces must be fully embraced (loved, if you like) by the artist, and be of the quality and riveting interest to hold his attention throughout the many repetitions of the same material. Also the variety of the instruments to be encountered in the course of the tour needs to be carefully considered. It is quite normal for a touring organist to find instruments of two, three or four manuals (keyboards) and the chosen programme must be able to be fully projected in all its varied character to the audience. This difference of size and character can also be of use to the performer in providing the respite from routine which the repetition of the same pieces might easily tend to engender.

There is one important difference between organs in the UK and the USA and that is in the balance of tone between the manuals and pedals. Traditionally, English organs have a stop named Great to Pedal combination coupler – rarely to be found in the USA. This useful device enables a correct balance between the main manual (the Great) and the Pedal department to be maintained throughout all changes of registration. But the invention of digital memory systems has overcome this lack of fixed balance between manual and pedal, and now virtually any combination of registers is available on almost any organ one may encounter – save one – an historically correct copy of a pre-twentieth century instrument, or one based on the same principles. Confronted with this situation the performer needs a knowledgeable assistant to help with any changes of stops. Unlike the piano, which varies only in depth of touch, or the violin, flute and the like, which the performer may carry around easily to his chosen venues, the organist has a fresh voyage of discovery to make on every new organ with each and every piece in his programme. And unlike every other performer the organist has to devote hours of practice time to working out the most suitable sounds for his programme as are available on each of the instruments he encounters. But of course this incessant difference between organs does mean that the player is kept freshly involved with his music as he endeavours to re-create it convincingly in each and every venue. So enough material has to be prepared to keep the performer's interest alive, and also to be performable on all of the instruments to be encountered. This can make the music case quite heavy on some tours, and this was certainly the case with the 2002 concerts! It has also become quite customary for recitalists to carry a box full of their CDs for sale at the concerts. This has something to commend it, though it is hardly feasible for artists travelling on their own, as I usually do.

As composition has been such an important aspect of my musical activities a recital tour is a natural opportunity for me to include some of this material in my programmes, as well as some of my transcriptions. On this occasion I gave the first USA performances of my Variations and Fugue on a theme of Henry Purcell – 'Wondrous Machine!' This work has a part for a narrator which of course would be something of a novelty in an organ concert. I also included several of my transcriptions – Mussorgsky's Pictures from an Exhibition, Bach's Chaconne in D minor (solo violin) and three movements from my Symphonic Suite 'The Fenlands'. Other works included Bach's Toccata and Fugue in D minor, Schumann's Sketches in C major and F minor, Mozart's Adagio and Allegro K.594, Cesar Franck's Choral in A minor and Elgar's Sonata No.2. It is important, I think, to play programmes which exploit the full range of organ colours, and also to base them on the substantial works of composers known for their works in the mainstream of music literature. I also featured three of my shorter pieces, Carillon on 'Orientis Partibus', Elegy and my well tried encore 'Etheldreda Rag'.

The first concert was scheduled for Friday, September 27th at Emmanuel Church, Chestertown, Maryland. I flew from London Heathrow Airport to Philadelphia on the previous Tuesday, which gave me all day on Wednesday to settle in from the long flight and time change, with Thursday and Friday available for some intensive practising. I had played the 1992 Harrison organ on my last tour four years previously, but it still took some time to feel really 'at home' with it. It is a beautifully voiced instrument which can deal with a great deal of repertoire, allowing for its limitation of size, and certainly greatly aided by its piston-setting mechanism. This was the programme:

Toccata and Fugue in D minor BWV565 – Bach
Voluntary in D – Handel
Two Pieces for an Organ in a Clock: Menuet and
    Allegro – Haydn
Two Sketches, Op.58 – Schumann (C major, F minor)
Sonata No. 2 in B flat – Elgar (Introduction – Toccata
    – Fugue – Coda)

Interval

Pictures from an Exhibition – Mussorgsky –
    Promenade – Limoges, The Market Place –
    Catacombae –
Sepulcrum Romanum – 'Con Mortuis in Lingua
    Mortis' – Baba Yaga: The Hut on Fowl's Legs –
The Great Gate of Kiev.
Elegy and Carillon on Orientis Partibus – Wills

This selection gave ample opportunity to exploit the available range of colour and dynamics, and the relatively small dimensions of the building allowed of a quite intimate relationship of performer, organ and audience. Of all instruments the organ is usually expected to keep its distance – "the mystique of the organ loft" is how a friend once put it, and this I think is one reason why today's audiences can find it a somewhat intimidating ordeal in a concert situation. A church service is a rather different matter, and here the organ can readily function as 'the voice of God' – overwhelmingly impressive in a large church or cathedral. But in Chestertown I was only a few steps from the front pews, and it was even quite possible to swing off the organ bench and talk from there without having to move further. I attach great importance to this opportunity to draw those present into the music and its historical background, and the choice of the first piece must create the right atmosphere of either gripping familiarity or an exciting surprise. The Bach choice was certainly right for this purpose, and I was able to mention its perhaps surprising version for solo violin, and also the fact that its compositional provenance has sometimes been called into question. The Handel and Haydn pieces were ideal for organ and the room, and again gave rise to the kind of instruments they were intended for. The Schumann Sketches likewise provided many ideas for the audience to ponder – the rehabilitation of Bach during the early Romantic period, led by Mendelssohn, Schumann and Brahms; the use of the pedal-piano at this time (and the fact that I had the use of one at home) and the relationship of these works to Schumann's piano compositions. The Second Sonata of Elgar is appearing more frequently in concerts these days. It is in fact more suited to the organ than its better known forerunner in G major, and being much shorter is less trying on the audience's attention span. It is a transcription by Sir Ivor Atkins of the Severn Suite which Elgar had composed for Brass Band in 1930 and dedicated to his friend Bernard Shaw. A comparison of this with the organ Sonata version, done by Sir Ivor Atkins with Elgar's co-operation, is very helpful for the audience, and greatly assists their understanding. After the interval the last section of Mussorgsky's 'Pictures' – beginning with the Promenade the composer re-worked from the opening of the piece – makes a really compelling experience for the listener, with some

167

introduction to the history of this work, which transcribes so readily from the composer's original piano version. Finally, two very contrasted pieces of my own – the Elegy from the mid-1950s and the Carillon from 1973. This last is based on an ancient tune often sung to 'Christ the Lord is risen again'. I introduced these pieces as contrasting ways of looking at death – regret at loss, but also final triumph to come. Then an encore – my own Etheldreda Rag, which always surprises, and generally captivates an audience – as it certainly did on this occasion.

But this visit to Chestertown was not just practising and concert – on the Wednesday I was taken round the historic centre and the waterfront, and every evening there was a dinner-party of great conviviality. All this readily arises out of a direct arrangement for the concert with the Organist and the hosts he arranges, thereby bypassing the expense and isolation of an agent and hotel accommodation.

The next concert was in a suburb of Washington, DC, Chevy Chase Presbyterian Church. The Organist had foreseen problems with the timing here as it was scheduled for their usual Sunday afternoon series at 4.00 p.m. but then changed to 2.00 p.m. on account of a concert at 4.00 p.m. at a nearby church. Unfortunately the church advertised the change correctly – but the newspapers didn't, with the result that there was a small audience for the 14.00 timing with a larger number appearing just as we were leaving for the reception after the concert. The concert had been advertised as including the USA premiere of my 'Wondrous Machine!' – Variations and Fugue on a Theme of Henry Purcell which I narrated myself from the console. It concluded with my transcription of three movements from my Symphonic Suite 'The Fenlands' for Brass band and organ. Many of the latecomers came to the Reception and eventually several asked me to play something from the programme, choosing 'The Fenlands'. At first I agreed to play the first movement of the Suite, but once I got into this I decided to play all three movements. But all ended happily when my host took me to dinner at an excellent Italian Restaurant in downtown Washington, followed by a tour of the capital, including a brief visit to the Episcopal Cathedral before it closed at 20.00. This visit brought back many memories of my first visit to the cathedral on my first USA recital tour in the Fall of 1969, when only the Choir and central crossing were complete. A very exciting encounter; meeting the Organist and Choirmaster Paul Calloway, John Fenstermaker his Assistant, Douglas Major, who eventually became the successor to Paul Calloway, and a host of other luminaries in the church music world of Washington Cathedral and the then thriving College of Church Musicians. It was especially enjoyable to spend some time with John Morehen, who was a guest lecturer at the College. In honour of us both there was a Reception at the British Embassy – a somewhat unexpected, but thrilling occasion!

The concert timing debacle is of course a rare occurrence on these tours, but it does serve to demonstrate the necessity for flexibility and equanimity when it does happen. The ability to cope with radically different (and sometimes problematic) organs is also an essential aspect of the touring experience. My encounter with the Washington Cathedral organ on that visit in 1957 was a somewhat less than an entirely happy experience – the organ was then in a state of being enlarged and generally overhauled. To my astonishment and dismay, the stop knobs bore but little resemblance to the registers they were apparently meant to control. How I managed I can't quite remember – but John Fenstermaker turned pages for me and was as generally helpful as he could be. In general you need to develop a mindset that will enable you to cope with any and all problems, and demonstrate to your audience that all is indeed for the best in the most intolerable of all possible recital situations!

The 1970s baroque revival instrument at Chevy Chase was in sharp contrast to the next organ on this tour. The First Presbyterian Church of Bonita Springs, Florida, was the proud possessor of a brand new Allen 'Renaissance' electronic instrument, with a 390 pipe division plus 61 Trumpet en chamade pipes on the front wall, and with four manuals and 100 stops, and an echo division at the back of the newly enlarged auditorium. This was an obvious candidate for my 'Wondrous Machine' as an opener, and as at Chevy Chase I narrated it with a lapel mike. The second half of the programme was given up to the Mussorgsky 'Pictures from an Exhibition' complete. All the variety of colour one could possibly want for this masterpiece was here in abundance. Also in equal abundance was the hospitality of my host Hank Hochstetler, a member of the Church Choir. He was an utterly delightful man – several years younger than myself and still active in business, though not without some health problems, and his wife had died just a few years previously. Nothing was too much trouble for him – temperatures were in the 90s and the Everglades beckoned. I had been to this nature reserve on a previous tour many years ago, but it is still a fascinating nature reserve to re-visit. The alligators exerted their usual mix of enticing compulsive horror!

Time for relaxation and sight-seeing is a very desirable aspect of touring and to be relished – it's not always possible with some schedules and the increase in tension is often noticeable. The day after the concert I had another lengthy flight back north to Akron, Ohio, with a change of planes at Charlotte SC. After the terrorist attacks of the previous year security had become a top priority at all airports, and I was a prime target for attention as I did not have any return ticket reservations, but I became used to the incessant searches of my person and luggage in time.

I was looking forward to the concert in St Paul's Episcopal Church with keen anticipation. I remembered playing there in 1983 when the Choir sang my Missa Eliensis in honour of my visit. The then Organist Robert Quade was the RSCM representative for the American Episcopal Church and a great power in the land! His successor Jamie Hitel had only been in office for a couple of years having previously been Director of Music at Waltham Abbey in Essex. I arrived in Akron at around lunchtime on Friday, knowing that this was to be a concert with rather less than ample time for rehearsal. After sunny Florida, Ohio proved to be cold and rainy though the following days were to be more enticing. The practice schedule was problematic with a wedding on Saturday, and I discovered that the church was required for photographs afterwards, with these taking almost as much time as the Service itself. Nevertheless, the large four-manual organ was capable of a wide range of repertoire, and 'Wondrous Machine' was an entirely feasible proposition. A particularly interesting feature of the inclusion of this work was that the narrator was to be Alastair Stout, an Ely ex-chorister who was now in charge of the music at a Methodist Church in the suburbs of Pittsburgh. He drove the two-hour distance after his morning Service and arrived a comfortable hour before my concert, enabling a useful rehearsal of the timing, volume, and the acoustical 'feel' of the building to be experienced. The organ console had been moved from its normal concealed position at the East of the Choir Stalls to the front of the Chancel, and at the conclusion of the rehearsal I was approached by a very imposing coloured man with a purposeful tread, who shook my hand and said, "I remember your concert here in 1983, and the encore you played – your 'Lullaby for a Royal Prince'." Goodness, I thought, they do take their concerts seriously here! And this was also born out by the size of the audience, one of the largest I encountered on this tour. I was being hosted by a couple of the Church members who let me use a self-contained flat on the upper floor of their house, very commodious with bedroom, sitting room, kitchen and

171

bathroom. It always takes a little time to accustom oneself to the available facilities, but the only problem I encountered was a toaster somewhat reluctant to be turned on. The first time I gave up, but the following morning I tried again with complete success this time – But! – I left it to its own devices, thinking that it would turn itself off as toasters usually do. Coming back I was alerted by an alarming smell and to my horror the toast was quite well alight. I turned it off and managed to extricate the bread with the help of a knife and fork. Nothing was damaged but the horrid odour of burnt toast haunted my rooms for the rest of that day. My hosts were not at all put out – "it's forty years old," they said, and undertook to replace it.

The next stage of the tour was two concerts in San Francisco – one of my very favourite cities, entailing a long flight over several time zones. I had allowed for the Monday as a day off in Akron for rest and relaxation and some sightseeing, and it was also a chance to spend some time with Alastair before he drove back to Pittsburgh. There is always the possibility of flight time changes or even cancellations, and this proved to be the case here, so that my hosts in San Francisco had some problems in identifying my time of arrival. After collecting my luggage I waited in the terminal building for several minutes, and then decided to wait outside. As I opened the door I was greeted by a familiar figure from England – Rogers Covey-Crump – a noted tenor and member of the Hilliard Ensemble. "Your car is here"! and so I was whisked off to my hosts in the suburbs.

The two concerts were on consecutive days – Saturday evening in St Bede's Episcopal Church, Menlo Park, where I had played before, very near to Stanford University – and the following Sunday afternoon in a very interesting venue new to me, the National Shrine of Saint Francis of Assisi, in the Italian-Chinese district of the downtown area of San Francisco. Both were two-manual instruments, but very different – St Bede's was an entirely mechanical instrument, with all couplers placed above the Pedals and in an only fairly reverberant wooden acoustic; whereas the Shrine Church organ was a 19th century French instrument in its inspiration, placed at the West End in an impressively tall and very resonant Gothic Revival Building in stone – the first church to be built in San Francisco after the Mission churches (1849). Jane McDougle was the Director of Music at St Bede's and was extraordinarily kind in not only arranging hospitality with two parishioners (I was to be there for six nights!) but also in thinking about my practice arrangements in two venues many miles apart in less than 24 hours. An old friend, John Fenstermaker, was now Organist at the Shrine Church after a very distinguished time in office at Grace Cathedral. He was away in Florida on this occasion, so that although all the arrangements had been put in place by him, details of transport between the two venues needed to be finalised and then be communicated to me. John had warned me that my concert was on the same day as the Columbus Day Parade – "this Italian area goes mad with delight!" he said. Well, that was indeed the case – swooping aircraft overhead, an amplified female vocalist and cheering crowds all accompanied my practice time between the end of the sung High Mass and afternoon Vespers. But that was it – all over before Vespers and as quiet as anyone could wish for the Service and my concert at 4.00 p.m. Rodgers Covey-Crump was my chief registrant at both concerts and in Elgar's Second Sonata (not a really good choice for the St Bede's organ) both he and Jane had their work cut out to manipulate the stops and couplers for me! But at the Shrine Church both Franck's Choral in A minor and my 'The Vikings' transcription sounded marvellous, with the Franck acquiring a spiritual ambience in that environment that I had rarely experienced before.

Five concerts still to go! I was looking forward to San Diego – the nearest I had been to the Mexican border. I was being hosted by Drs Ty and Penelope Smith, retired hospital medics who had turned all their energies into forwarding the cause of church music in the Pacific area. Their efforts went under the title of PACEM (Pacific Academy of Ecclesiastical Music), and their office and library are located in St Paul's Episcopal Cathedral, where I was engaged to play my concert. The Director of Music – Edgar Billups – had been unwell for some time and the music was in the charge of his Assistant Martin Green. Martin had previously requested that I should find time to work with the Boys' Choir and I was happy to do this, of course. It was brought home to me once again how all children's activities in the USA are dependant upon what are derisively called 'gasguzzlers' in Europe. In fact nothing would be able to happen without these vehicles, and my admiration for both parents and children – and the musicians who have to inspire their loyalty – was aroused once again. The cathedral organ was a large four-manual instrument which was brought out into the front of the chancel for the concert, and so allowed me to narrate 'Wondrous Machine' from the console.

There was little time for sight-seeing on this visit to San Diego, but the Smith's house was wonderfully situated on the hills surrounding the harbour and by day and night gave marvellous views of the city and its harbour – also an important naval base, the existence of which I had not previously been aware.

Then on to Los Angeles – always a fascinating city to visit and only a short commuter flight from San Diego. Here the venue was All Saints' Parish Church, Beverley Hills, where the organ was from Schlicker, 1988. The Organist there is Thomas Foster, who I remembered meeting in the 1960s when on a previous visit to the 'City of Angels'. I was being hosted by Ivy and Leo Chu whose house was situated a short walk from the church in North Camden Drive. Ivy was a keen musician with a piano and house organ, both clearly in frequent use, though it was clear that she and Leo were very absorbed in their business activities, and I did not manage to see a great deal of them, apart from an enjoyable Saturday breakfast at a local restaurant. I found the organ and acoustic very manageable, so much so that I was able to find time to spend the Saturday afternoon visiting the Santa Monica Beach and the famous Third Avenue with its Mall and market ambience. At the Sunday afternoon concert a lapel microphone was available for 'Wondrous Machine' so I was very happy with this – and also the enthusiastic audience – the most uninhibited I encountered on this tour! A dinner had been arranged for after the concert, and our number was joined by Martin Neary who had noticed my presence in L.A. He congratulated me on my ability to 'draw the audience into the music' with my spoken introductions, and was a lively conversationalist at the dinner – to the interest and amusement of the other guests!

Monday morning saw my embarkation on the longest flight of this tour, from the West to the East coast – California to Georgia – from the worldly sophistication of Los Angeles to the deep Southern mystery of Savannah, with its deep rich heritage of plantations, and its abundance of old world mansions. Arriving at 22.30 hours, I was met by the Director of Music, Mark Williams and his wife Tina. They drove me to the house where I had the lower floor completely to myself, including two bedrooms, a sitting room and small kitchen! After the long flight I needed a day to recover, which was just as well as the situation with the organ to be re-dedicated was, as it so frequently is on these occasions, a long way from it being usable.

My concert in Christ Church was scheduled for Friday evening, and its purpose was to dedicate the rebuilt Harrison organ, first installed in 1972, when it was dedicated by the Bishop of London. My Missa Brevis for unison voices was sung at this Service, and the recital was played by E. Power Biggs – one of the great personalities of the American organ fraternity! For my dedicatory concert, 'Wondrous Machine' was an obvious choice for the first piece in the programme and I suggested to Tina – a professional singer – that she might like to be the first woman to narrate it. She was enthusiastic about this and did it superbly well on the day. Nevertheless, I was increasingly alarmed at the slow progress of the completion of the work on the organ, and it was not until the morning of the day of the concert that I was completely satisfied that it would be ready. (I was reminded of a similar occasion in 1980 when I was scheduled to open a new organ in Wellington Cathedral, New Zealand on a Sunday afternoon. The organ was still not quite ready after the morning Service – and the concert was to be broadcast live! Still, the day was saved, and I travelled on to Christ Church immediately afterwards, where on my arrival I was congratulated by the organists who had heard the broadcast!)

The rest of the tour was a fairly hectic business – my next venue was in Tulsa, Oklahoma, at Trinity Episcopal Church and scheduled for Sunday evening. This entailed a flight leaving Savannah at 9.05 on Saturday morning; this doesn't sound too bad, but bearing in mind that security arrangements meant arriving at the airport two hours previous to departure was a rather strenuous early get-up! But I was assured that at a smallish airport such as that at Savannah I could be rather more relaxed about my timetable in order to get through security. Though I needed to change planes at Atlanta, so that I was relieved when I arrived at Tulsa on time at 12.28 to be met by the Assistant organist Casey Cantwell. Lunch was the first requirement and then an afternoon getting to know the organ, which was a four manual instrument by Moller installed in 1962. I had played many Moller organs in the course of my travels and had formed a not entirely favourable opinion of them, but this one was of interest from its seven divisions spread over four manuals, and an apparently favourable acoustic. An organ of 80 speaking stops takes some time to arrive at a satisfactory scheme for five major pieces, and I was only halfway through the programme when it was time to stop and be taken to my hosts who had arranged a dinner party of some dozen guests. I attended the Eucharist the following morning and was somewhat surprised to be joined in my row by a lady who had attended my concert in Adelaide Town Hall in September of 2000. The Organist Stephen Tappe expressed a wish to narrate 'Wondrous Machine!' from the Lectern, which he did with great aplomb after I had introduced the work.

Finally, the following day I flew to Dallas, which was the original starting idea for the whole tour. The previous year I had been commissioned to compose a Latin Mass for the Church of the Incarnation – the Missa Incarnationis, and it was agreed that I should play a concert in the Fall of this year. The Organist, Kevin Clarke, had agreed the date of 29th October, and deciding on this as the final concert of the tour was the mainspring of the whole venture, once I was assured of the first recital date at Chestertown in late September. As was the case with the Tulsa concert it was a question of travelling one day and performing on the next. The three-manual organ was well suited to an elaborate and colourful programme which included the complete 'Pictures from an Exhibition' as well as 'Wondrous Machine!' but it nevertheless takes a long time to decide on the precise colours from the particular range of stops and the dynamic range available. Nevertheless, all was ready on time and it was agreed that I should introduce the programme from the organ loft, which was placed above the choir stalls as is the case with the English cathedral tradition – and also of course narrate 'Wondrous Machine!' from there. On this occasion, the microphone was not at first reliable, and some adjustment was needed after a first attempt. After that all went well and I was mainly happy with this my final concert of the tour. A visit to a local seafood restaurant rounded off the visit very satisfactorily! All in all then, a very enjoyable outcome in every way.

A diversion from touring greeted me on my return home – my wife had already alerted me by telephone to be prepared to deal with an invitation to supply some organ music for a Short Film – *The Goodbye Plane*. She had already told Kewhaven Pictures "He will do it!". The world of short films was certainly a new field of interest – in order to raise sponsorship the film is made in support of a good cause, in this case 'The Royal Star and Garter Home' for Disabled Ex-servicemen. It will then go the round of Short Film Festivals to arouse interest in the quality of the product. As it is for charity, all expenses incurred, but no fees, are paid to the participants in the endeavour.

On two occasions I was fetched by car from Ely to Chiswick, in West London where the Parish Church and its surround was the centre for much of the film. It was mid-morning before we arrived, but I managed to begin to get to know the three-manual organ, and even to start recording. In any film much of what is taken inevitably eventually ends up on the cutting floor, as it is always a piece of creative work in progress, rather than the simply filming of a determined piece of work. Therefore the list of pieces I was asked to prepare and record, mostly excerpts, might never be used in the final filming. For instance it was a matter of regret for me that Karg-Elert's Nun danket alle Gott which was recorded complete, and which I considered one of my best performances, was not used at all in the finished film. But the opening music, which emerges from a pianissimo distance effect was the final two pages of the J.S. Bach Passacaglia and Fugue, a stunning climactic effect, including an improvised cadenza after the indicated pause chord. A balletic sequence required the first two pages of the Finale from Guilmant's 1st Sonata – more than one go needed here to get every semiquaver into place! Then, short excerpts from Mendelssohn's Wedding March and the Hornpipe from Handel's Water Music completed the material required for the finished product. The private premiere screening of *The*

Goodbye Plane at The Royal Star and Garter Home was on the 20th July 2003 – quite fascinating to see how the playing was integrated into the visual experience.

My first visit to Australia and New Zealand in 1980 (the first of four tours, two of which also included New Zealand) was also very enjoyable, and of course highly informative, as these travels invariably are – indeed one could write a book entirely devoted to such experiences. I left for London/Heathrow on Sunday July 13th, having spent the first three days of the previous week recording my transcription of Mussorgsky's Pictures at an Exhibition for Ted Perry and his new label Hyperion, followed by the usual two days at the RAM, dealing mainly with the end of year B.Mus. results. I travelled with the great cellist Paul Tortelier from Heathrow to Perth, and we had a long conversation during the stop-over in Bombay, with the rats scurrying along the rafters above our heads! His itinerary more-or-less mirrored mine, which meant that I was able to pick up several of his appearances en route. His wife would appear for the encore and join him for 'Otters' – a scampering duet – his own composition I remember him telling the audience.

I played two concerts in Perth, both at the Winthrop Hall in the University of Western Australia. the first was a lunch-hour event, sponsored by The Swan Brewery Company Ltd on Thursday (allowing Wednesday free to recuperate and a little practice). The main concert was on the following Sunday afternoon and included the Liszt Fantasia and Fugue on BACH, two of Franck's Three Pieces, the Elgar Sonata Op.28 and two of my pieces from the seventies – Variations on 'Amazing Grace' and Resurrection. In between, on the Friday evening I attended the Tortelier concert with Prof. David Allen-Williams. Any recital tour of Australia tends to be a trawl along the coast either from Perth to Brisbane or the other way round. On this occasion, after playing in Adelaide Cathedral, where Prof. David Swale of the University of Adelaide was the organist, he introduced me to some of the natural flora and fauna in the great Park – notably the trees and the Koalas!

Before going on into Victoria State I also visited Tasmania, taking in Hobart – St David's Cathedral; St John's Church, Launceston and St George's Church, Burnie. Then back to the mainland Melbourne, and straight on to Geelong for a concert in the famous Grammar School Chapel the following evening. An Ely connection here – the then Headmaster at the King's School, Hubert Ward – had previously taught at Geelong. Back to Melbourne where I played a lunchtime concert in the University's Melba Hall, heard June Nixon's Cathedral Choir sing Evensong, and also spoke at a Dinner held at Monash University at which I was able to express my admiration for June's ability as a Cathedral musician – all this not on the same day of course! Her Choir happily conducted itself while June played for William Mathias' setting of the evening Canticles: The 'Jesus' Service – not the easiest of settings. Bill James was at the Dinner – he had sung in the Ely Choir and was also Director of Music at the King's School for several years – in between Gerald Gifford and Steven le Prevost.

Next, on to Canberra, where Jack Barratt was Organist at St Paul's Church, Manuka. Jack's enthusiasm was as much in evidence as always – he was also in charge of the City Carillon and made it his business to show me round this impressive structure, and also took the opportunity to perform several of his favourite items. Regrettably Jack died in 1983, but it was some satisfaction to have been with him for those few days, when we could enjoy recalling many good times together thirty years earlier in Canterbury and Ely. I conducted an RSCM Festival for him, and the concert I gave in St Paul's Church included my 'Amazing Grace' Variations.

My next concerts were in Sydney – an exciting prospect! I was driven by car from Canberra by Alan Moffat, who was the Branch Secretary of the RSCM in New South Wales.

During the journey he phoned ahead to give the estimated time of our arrival – and was given the news that the Cathedral Organist had died that morning – in the course of a Choristers' Practice! Needless to say, the rest of the journey was somewhat fraught in atmosphere. Alan had arranged all my venues, and also my hospitality arrangements with Peter McMillan, the Organist and Choirmaster of St Paul's Church in Burwood. (As a result Peter was to play an essential role in my return visit to Sydney five years later.)

But now the full itinerary began (after a free day to settle in) with a lunch-hour recital at St Andrew's Cathedral. Incredibly, that evening at 6.15 p.m. I also played a concert on the famous Town Hall Organ noted for its 64' pedal stop. The audience particularly enjoyed my 'Amazing Grace' Variations, and I also included my Mussorgsky 'Pictures' transcription. The following evening venue was St James Church, King Street – a very famous centre of Anglo-Catholic worship – I suppose the 'All Saints, Margaret Street' of Sydney! The vicar was the Revd Howard Hollis (who I remembered from St Mary's Church, Primrose Hill where I played a concert in the early seventies) and the organist was Walter Sutcliffe, who also led the double-basses in the Sydney Symphony Orchestra. They proudly admitted to featuring my Missa Eliensis on a regular basis – indeed I was encouraged to discover that it was in the repertoire of most choirs in Australia capable of doing it justice. Alas – I revisited St James in 1992 – and even succeeded in playing a concert there again, but suffice it to say things were not at all what they had been just twelve years earlier. Sad – how can the Church so readily acquiesce in its own demise? The day following was given up to an RSCM Festival in the Cathedral. This was still not the end though, on the Tuesday evening I played a three-quarters of an hour concert in St Mary's Catholic Cathedral – an atmospheric venue (of course!) and resonant building. After that I was driven by road to Newcastle NSW for a concert in Christ Church

Cathedral the next day, which was to be recorded for broadcasting later. The organist there was of course Michael Dudman, who had been my Assistant for three years at Ely. But the next day back in the sky to Brisbane Q, with its sub-tropical climate. Before talking further about music I must express my avid enjoyment of the seafood restaurants in that coastal area – Sydney/Brisbane; – the oysters! – words fail me!

Having recovered somewhat from these culinary musings, my first concert was at Brisbane University's Mayne Hall, which possessed a classical style organ, and there I played my second Trio Sonata. The following day a lunch-hour concert on the St John's Cathedral organ – gorgeously Romantic. The Organist there was Robert Boughen – certainly Mr Music of Brisbane I was assured! And then – off to the airport to fly to New Zealand! – what else? – this is a concert tour of course. A febrile mixture of work and pleasure – I thoroughly recommend it.

The next day (Sunday) I was in Auckland, with an afternoon concert in Holy Trinity Cathedral (Organist Anthony Jennings) to prepare and deliver at 2.30 p.m. A large and resonant building, it has since been re-modelled but not entirely satisfactorily to my mind – there is a central space with no really convincing reason for its existence. I was to encounter Anthony Jennings again in 1992 at Newcastle University where he had become a Lecturer in the Early Music Department. It was good to be commissioned to compose a Communion Service setting for the Auckland Boys' Choir by their Director, Neil Shroff, as a result of this visit. On my return to Ely I must have got on with it more or less straightaway, as it was in Neil's hands by mid-October and he premiered it in a Celebration Concert held in Saint Matthews-in-the-city on November 2nd. There were three other commissioned works also premiered in this concert! Impressive by any standards.

The itinerary for these tours often looks frightening in retrospect! After one full day in Auckland, with its afternoon concert, I flew to Tauranga (with its hot springs!) the next day, leaving Auckland at 6.30 a.m. and arriving at 7.10 a.m. in Tauranga. Besides a visit to the Springs (very worthwhile) I prepared and played a concert that same day, going on to Hamilton by road the following day and playing a concert in St Peter's Cathedral there. Napier was the next venue – I flew from Hamilton at 9.45 a.m. arriving at Napier at 10.40 a.m. Fortunately this was a 'free' day, so slightly more relaxed. (Not entirely so of course – when you are 'on the trail' the next concert is 'always on your mind'.) The Cathedral Church of St John the Evangelist in Napier is an extraordinary building, and very striking in its architectural modernity. It is the third church to be built on its site, the second having been completely destroyed in the earthquake of 3rd February, 1931. Also remarkable is the city's post-earthquake history – more land had emerged from the coastal waters, and eventually was built upon in a significant enlargement of the available housing resource! As always, I would have preferred more leisure time in which to explore this fascinating city, but not so – Wellington now beckoned, with the prospect of a newly rebuilt organ and a broadcast recital to boot!

Stanley Jackson was Director of Music at Wellington Cathedral and we both had enjoyable memories of the far-off days when we had spent a year together at the College of St Nicholas at Canterbury. The organ had been enlarged from two manuals to four with a consequent doubling of the tonal resources now available. Radio New Zealand had arranged to broadcast the Dedication Service and recital on the Sunday at 2.00 p.m. and did so, but I recall that even after the Morning Service some final completion of the builders' work was still taking place. The recital programme as printed in the Order of Service ends with my Homage to John Stanley – which is a work for manuals only. This seems an unlikely item with which to conclude an organ concert, especially on this occasion. My recollection is that I concluded the concert with my 'Resurrection' – a far more appropriate character piece for this occasion! Then my diary tells me that I took a boat from Wellington at 15.45 p.m. and arrived at Christchurch at 16.30 p.m. where I was welcomed enthusiastically on arrival by David Childs and several other organists from that city!

The Cathedral in Christchurch is a magnificent building of Gothic design and resonant acoustic, and I recall giving a talk to the Organists' Association that evening before devoting Monday to rehearsing and the concert in the evening. Knowing that I was to conclude the tour at Dunedin it was suggested that I should buy some Jade ornaments for my wife, and also make a point to look due South from the City waterfront – next stop Antartica! In those days planes did tourist flights – but eventually stopped after a disastrous accident. The flight from Christchurch to Dunedin is spectacular for its mountainous scenery and the city rises sharply from the seafront, with the cathedral occupying a prominent position at the top of the hill. Raymond White had only recently moved to Dunedin from Nelson, and so was full of energy and enthusiasm for this new position, and I greatly enjoyed his hospitality. Alas, when I revisited Dunedin in 2000 he was no longer in office at the Cathedral, though still living in the City – his longheld opinions on what the music should be there being no longer 'relevant' to the current situation in the Church in New Zealand. Much the same kind of wilful discarding of a great tradition that I had witnessed at St James' in Sydney eight years before. Do I remember reading somewhere that an Empire in decline begins to fray first at its far outposts? But happily, nothing of the kind was being dreamt of in 1980, so after a stimulating visit with plenty of time for sightseeing, the purchase of some Jade and a final recital, I flew back to England via Australia, arriving back at Heathrow on Saturday – just in time to get my breath back for the start of the Autumn Term with Men's Voices Services the following day! This first Antipodean tour had been a great experience in every way, and had been an encouraging start to many new friendships, and very useful ideas and contacts for the future. One very exciting development was the possibility of a concert in the world-famous Opera House, and this was much in my mind over the next year or so, and was to be eventually realised in 1985.

In those years when I did not go abroad for a recital tour the summer holiday break might well be used for a combination of the two activities in this country, sometimes with a hired caravan. August 1981 was one such arrangement, and Mary and I left for Bridgewater in Somerset on the 8th to visit Michael Martin and his then wife Lizzie. He had been an organ pupil of mine at the King's School in the 1950s. This was a resting place en route to Exeter where I played a concert in the Cathedral on the 12th. Then on to Stoke, Hartland – on the North Devonshire coast – a truly delightful spot unspoiled by the ravages of so-called progress. The famous village of Clovelly was just a few miles down the road. The organist at the great Parish Church of St Nectan, Stoke, was Sidney Perrin whom I had known well in Cambridge, where he was Organist of Holy Trinity Church and a salesman at Millers Music Shop. A truly delightful man, he eventually felt that his move to Stoke – in his words – 'had been a disaster'. Financially maybe, but he in fact had the personality to make things happen, and he had soon set up – from 1971 onwards – an annual Summer Festival in this tiny coastal resort, in which I must have participated four or five times over the years. For a time he also conducted a male voice choir, which sang in one of the festival concerts in which I played, and I eventually asked for and received honorary membership, signified by a delightful badge which was worn with pride when sewn on to a couple of sports jackets! Having played there on the 15th and enjoyed the Perrin's superb hospitality for another day, we motored to Wells where I played in the Cathedral on the 20th. The next, somewhat intriguing venue, the following Saturday evening was at the village of Stogursey, where there was provision for regular organ concerts established by the Countess of Dawlish. These always attracted large audiences, and the organ was fully equal to the demands of my transcription of Mussorgsky's Pictures from an Exhibition. The next day on to Dorset and Wimbourne Minster, where I played the fifth and final concert on the 26th at the Minster Church. Two days later we were home, had returned the caravan to Cambridge and collected our dog from the Kennels. All in all a very nice combination of business and pleasure, repeated on many such holiday breaks over the years.

Other countries I have visited as a recitalist include, notably, South Africa in 1984, with concerts in Johannesburg, (St Mary's Cathedral and a broadcast from the Radio Studio plus an RSCM Festival); two concerts in Durban Town Hall (and I managed to fit in a two-day Safari in Zululand!) and the Anglican Cathedral in Cape Town as well also as concerts in Grahamstown and Port Elizabeth. Again, there can be no finer way of combining business with pleasure – would I have visited Table Mountain, or Soweto Township without the musical connections which provided the helpful hospitality and necessary contacts? And I came home with ideas for a new guitar piece – Suite Africana in three movements, published in due course by OUP.

In 1985, the prospect of a return to Australia during August was immensely appealing, especially as this time a concert in the Opera House had been being arranged. I was to be away for most of the month, but before leaving I managed to fit in a concert in Durham Cathedral on the last day of July. The following day I drove back to Ely, and I left Heathrow for Perth on Saturday 3rd August, arriving the following day. I played a concert in Guildford School on the 6th and did an interview for the Australian Broadcasting

Corporation on the 9th, to my amusement being preceded by Woody Hermon! That first week in Perth seems to have been an unusually relaxed one, as I didn't leave for Adelaide until Sunday the 11th. I was being hosted by Prof. David Swale again, and there I again played a concert in the Elder Hall at the University and gave one of the first performances of my Suite: 'The Spirit of Elgar' – three pieces for organ manuals, with optional pedals, all named after houses where Elgar once resided. The review by Stephen Whittaker for the *Adelaide Advertiser* didn't touch on this work, but did mention my transcription of the Bach Chaconne, adding the comment "Dr Wills clearly aims to be the Busoni of the Organ."(!)

I also directed an RSCM Festival in the Cathedral before leaving for Canberra on Sunday 18th – a move which initiated a much less leisurely period of activity. On this occasion I played in St John's Church, Reid, in an event sponsored by the Canberra School of Music and the programme included one of the first performances of my Lullaby for a Royal Prince – a piece for manuals which was intended to enhance the RSCM's new initiative of encouraging pianists to learn the organ. The title was a timely response to the birth of Prince William, but a secondary idea was its possible use at the Christmas season!

Then on to Sydney the next day for the long anticipated concert at the Opera House on the 'Concert Hall Grand Organ'. It was arranged in conjunction with the participation of the Choir of Saint Paul's Burwood, and their Director Peter McMillan. My solo rehearsal was timed for the early morning – 7.00 a.m. is in my memory! My solo items were the Bach/Wills Chaconne in D minor, Mozart's Fantasia in F minor K.608, the Final in B flat by Franck, my Tongues of Fire and after the interval my transcription of Mussorgsky's Pictures at an Exhibition. The Burwood Choir sang three groups of anthems, including my carol 'Sweet was the song', and also programmed was Purcell's Trumpet Sonata in C, played by Linda Bacon. The critic Fred Blanks was somewhat sniffy about the inclusion of the two transcriptions (he failed to notice a third – the Mozart was originally written for a mechanical organ in a clock) – the headline was 'Poacher (!) demonstrates impressive technique' and goes on: '…evident even on an instrument whose acquaintance he had made less than 24 hours previously.' Rather less than 12 hours previously to be accurate! The keyboard touch was uncomfortably heavy, and in tonal effectiveness the instrument did not really justify its large specification. But one has to remember its history. Begun by Ronald Sharp, whose previous experience had been whetted on some superior but comparatively small instruments, the emerging problems he encountered necessitated his relinquishing the task to the more experienced Rieger firm. Nevertheless, the total experience was exhilarating in the extreme and certainly comparable with the 'buzz' I experienced in my Festival Hall concert in 1967. And an excellent party afterwards!

The following day (22nd) I played a lunch-time concert in St Andrew's Cathedral which included all Eleven Transcriptions in the Arthur Wills Bach Book which I had recorded for Hyperion Records the previous year. Fred Blanks was not present to give his opinion on this piece of programming! Though more of him later.

On my way to Brisbane the following day, where I was scheduled for two concerts. I practised most of Saturday for a Sunday afternoon concert at the Conservatorium – all music by J.S. Bach including some of my transcriptions, but also the Prelude and Fugue in C major BWV 545 to begin with, and that in E flat BWV 552 to conclude the concert, as well as the Fantasias in G major and C minor. I played my second concert in the University Mayne Hall the following Wednesday – Bach transcriptions, Mozart, Schumann, Wills and Mussorgsky/Wills. I must have had plenty of time for sight-seeing and seafood at this stage of the tour – and left for London, via Sydney on Friday 30th arriving in London the following morning at the usual eye-watering time of 6.55 a.m. One thing riveted my attention on those two homeward flights – the Australian newspapers were full of articles on the rapid spread of the Aids virus – something that had completely escaped my attention so far in the UK.

My next Australian tour in 1992 was suggested to me by Michael Dudman, who had resigned his Cathedral post in Newcastle, and now was Professor at the Conservatorium of Music in the University of Newcastle. Having retired from Ely Cathedral in July 1990, and the RAM in July 1992, I was now free to undertake overseas tours without let or hindrance. Michael had instituted a bi-annual Keyboard Festival at the University and now invited me there in August (24th–29th) 1992 to participate as Guest of Honour, commissioned Composer, Performer and Adjudicator. He also asked me to give the Keynote Address, which I did on the topic: '20th Century Music – The Beginning of The End?' I was also asked to provide two substantial pieces; one for the Opening Concert of the Festival, for which I composed Choral Concerto: 'The Gods of Music' for Chorus, Solo Organ, and Brass and Percussion Ensemble. Michael conducted the work and I played the solo organ part. This is the note on the Concerto that I provided for the programme:

The impulse behind the composition of this work arose from the circumstances of the commission for the keyboard festival itself: A solo keyboard part for myself to play, the participation of the Faculty Chorus, and an orchestral group which would play an individual role and yet combine with and set off the organ and choral sonorities. I had to provide the text myself simply because I could not find just what I needed in either theme or length elsewhere. As the opening Festival work I considered that a ceremonial character was appropriate; the Odes to Music and St Cecilia composed by Purcell and Handel came to mind as models for inspiration. I chose the unusual title Choral Concerto for several reasons.

Beethoven's use of the title Choral Fantasia for a work with solo piano, chorus and orchestra was an obvious pointer, and I also had in mind the Baroque use of concerto for pieces combining vocal and instrumental sonorities, as in certain Bach cantata movements. The words deal with the art itself in its perpetual search for an equilibrium between order and chaos, unity and variety, and give a prime position to the organ as a single voice in itself and the integration of many voices. The chorus is used to convey the point of the work though the text, and is also used as a sonority in the texture, either vocalising or humming. My primary concern was that the music should make its message understood with or without knowledge of the words. The solo organ part provides technical challenges, but is not fashioned as a dominant virtuoso element – rather than as one powerful voice among equals – the baroque influence! the work is organised as a single movement in several sections, contrasting its Apollonian and Dionysian aspects. Order and unity are symbolised by the use of a single pulse duration as the basis of many highly contrasted rhythmical ideas, and also in the symmetrical placing of the sections in contrasted tempi. But enough of analysis – the sound of the music is its meaning!

As in 1985, Fred Blanks again represented the *Sydney Morning Herald*: – "the work is a mighty, eventful, joyous choral fanfare with brass, percussion and organ solo. Its text is by the composer, and it is 21 minutes long and about 18 minutes loud."(!) Rather more interesting, though still not flattering, is this from Barry Walmsley in *The Newcastle Herald*: – "one has to suspect that there is a little bit of the cultural cringe at work here. In all the commissioned works for this festival, why is there not something of Australian origin? He writes of the Choral Concerto as – 'having the air of a ceremonial piece. It contained many imposing and challenging sections. The over-indulgent sound from much of the tutti sections was thankfully offset by a beautifully languid middle section."

The following day I adjudicated a composition competition in the afternoon, and then in the evening played a solo organ concert in the Conservatorium Performance Hall which was recorded for later broadcast by the ABC. Works of my own in the programme included Tongues of Fire, Icons and Suite: The Spirit of Elgar. This was followed with a concert by Michael the next day entitled Organ Music from Paris and Ely. His programme consisted of Widor's Symphonie No 5 in F minor and my Variations on a Carol.

At a lunchtime concert the following day my other commission for the Festival was given its first performance. The programme was entitled 'Vocal Music from Four Centuries' and was given by Katherine Capewell – Contralto accompanied by Anthony Jennings – Harpsichord, Helen O'Brien – Fortepiano, David Miller – Piano and Michael Dudman – Organ. My piece was entitled Eternity's Sunrise – (Three Poems by William Blake) and included settings of The Lamb, The Tyger and Eternity – all inspirational poems crying out for music. During that afternoon I adjudicated an organ competition; the following morning I lectured on Composition and Cathedral – An English Tradition, and also did some practice on the Newcastle Cathedral organ where I was to play the Eucharist on Sunday morning.

To round off the Festival, Michael conducted 'The Messiah' at the Saturday evening final concert. All in all I felt that Michael had paid me a great compliment with his Guest of Honour invitation, and certainly that in all the events of the Festival in which I actively participated. On the Sunday morning I'm pretty sure that the Eucharist setting I accompanied was my Missa Eliensis and I also played a short recital after the Service. This was followed by Lunch with the local Organists' Association and then a short talk, followed by a discussion. I then had some time on my own to await a taxi to take me to the airport for an evening flight to

Sydney, and I remember working on a Christmas carol for the Church Choir on the Island of Sark in the Channel Islands – Love came down at Christmas – with its beautiful text by Christina Rosetti. It is quite normal to take such work as this on tours – hours spent in aeroplanes are very conducive to composition. (My 'Song without Words' was begun in Ely on 7 June 1994, continued whilst flying to the USA over the North Pole, and completed and premiered (as an encore) in St Andrew's Cathedral, Honolulu on 22nd June 1994.)

Of course it would not have been economically viable to travel to Australia, even for such a prestigious event, without other engagements, and in any case one always desires to see as much as possible of such a fascinating country once you are there! So, on this visit I began as in 1980 at Perth, with a concert in St George's Cathedral on Sunday afternoon. At the Reception afterwards I met a young man with his mother, who said that he remembered me from my first visit in 1980 when I had rehearsed Missa Eliensis with the Choristers at their Friday evening Choir Practice! "I remember that well," he said – so did I, as one of my many somewhat heated experiences! Then on to Victoria State with a recital in Geelong, this time in St Paul's Church.

The next day to Melbourne, with an RSCM Dinner at 7.00 that evening, and a concert in St Paul's Cathedral the following day. The organ had by now been rebuilt by Harrison's and sounded magnificent in that reverberant acoustic. I also remember that the retired Organist of St Paul's Cathedral in London was present. After the great Newcastle Festival I flew back to Sydney for concerts in St James' Church (then a pale shadow of its former excellence in music and liturgy) and the Cathedral (lunchtime the following day) and then on to Brisbane for a concert in St Andrew's Presbyterian Church. The Minister took me out the following day to the beach in the 'Sunshine State'. (Interesting both for the surfing delights and the conversation!) Then back to England and Ely on the 8th September.

I mentioned the Dame of Sark and the carol I was working on in Newcastle NSW, and the reason for this was the tour of the Channel Islands I undertook with my wife towards the end of July this same year. I played a concert on each of the four Islands, visiting Alderney and Sark for the first time for this purpose. My work at the RAM was concluded on Graduation Day on Friday 3rd July, and so a new era of freelance activity now beckoned. It is true that I regretted the loss of the weekly contact with London life and its feverish activity – and also the fact that the old dispensation at the London Colleges had a history of a 'job for life' valued by many, and not just by those professors immediately concerned. It is true also that some professors found it difficult to get up the steps into the Entrance Hall at the RAM, and then received a mere pittance for their time and trouble, but some great names – Herbert Howells at the RCM comes immediately to mind – were able to go on teaching into their seventies and eighties, and the sense of historical continuity thereby imparted was important and significant to many students, professors and general observers. On the other hand of course the salaries were greatly improved, and there were pension rights rather better than those under the former dispensation. But this release from the ties of my last regular employment commitment meant that I was now free to undertake any Overseas Tour that the Associated Board were prepared to offer me. Hence, less than a month after my return from Australia, I took the flight to Hong Kong for a two months' Examination stint.

I had always imagined that this venue would be one of the most attractive Overseas Tours available, and my appetite had been thoroughly whetted by the Hong Kong Schools Festival that I previously undertook in February 1988. Another reason for my attraction to Hong Kong was the fact that there were two very interesting Reiger organs installed there – one in the Academy for Performing Arts (Three-manual), the other in the Cultural Arts Centre (Four-manual). The Advisor for both had been Geraint Jones, who had often talked about these projects with me in the Canteen at the RAM when we occasionally met at tea-time. On this Schools Festival visit I heard Simon Preston play an organ concert on March 8th at the Academy, sponsored by Lloyds Bank. I remember that he began with Elgar's Imperial March (a nice choice with the imminent return of the Hong Kong Dependancy to China!) and his second half consisted of Guilmant's First Sonata. I was there with Michael Rippon, Head of Voice at the Academy (whom I remembered as a Choral Scholar at St John's College, Cambridge). We both went to the Reception afterwards and then decided to take Simon out to dinner – as usual a very convivial occasion. I played a concert on March 15th and then flew back to Heathrow on March 20th (Mary's birthday) and began an Easter Day *Songs of Praise* recording for the BBC the following day! The frenetic pace of activity in my life then seems almost unbelievable now.

In addition to the *Songs of Praise* programme, we had also been asked to record an *At Home on Sunday with Mary Archer* programme, and I had also been booked to record Cesar Franck's Choral in A minor for a solo television slot on Maundy Thursday afternoon! (Get as much in as you can while the equipment is still around!) This kind of thing just doesn't seem to happen nowadays, and I remember getting some practice done on the Franck Choral on the Academy organ in Hong Kong. The 'Mary Archer' programme was 'In the Can' on the first evening, plus I think the carol 'This joyful Eastertide' for the Choir spot in the *Songs of Praise* recording. The congregational rehearsals on the Tuesday and the recording on Wednesday were enjoyable as all such events are – "Like Cardiff Arms Park!" remarked Dean Pattison. One contretemps concerned a point in the rehearsal in which some choristers from local churches in the far distant South Transept were perhaps less attentive to my beat than I judged was needed. "That girl in the yellow anorak is not watching the beat!" I thundered. She did after that, as did all her companions, and this incident seems to have stayed in the mind of many of those present many years later! The search for 'ratings' and the supposed need to always be 'entertaining' has ruined the contemporary *Songs of Praise* format – especially the strange notion that hymns must be sung as fast as possible and 'glamorised' with outlandish harmonies and arrangements. It surely will not be long before a percussive 'beat' will be deemed necessary, and the arm waving of scantily attired female teenagers will follow – this for a congregational 'Service' of course. But for occasional added 'glamour' we are sometimes regaled with a semi-professional young adult choir, chosen as much for their looks as vocal ability, and directed(?) by a writhing, equally professional conductor. If it's television it must be visually glamorous – 'What? – a traditional surpliced choir of boys and men? – good God – No!'

All this may seem a diversion from 'paths my feet have trod' perhaps, but not entirely so, since on Easter Monday Mary and I flew out to Gran Canaria for a much needed brief holiday of one week's duration. The day after we returned I was at the RAM for next year's intake auditions. The 'paths' do need to be trodden speedily!

But on (or back) to 1992 again – we examiners arrived in Hong Kong on October 6th and learned that our residence would be divided between two hotels – City Garden Hotel on Hong Kong Island, and the Royal Pacific Hotel in mainland Kowloon. My fellow examiners were a lively bunch – some perhaps with a somewhat jaded and cynical approach to the examination process, at least in conversation – it is in fact possible to make a full-time activity from examining, and many do this for at least part of their professional career – perhaps after a rather too onerous time as an orchestral player. For instrumental teachers, whether private or institutional, it is a natural extension of their main activity. Some on this tour considered me something of a 'swot' and a 'go-getter' when they became eventually aware of my persistently hectic and varied life-style! This two-month stint was in fact just as much fun as I had anticipated – with several parties each week, and excursions to well known and favourite venues. One of these was Lamma Island where there was a restaurant with a pigeon dish speciality – absolutely delicious I thought, though my taste was not shared by all my examiner companions on this trip. But I did several journeys to that eatery! In the City Garden Hotel I encountered for the first time an unexpected phenomenon – once or twice each week the room lights would go out, presumably in a power-saving exercise. I found that the same was true in Malta, where I was examining at the same time the following year.

Once settled in I was keen to play a concert on the organ at the Academy of Performing Arts, and this was eventually arranged for Monday evening at 6.15 p.m. on October 26th. I included my Tongues of Fire and I think that this made a definite appeal to those Chinese present! It is something of a strain to perform before an audience with a strong examiner contingent present – the Board does warn you against too readily subjecting yourself to a critical appraisal of both your colleagues, and possibly of course, some candidates for the examinations. The enthusiasm for music as a career is tremendous in the Far East, and it is impressive to witness the dedication of the students of all ages. After my concert I was questioned on many aspects of organ playing by those students present. A career in the West beckons for very many as a dream to be pursued, but rarely realised. The number of entrants for the Associated Board Examinations – and the Schools Music Festivals (several hundreds in each Class for these) – demonstrates the commitment of the Oriental to the desire for success (or Face in their society). Exceptionally cramped living quarters – even sometimes squalid in appearance by Western norms – do not prevent children emerging each day looking immaculately clad, and ready for further progress in their schooling at whatever age and level they have reached. And it is a welcome surprise to witness a thousand or so children entering one of the great assembly rooms in Hong Kong in complete silence. What a good idea! – for without it the din would be intolerable.

On November 1st we changed domicile with our colleagues and moved to mainland Kowloon and the Royal Pacific Hotel on the Canton Road. Somehow one's imagination was sparked by this new address! The hotel lighting here was totally reliable and there were many more walking possibilities. Amongst the many and varied culinary delights of Hong Kong the Oyster Village at Lantan proved irresistible for a couple of visits, in spite of a long and somewhat dreary bus journey; and a one day trip to Macau on the Central Ferry Jet Foil proved a sheer delight, with lunch at the Hotel Bella Vista as its supreme consummation! Although the hours spent in the examination rooms were long and somewhat daunting, the overall experience has to be considered as extremely rewarding. (One somewhat hilarious but serious matter – always carry some toilet paper with you on your perambulations – unless conditions have improved since then!)

As always in any examination session there are absentees, and in this lengthy stint, as was my custom I had at the ready plenty of MS paper for composition work. For a very long time I had in my mind a wish to set passages from The Light of Asia by Sir Edwin Arnold – a translation of the Life and Teaching of Gautama (As Told in Verse by an Indian Buddhist) which seemed to me to demand to be set to music. So it seemed appropriate to begin work on this projected four-movement work for Tenor Solo, Chorus and Orchestra whilst in the Orient. I decided to compose the fourth and final movement first, which culminates ecstatically with the chorus entry: The Dew is on the Lotus! – Rise, Great Sun! I did finish the first draft of this movement but the whole work was not completed even in sketch form until 1994 – always in the case of a long work other shorter pieces intervene. And in those two months I also composed Rabbi Ben Ezra – the poem which eventually became the second song of Dramatis Personae: Two poems by Robert Browning – I really must have kept myself busy!

As the examination tour drew to its close there seemed to be parties almost every evening but I attended the Advent Carol Service in St John's Cathedral (nursing a cut thumb got whilst trying to open a jar of caviar – that's what examining in Hong Kong does for your culinary tastes!) and there met up again with Michael Banyard who now sang in the Cathedral Choir, having moved from Cyprus to the St George's Army School in Hong Kong. Things were moving apace now, a final visit to Lamma Island for a last pigeon lunch before the Carol Service, and the next day I visited Lantau to see the Great Bhudda statue – overwhelming in its presence and sheer size. On Friday there was a final party in the City Garden Hotel on the island and Jean Cooper asked me to write an organ piece for her. It was finished 7.2.1993 according to the score – ORIENTAL Three variants on 'Entrance Hymn for the Emperor' (a Chinese melody c.1000 BC) – and I heard it played at the Lunch Hour Recital at St Michael's, Cornhill on Monday 27th September that year. The previous day I had collected a large photo Jean took of me at one of the parties – looking lubricious in the extreme! Nicely framed, it now hangs in our hall. On Saturday we flew back to the UK which already promised short and frosty days in contrast to the balm of the South China Sea. Mixed feelings – but another Schools Festival in Hong Kong was looming in the next year – some consolation here!

It was good to be home at last, and Christmas came and went – when put like that it appears to be a less than enjoyable experience, and I must articulate what I suppose every retired Cathedral Organist feels at this time – a total emptiness. The two Great Festivals of Advent and Christmas, Lent and Easter are so satisfying on a musical-dramatic-emotional level that without them as a full participant you feel completely bereft. When in my retirement speech I said that sometimes I would have done this job for nothing (and that sometimes I did do it for (virtually) nothing – joke!) it was those experiences I had mainly in mind, and to my dying day I expect to feel the same void at those two great seasons of the year when the Church and the Theatre merge unforgettably through the power of music and liturgy.

But soon there was the Hong Kong Schools Festival to begin in mid-February and the renewal of remembered delights to look forward to. As we were to stay with Michael Banyard in his spacious flat courtesy of St George's Army School, the hotel accommodation costs could be diverted to pay for Mary's flights, a very agreeable solution for all concerned. And this time Michael had arranged with the Cultural Centre's administration that I should play a lunch-time organ concert on the magnificent four-manual Reiger organ on Saturday, March 6th. For this half-hour programme I chose my transcription of Mussorgsky's Pictures from an Exhibition with Etheldreda Rag for the encore. This was to prove an exceptionally busy year for travel, with Associated Board tours of Greece and Malta to look forward to. Back from the Hong Kong Festival on March 15th it was necessary to plan for the flight to Athens on the 4th April to be preceded by a Council Meeting at the Royal College of Organists on the previous day.

Athens was not new to me, as Mary and I had holidayed there many years before. But it is a fascinating place simply to walk around again, and the tourist crowds had fortunately not yet arrived. I examined in Music Store Centres and Schools for four days and then flew on to Thessaloniki for two days' work at the Academy of Music. This was a fascinating visit – in the steps of Saint Paul!

Macedonia was just over the border, the Balkan conflicts were reaching fresh heights of ferocity, and my Steward informed me that he might well be called up for military service if Greece was eventually drawn into the war. Of course this did not happen, but the tense atmosphere was palpable, and the Thessalonians walking the streets in the brilliant sunshine could have come from any of the Balkan States then involved in such frightful strife – and the mountainous Home of the Gods loomed ominously in the clouds over the harbour. After the work there I flew back to Athens, and the following day on to Malta via Rome – more Pauline journeys! This first visit to Malta was quite riveting, one free day to look around and discover the chronic unreliability of the Bus Service, but very useful in view of my Examination tour there in the Autumn. Just one day's work to come, but I met up with my lady co-examiner in the evening to prepare for the Diploma Examinations the following day. Both Greece and Malta are now lined up ready to be admitted to the European Union, and their eagerness is certainly understandable.

Diary entries for the next four days reveal a concentration on the marking of Theory Papers – not the most interesting of tasks, but when a musician's life revolves around a good deal of freelance work as mine did, you tend to take on what is offered until it becomes unbearable in the growth of official requirements which lead to an inordinate amount of tedious form filling. (The only period in which I found it at all tolerable was 1978 to around 1995, when it could be done over afternoon tea watching TV, with my wife present to check my totals!) There followed a two-week visit to Scotland with recitals at Lorettos School, (arranged by Alastair Stout, my ex-head Chorister, who was then Organ Scholar at the School) and Dunblane Abbey.

Then back to Ely via Newcastle, where Colin was working at that time. My next concert of unusual interest was featured in the Leeds Summer Heritage Festival on Sunday

27th June in All Souls' Church, Blackman Lane, Leeds. This featured my Choral Concerto: The Gods of Music – its first performance in England after its Australian premiere in Newcastle NSW. As then I played the solo organ part and Simon Lindley conducted his St Peter's Singers and Brass Players. It was a very reasonable performance, given the amount of rehearsal time available for this quite rhythmically complicated piece.

There was to be no organ concertising in my Malta visit for the Associated Board, though there were a few organ candidates to be examined in the Cathedral at Valletta. If the question was to be posed – 'Is the country Catholic?' – in my experience the answer would have to be the Island of Malta, and this in the most natural and unforced manner. Church attendance must be the highest per head of population anywhere in the world, and it is a moving experience to visit a Basilica during Mass, full of worshippers of all ages, and so happily redolent of the Kingdom of Heaven. Some might find this surprising – after all, in the siege of Malta 1940–43, were there not almost 7000 bombs dropped on the Island in April 1942? And, its buildings flattened, were not its inhabitants forced to live in cellars and caves? Nevertheless, 'faith, hope and charity' not only survived, but strengthened under hardship. Today, this Island in the Sun is a well patronised holiday resort, though there are few beaches of any size, and it's certainly not a natural Club Med habitat. This of course is its appeal – a bit behind the times perhaps? – but all the more refreshing for that. The author of the above quote was famously ship-wrecked on the Island, and that site is well marked with the Grotto where he was sheltered and of course a splendid Church. That shipwreck poses no difficulty to belief – mostly blessed with sunny weather, storms can swiftly arise without much warning, as happened in early November, when a leisurely evening meal in a restaurant near the sea-wall beginning in a peaceful sunset ended in torrential rain and high winds – and a taxi for the short distance back to the hotel!

I made two visits to the sister Island of Gozo, one to examine in the Schools, the other with Mary when she came out for our Wedding Anniversary on November 14th. That day trip visit to Gozo was after another torrential storm and much of the Island was a sea of mud, but we still managed to find a good restaurant for lunch – treading carefully! On an earlier free day I took a day trip to Sicily, taking in Mount Etna (nicely quiescent) and a meal along the coast in the delightful Resort of Taormina. So, no organ playing, but the examinations were held in the hotel where I was staying, so I had brought along some Chopin and Liszt to help maintain and improve keyboard technical prowess.

1994 saw an especially interesting tour of the USA, starting in St Mark's Church, Portland, Oregon. I had played there many years before, and now the church was unmistakably suffering problems over the admission of women to the Clergy – very sad to see such divisions arising. During my stay I managed to find time to work further on my latest work 'Song without Words' which was now reaching completion. The next morning a short drive to Salem – St Paul's Episcopal Church, where I practised immediately and played the concert that same evening – a most unusual procedure for me then, but needs must sometimes! An excellently large and enthusiastic audience. The next day back to Portland to catch a plane for Seattle where I was to play at Emmanuel Episcopal Church, Mercer Island, Washington. A one-night stand there, and then on to San Francisco the following day. Grace Cathedral is one of my very favourite venues – a wonderful acoustic (infrequently found in the USA) and a very cultured community which supports concerts and all the arts with the greatest enthusiasm. John Fenstermaker was there to welcome me, and took me down to Fisherman's Wharf for an excellent lunch of the finest oysters – it's ridiculous, but I have never been able to find that restaurant again on my own, and even more sadly, John is now no longer in office at Grace to host me. My favourite US city? – it has to be either New Orleans or San Francisco, I have to conclude that the latter wins by a very short head! Also memorable was my dinner in a restaurant with the TV News relating the chase of O.J. Simpson along the freeways of Los Angeles by the Police!

And then on to Honolulu and St Andrew's Cathedral. I think this was the visit in which I obtained a virtually full audience for the concert, and I premiered as an encore 'Song Without Words' which is dedicated to the Organist John McCreary. The reason? – a large poster advertising me as 'Sir' Arthur Wills – it does help! Then back to California for the final concert in St Mark's Church, Glendale L.A. (A second performance of 'Song Without Words' for the encore.) A barbecue supper followed the concert – an unusual but excellent idea! The following day, instead of getting the first plane back to the UK, a friend had offered to drive me around some of the not to be missed scenic sights of the South Western States, an experience I had welcomed, and greatly relished.

So the next morning the freeways of Los Angeles beckoned and we began the long trawl through the Mojave Desert to Bullhead City, our first stop overnight. As is the case with so many desert cities the only interesting feature appeared to be a casino, the number of people engaged in playing the machines equally astonishing and depressing. But you could also get a decent meal there. The next day on to the Grand Canyon and its Village – that incredible prehistoric deep-down river bed. So huge that it remains peaceful in spite of the hordes of visiting crowds. Then on to nearby Las Vegas, best experienced at night – and it is only a Strip – but unique in all possible senses! The following morning a left turn into Death Valley, the graveyard of the great 19th century Gold Rushers – a salutary lesson, and an apt illustration of the Valley of Dry Bones.

A long way north on the map I even spotted an Ely(!) – on the edge of The Great Salt Lake Desert – and much further West, on the far coast more or less in a straight line, was San Francisco. An overnight stay in Yosemite (those huge Sequoia trees!) and then on to 'Frisco' – only used, John Fenstermaker once informed me, "by sailors long at sea"! In early January the San Andreas Fault had erupted, with some damage to both San Francisco and Los Angeles; but almost six months later there was virtually no evidence of this in L.A., yet some roads in San Francisco were still awaiting repair. There was time for a visit to the Redwoods, which I had visited on an earlier occasion, and also to the Prison Island of Alcatraz – now just a fascinating tourist attraction, but the real delight was our leisurely drive down the coast road on our way back to Los Angeles via Palo Alto, Santa Cruz, Monterey, Carmel, Big Sur, Santa Barbara (for the Fourth of July celebrations – quite quiet actually), and finally Santa Monica and L.A. in order to fly back to the UK arriving on the 7th – quite a trip, and a nice change from practising and playing recitals!

Later that month I did a mini-tour of three concerts in the West Midlands – Stratford-upon-Avon, Leominster and Ludlow. At Stratford Mary and I stayed with the Organist Peter Summers, and he suggested that I might like to provide the anthem (always newly commissioned for each year) for the Service on 'Shakespeare Sunday' – that one following the Birthday celebrations. This greatly appealed to me, with my love of Shakespeare and my family Warwickshire connections, and for the text I chose John Donne's 'At the Round Earth's Imagin'd Corners'. We were there to hear it at the following year's Service.

Another trip to hear a commission's first performance took Mary and I to Hinckley in Leicestershire, where James Bowman was President of the Music Club. Here, on the 24th September, in Holy Trinity Church Hall, he had arranged a concert in which he premiered 'A Toccata of Galuppi's.'

This was attended by Maxine Handy, who had commissioned the work in celebration of James' 50th birthday, with her family among the audience. James had requested a work with accompaniment for string quartet, and I acquiesced, but Browning's great poem is essentially about mortality glimpsed through the work of a keyboard composer, so I should sometime do a keyboard version – if Browning's 'Grow old along with me' prevails, and I survive!

Tours of some length in far-flung continents were usually spaced at two-yearly intervals, but itchy feet often suggested more frequent ventures. Hence in 1995 a the idea of another visit to Norway and Sweden eventually became irresistible. In the 1960s–1970s there had been a very flourishing organ culture in Scandinavia, clearly well supported by State funding. In my preliminary enquiries to previous contacts it very quickly became clear that this was no longer the case – 'The good times are over!' was one laconic comment I received.

Nevertheless I decided to go ahead, if only on the basis of interest and curiosity, and of course both countries are delightful holiday venues, so we decided to take the car on the overnight ferry Harwich–Gothenburg on Sunday, 13th August. We didn't arrive until 4.00 p.m. the following day; it was the rush-hour and it took quite a little time to get out of Gothenburg and on to the Stockholm motorway. This was fine for a time, but eventually the motorway petered out into a country road not unlike the more remote areas of the Fens, more than a little disconcerting! Then patches of fog were encountered... There were two concerts in Stockholm the next day – lunchtime and evening, and we had to get there, find our way around the city centre and locate the hotel – and then get some sleep! As I remember, we did just manage to get to bed before midnight, but it was a 'damn close-run thing'. Fortunately the hotel was only a short walk away from St Michael's Church, so that the two concerts were quite viable in terms of practice time, but I have to say that neither was well attended. Compensation though lay in the provision of lavish hospitality, and the interesting guests we met. The 'good times' were not over – at least not in that sense! And so to bed.

Another day, another concert – this time in the great Cathedral of Uppsala. After an early start got us there in time for coffee, my anxiety to get on with practice was not matched by my hosts' similar sense! Fateful words – "There is a midday Service soon – plenty of time after lunch!" I experienced something like panic when I climbed the stairs to the organ loft. The very splendid organ console was French in character, with no settable pistons and only foot combination pedals. And it was short manual compass – to F as I remember. I had toyed with the idea of including Schoenberg's Variations on a Recitative in the programme – a work I had recently played at St Michael's Church, Cornhill – and the organist had said, "It might work" – but it was now clearly not viable on grounds of compass alone. So I substituted – Franck's Choral in B minor, I think. Even that would have posed problems for me given the amount of time left for practice, but the Assistant Organist saved the day – an agile girl who skipped around the console with the greatest aplomb, and seemed to grasp my requirements before I hardly knew what they were! There was a splendid party after the concert with many English people present – somewhat to my surprise.

Another concert the next day at Finspång, a tiny church and a tiny audience. I think it was here that we camped out on a kitchen floor in a sleeping bag for a couple of nights – it is always as well to be adaptable! We went back to Stockholm for the weekend in order to have a rest from incessant driving and performing, and also to have a good look around this very beautiful city. There was a Water Festival in progress, and the illuminations at night were quite entrancing. We drove around the city and also enjoyed a boat trip – somehow it's quite bemusing to gaze out across the

Baltic and realise that the next landfall would be Poland. On Monday we set out for Vansbro, the last Swedish venue, and situated just about halfway between Stockholm and the Norwegian border. Wonderful scenery, but the amount of driving was beginning to tell on both of us, but we got there in time to do some practice that evening. (Perhaps it was there that we slept on the floor!)

A concert on Tuesday is rather blurred in my memory, but it was the next day's journey from Vansbro to Haugersund in Norway that has stayed permanently etched on my mind. We arrived at the Oslo ring road around lunch-time and glanced at the map over a quick snack. We had still to drive the width of Norway and it looked pretty hilly terrain. Not just hilly we discovered – positively mountainous! It rained, and eventually we reached the snow zone – but fortunately the road surfaces were mostly clear – it was towards the end of August after all. Of course about 8 p.m. we needed to stop for supper, and after that eventually arrived at the church (Var Freisers Kirke) at about 10.00 p.m. – to be met by the Organist. "Would you like to practise?" he asked. He was so kind – but I said that just a quick look at the instrument at that moment would suffice! In fact it was a fine instrument of a reasonably romantic cast, and I was able to encompass my 'Fenlands Suite' (three movements arranged for solo organ the previous year) quite easily. It turned out that many years before I had played a concert for my host when he was in post in quite a distant area – a fascinating revelation!

Came Friday morning and the last venue – Stavanger – now beckoned, reasonably near as the crow flies – but we would have to take the ferry. We arrived at the harbour in time for a delicious lunch of reindeer, our first experience of that dish, and the Domkirke (cathedral) was reassuringly in sight! Our hotel had been arranged for us, gratifyingly quite close to the Domkirke. The concert was at Noon on Saturday, and the West End organ in the gallery was a faithful (down to the last detail so far as I could remember) recent copy of the world-famous Schnitger organ in Alkmaar. I had my Prelude and Fugue (Alkmaar) with me, as a suitable piece for historic organs (or copies thereof) so looked forward to hearing it in this favourable environment. It was indeed an interesting experience to play that piece on that organ! Even with Mary constantly on the move to change stops, it was brought home to me that two assistants were ideally necessary to obtain the necessary fluency of timing the changes. But all went well with a considerable audience that came in all together, as if from a boat or coach. I sensed that the longer than usual gaps between pieces created some unease in the listeners as to whether or not more was to come – I assume that they had programmes – but at that distance from the gallery you couldn't be sure.

On Sunday we started our long drive back to Gothenburg, with an overnight stay near Oslo. These Scandinavian trips are great fun in Summer – the weather reliable, the food excellent (steak on a wooden platter!) and the scenery magnificent. But financially – as the man had said – the good times are over. But after all, this trip was a kind of afterthought – more for fun than profit, or as in the faux-Biblical phrase – 'Yea, and more than a profit!'

The Canadian tour for the next year of 1996 had already been planned as a major event – September through October, fourteen concerts with ancillary events, from British Columbia right across from West to East to Saint John, New Brunswick. The first event was the opening of a newly rebuilt organ in Holy Trinity Church, Vancouver. Ted Quinton, the Organist, met me at the Airport and settled me in at the Rector's House. He and his wife were from England and knew much of the Cambridge scene, and the Fen Country folk. The Quintons took me out on the next morning to show me some of the sights of Vancouver – vastly changed and improved since my last visit. Fascinating though all this was, I was anxious to have a sight of the organ, but there was some reluctance on their part to take me to the church. Eventually they did, and I at once understood their somewhat diffident attitude – the organ was nowhere near ready for use!

Their son John was in charge, with just one helper, and the organ was strewn over a wide area. Admittedly there were two clear days before the opening concert, but the outlook for both the instrument and adequate practice for me was decidedly unpromising I thought. It was a three-manual instrument on a movable platform, and the room was decidedly dry acoustically. You couldn't get away with much there, and the large audience which always turns up for the opening concert on a new or refurbished organ would render the room even less forgiving.

The first concert of a major tour is always a somewhat nerve-racking experience, and my first piece was the D major Prelude and Fugue of J.S. Bach – a work with several exposed and hazardous passages on the pedals. Somewhat idiotically I had altered the footing for some of these passages from toe and heel to toes alone, including the first very exposed page of the music. Any change in fingering or footing takes a great deal of time to become completely reliable, so I pressurised the builders to get the instrument in some condition for my use, and by the morning of the concert it was all useable – except for the piston mechanism, which resolutely refused to work. Without this every stop had to be manipulated by hand, and there were at least fifty. "I won't play unless you explain to the audience the registration problems I am having to cope with," I told Ted. He could see I was in earnest and said, "We can say it was an electrical surge that caused the problem." "Tell them what you like!" I said, not in the best of humour by now. Of course by now I could see that I would have to manage as convincingly as I could, and do what might be possible to rescue a potentially very difficult situation. So that was the scenario we followed. After Ted's introduction and explanation for the absence of pistons I weighed in with the story about Sir Walter Parratt

(Organist at St George's Chapel, Windsor Castle) who was frequently asked to open organs, but was heard to say that very many times he would prefer to close them! This was received with much mirth, and in that relaxed atmosphere I launched into the concert which then went with surprising ease, and to considerable acclaim.

The next day I took the Ferry Bus to Victoria, Vancouver Island B.C. where I was to play a concert in Christ Church Cathedral in aid of the Organ Fund-Raising Appeal. Again an instrument in a less than ideal condition, but once on tour you do learn to make the best of whatever difficult circumstances arise. Again, the reception was gratifying, and resulted in a 'generous donation to our Fund-Raising Committee' – as well as a (smallish) fee for my efforts! And then on to Lethbridge, Alberta – a new venue for me – to play in Southminster United Church. Here I was able to include in the programme my 'Concerto for Guitar and Organ' as Dale Ketcheson, a teacher at the University, had noticed the work on my web site and offered to perform the work with me. We managed on just two rehearsals to give a very convincing account of the piece, and I was grateful for the opportunity to perform this really quite difficult work. It doesn't set out to be immediately attractive, and in many ways is somewhat forbidding in its technical and interpretative demands. (It's paired with the Rodrigo on the demo tape/CD, and it was never my intention to try to compete with that delightfully attractive piece!) I was glad to make the acquaintance of Lethbridge – one of the smaller venues on this trip, but with many attractive features in the early Fall.

Calgary was next on the itinerary, and I recalled playing there on my first North American visit in 1967. Then it was mainly noted for the Calgary Stampede, nowadays it has oil as its main economic underpinning, and that also supports the International Organ Festival, held at the Centre for the Performing Arts. I recall playing in the Cathedral series on that first visit; now, for the Calgary Society of Organists my concert was to be held at Knox United Church. Mary had secretly informed the Society of the proximity of my Seventieth Birthday (the day before) to the concert, and they had provided a cake and wine for a party afterwards, much to my surprise. I have mentioned that the Bach D major Prelude and Fugue featured on all my programmes for this tour, and my changed footing for it. The atmosphere of the Calgary concert played havoc with my poise, and as a result the first page of pedalling was messy to say the least! My visit also coincided with the setting up of the Organ Academy at the Mount Royal College Conservatory, and it was decided to ask me to take a Master-class in Improvisation the day after my concert. This I did, but as usual there were few takers, and those very inexperienced. In the afternoon Simon Preston took a spirited Performance Master-class, and in the evening the new Organ Academy was officially opened, with its fine new instrument by Letourneau. This ceremony included a performance of the fun-piece William Albright's 'The King of Instruments' by Terence Fullerton (organ) and Simon Preston (narrator and maracas!). We all stood around with a glass of wine listening to this, and the evening was made for me, when after that performance one of the principal donors shouted – "Play us some Bach, Simon!" He wouldn't – and the evening concluded on a somewhat disconcerted note. A case of he who pays the piper somewhat lavishly, boldly calls, but may not always be satisfied? – I suppose.

The following day I moved to the Prairies, with the next concert in Regina – the venue being the Catholic Holy Rosary Cathedral. Here Dr Thomas Chase was the organist and he was also interested in interviewing me for an article on my work as a composer. He had pointed out that 1996 marked the 25th anniversary of the death of Marcel Dupré, and the 10th of the death of Duruflé, suggesting that my programme should contain some recognition of this. Accordingly I included in my programme for the tour Dupré's Carillon and Final Op.27, and the Scherzo Op. 2 by

Duruflé. Once again my memory of the unease of my performance in Calgary marred my Bach performance.

The next move was to Saskatoon – the Northern-most point of the tour, and my first encounter with snow – it was the 27th September. Here, I thought, I must put a stop to this nonsense, and I worked on that first page of the Bach until I just couldn't get the revised pedalling wrong, however hard I tried! And in the concert it was secure. The day after the concert I took a workshop/rehearsal with singers from the area in readiness for an Evensong the next day. Mr Music in Saskatoon is Bernard Wesselingh, who was milk-farming ten years ago, and now I gather is more concerned with the transportation of it by road through the vast prairies of Saskatoon. He had gathered together most of those singers in the Anglican tradition he knew would be interested in singing an Evensong, and in preparation for that, participating in a Choral Workshop with me. For the Service we agreed on music by Ely composers. Tye's O come, ye servants of the Lord – my Evening Canticles in D with a congregational part, and Sidney Campbell's anthem Praise to God in the highest. For the Workshop we also looked at music by Hilton, Attwood, Bruckner and Britten. My next move was to St James' Cathedral in Toronto, but first I had a free day in Saskatoon, and Bernard had asked the recently appointed Cathedral organist – a lady named Ondrea – to show me around the area, including the Indian Reservations and other interesting features of this area.

To go from the Outback to the metropolis of Toronto was a considerable jolt to the sensibilities, but it has to be admitted that Toronto is nothing like New York – a good thing, many Canadians would say, I'm sure! Nevertheless St James' Cathedral has a remarkably fine building, and also a Choir of Men and Boys comparable with many in England – I well remembered playing there on my first North American tour in 1967. Giles Bryant was Director of Music now, but was looking forward to his retirement soon, and Christopher

Dawes was his lively and forward looking Assistant. I had earlier this year acquired an Acorn computer in order to use the Sibelius 7 Software for music processing, but Christopher was already an adept user of the Internet and its e-mail facilities, and played a very useful role in sparking off my own eventual usage of all this then very new technology. Giles mentioned his wish to include an improvisation on a Gregorian Hymn melody in each recital of the concert series, so I readily agreed to do this. The audience was one of the largest I had enjoyed on this tour, and as the concert was well supported by many of Toronto's renowned organists it had to be a stimulating experience for all concerned. My transcription of 'The Fenlands Suite' and Venus and Jupiter from Holst's Planets Suite were both well appreciated, and afterwards my delight in a Thai Restaurant cuisine was commented on as being slightly surprising for an English Cathedral Organist – I wonder why?!

On to Hamilton the following day (Saturday) by GO Bus in readiness for a master-class sponsored by the School of Art, Drama & Music at McMaster University, and organised by William Renwick, the Chair of the Hamilton Centre of the RCCO. This was scheduled for the following Monday at Central Presbyterian Church, but on the Sunday, at the suggestion of my host I attended Binkley United Church where he was organist. There was a distinguished visiting preacher whose sermon certainly made the attendance worthwhile, with a very pleasant reception afterwards, and the next evening there was a good attendance at the master-class – I remember playing my Tongues of Fire at the conclusion of the evening.

Then on to Belleville the following day. This necessitated getting the GO Bus from Hamilton back to Toronto and then getting a VIA Train to Belleville. (Juggling transport times and means is all part of the fun on a longish trip like this!) The recital was in Bridge Street Church, and the organ was placed near the edge of the stage for my concert (excellent for audience contact, but slightly off-putting for manoeuvring on and off the console!). I was interviewed by the local paper *The Intelligencer* on the morning of the concert, and there was an interesting approach to the critic's review the next day. After a generally laudatory comment on the programme and my performance, he concluded, vis-a-vis the programme note about the anniversaries of Dupré and Duruflé – "Neither have any type of anniversary this year but Dr Wills missed a golden opportunity in that the same day that he appeared here (October 11) was the exact 100th anniversary of the death of perhaps the greatest organist of the 19th century – Anton Bruckner." What was he thinking of? The answer to that is that Bruckner was certainly the organist at Linz Cathedral from 1855–68, but the main outlet for his creative genius lay in his inspired improvisations – he left no important organ compositions worthy of including in a recital programme – more's the pity!

On to St Paul's Cathedral, London (Ontario!) the next day. This venue was of special interest to me as John Cooke had made his move from Stratford-on-Avon to North America via this Canadian Cathedral. Angus Sinclair was Interim Organist and Choirmaster at the time, and he is now Assistant. He asked me if I would give him some advice on my 'Alkmaar' Prelude and Fugue on which he was currently working, and also offered hospitality with him and his wife at their home. This visit coincided with the North American 'Thanksgiving Sunday' Anniversary and I was driven through roadside fields of pumpkins to a family gathering for the traditional 'Pumpkin Soup and Turkey Lunch'. The large number of squirrels to be seen on the walk from my domicile to the Cathedral has also stayed in my mind.

Next stop: Christ Church, Niagara Falls. I had visited the Falls on several occasions from both the American and Canadian sides, but the prospect is always exciting, and so it was this time. It had been arranged for me to stay with the Rector Duncan Lyon and his wife. They had previous associations with the Diocese of Ely, so it was pleasant to chat about mutual acquaintances – especially over dinner at the local Red Lobster Inn! After the other Ontario organs I had encountered this was rather less well endowed (two manuals), but the chosen programme proved perfectly possible, and the audience was warmly appreciative.

Still in Ontario, the next stop was Kingston where I was to adjudicate a Choir Festival and also play a recital in St George's Cathedral. The newly appointed organist at St George's was Robert Bell, whom I had first met at the Cathedral in Calgary on my first visit in 1967. He then moved to the famous High Anglican Church of St Mary Magdalene in Toronto, following on from the renowned Healey Willan. He had recently been appointed to Kingston, and I enjoyed dinner with Bob and his wife on the Saturday evening of my arrival. On Sunday morning I heard his Girl's Choir sing the Fauré Messe Basse. Very beautiful, but what is happening to the traditional Male Choir heritage? As in Australia and New Zealand its hold on the public imagination is gradually being weakened, and in some quarters you may now hear the assertion "Well, they make the same sound anyway." They don't, and in any case where is the next generation of altos, tenors and basses to come from? The Choir Festival was held in the afternoon and culminated in a performance by all the choirs of my unison anthem 'Sing a new song to the Lord'. My organ concert on Monday evening was well attended, and my page-turner was a teenager, (and I'm sure was a former chorister) who made the point, "I haven't heard the organ played like that before!" The same comment was made on my Australian/New Zealand tour in 2000 and I'm sure it's the repertoire, and perhaps especially the transcriptions that I include in my concerts that the listeners find so refreshing.

Then the flight to the most far-flung of my venues on this tour – from Kingston to Saint John, New Brunswick. A new venue for me, it was suggested by an old friend from

Montreal – the organist George Chubb, with past Ely family connections and now living in Burlington near Toronto, and his Vicar – the Revd Canon Brian Campion, with his wife Ann. Now in retirement, they lived on the Bay of Fundy, about thirty miles from Saint John. I enjoyed their hospitality on at least two occasions before when I played in Montreal, and they now kindly offered the same, which I gratefully accepted. What a different feel this place has – with the wind cutting across from the Atlantic – bracing to say the least!

Once you have acquired a taste for being 'on the road' and enjoying the pleasures and the uncertainties of touring, it becomes a yearning hard to break! Signs of the times though – I heard from Brian this year (2003) that the organ I played in Saint John has now been sold to a church in the USA and the church closed. What is one to say to this? The traumas of the 16th century English Reformation and the 17th century Cromwellian Revolution were of a different order to those of the endgame we are now witnessing in the New Millennium. 'O brave new world – with such people in it' – how did Shakespeare manage to get his meaning and his words so precisely apt? After the concert Brian and Ann hosted a really excellent party, with a full house prepared to drive those thirty miles to be present!

On to the last venue – Christ Church Cathedral, Ottawa, where Frances Macdonnell was Organist and Choirmistress, and extraordinarily efficient in both roles. There was time for some sightseeing and Frances drove me around the very beautiful parkland and pointed out the sights – "That's Quebec Province just over there!" for instance. The audience was one of the largest of the tour, and at the Reception I was asked about the full score and parts for 'The Fenlands' by the conductor of a Brass Band who already knew the Hyperion recording. So, a very enjoyable end to a tour of almost two-months' duration – it has to be my longest to date I'm sure. BUT – that was 1996 – this is 2003 as I write, and I have just received a letter from Frances telling me that she is resigning from the Cathedral – as she puts it: "taking early retirement effective the end of August." One more very successful choral establishment in the Overseas Anglican Church hits the rocks, and looks likely to sink with all hands on board. What a downbeat way to have to finish this otherwise so interesting and successful visit.

In 1998 I did a rather shorter tour of North America, which included Vancouver and Victoria once more. Two memorable side tracks were a visit to Pearl Harbour, when I was in Honolulu again at St Andrew's Cathedral, and a visit to the Paul Getty Museum when I played in Glendale, L.A. Being an organist on tour is not all work and no play!

Finally, New Zealand and Australia claimed my attention again in 2000. One disagreeable aspect was that I was suffering from an excruciating bout of sciatica (I blamed the marking of too many Associated Board Theory papers!) which refused to relent whatever the treatment. These tours do always succeed in demonstrating something useful – in this instance that one could be at work fulfilling one's obligations for five weeks on the move with fourteen engagements – all involving some really excruciating pain. But I must make it clear that it was only walking, or sometimes even just standing that involved the pain – fortunately, once seated on the organ bench the pain was completely absent, and my pedalling was just as fluent (or otherwise) as usual! The problem began on July 5th and lasted well into the following year, only abating by the beginning of April.

I flew to New Zealand via Singapore arriving at Auckland on Thursday morning and I was met by my host Margery Glasgow and driven to her house for a day's recuperation. I was ready to practise at the Cathedral the next day and enjoyed the spacious feel of the greatly enlarged building since my first visit in 1980. Peter Watts was the Acting Director of Music in the absence of Peter de Blois, but Stanley Jackson had moved from Wellington to Auckland,

and he and his wife asked me to lunch on Saturday – a most enjoyable visit on every level.

My host now was Margery Charlton, and in the evening I was taken to a concert of English choral music at the University Concert Hall. This had tiered seating, and shortly after I had taken my seat a girl came to the seat adjoining. "Hello, Dr Wills," she said, "I sang in your Choral Concerto in Newcastle in 1992!" "What a coincidence!" I said. We then talked about Michael Dudman and his untimely demise – "It was his own fault – he couldn't control his temper," she said, "His heart just couldn't take the stress." Just a few moments later a youngish man came and sat in the row in front, and at once recognised me – "I used to record your Psalms at Ely in Ian Harwood's time!" Ian sang alto for some ten years or so from the early sixties onwards. There wasn't a third coincidence, but those two were unlikely enough!

I played the concert on the Sunday afternoon, and it was very well received. The usual reception followed in the Cathedral restaurant, and being in my usual agony I looked for a chair in which to sit, spotted one and rushed for it, thereby smashing the frames of my spectacles on collision with large glass doors. I had my playing glasses, so was not entirely devoid of sight, but it was a somewhat inauspicious start to the tour! Monday morning I was taken to an optician by Stanley Jackson and the spectacles were ready after a few hours which I had used practising at the University Church for a lunchtime concert on the following day.

My host now was John Wells, the University Organist, and a gifted and prolific composer. When he was working in Cambridge in the eighties he organised that year's summer concerts and asked me to play a concert in St Catherine's Chapel. For this second concert on a two-manual organ I needed a different programme and chose: Handel: Voluntary in D, Haydn: Two Clock Pieces, Bach: Dorian Toccata and Fugue, Messiaen: Les Anges, Mulet: Carillon-Sortie, Wills: Elegy, Etheldreda Rag, The New Millennium Rag.

The following day an hour's flight took me from Auckland to Wellington, where I was met by Andrew Cantrill, the Cathedral organist. This of course was where I had opened the re-built organ in 1980, and I was intrigued to receive a message from Celia Lampe with an invitation to lunch on the day of the concert. Celia was the daughter of Canon Geoffrey Lampe, the Ely Professor of Divinity in the mid-sixties. It was fascinating to recall those far-off days – the gradual demise of Dean Hankey's reign and the new dispensation of Dean Carey. She couldn't attend my concert which was in any case rather poorly attended – unfortunately it clashed with a performance of Vaughan Williams' Sinfonia Antartica by the Wellington Symphony Orchestra.

On Saturday 26th on to Christchurch where I was in a fine hotel in the Square opposite the Cathedral. Chris Oldham was my host, due to the sad demise of David Childs. I attended the Sunday Morning Eucharist and then practised until the afternoon concert at 2.30 p.m. After that, to the airport for the flight to Nelson – where I alighted from the plane, but my luggage failed to accompany me! My host was the organist Roger Williams, who did all he could, but the concert in the Cathedral was on the following evening and the next day I was leaving for Dunedin – the final recital in the New Zealand leg of the tour. The Airline officials provided vouchers for basic needs (as usual) and I obtained a rather nicer pair of slippers than the ones I had brought with me – every cloud must have a silver lining, I suppose! Practice time was somewhat limited but the organ possessed a sequencer device with which I was not familiar, and the young Lady Assistant Organist offered to set that up and then used it to excellent effect. Nelson is a very attractive Cathedral City and I would have liked to have had more time to look around, but the next venue inexorably beckoned!

Dunedin was a somewhat sad experience – the New Zealand winter at its worst – a cold wind and persistently rainy. This time I didn't venture down to the seafront to gaze at the expanse of water between myself and Antartica – the weather and my sciatica effectively killed off any such notion! David Burchell was out of town but the Dean's entertainment was more than adequate, yet the unhappy estrangement of himself and Raymond White (the Organist who had just moved to Dunedin from Nelson Cathedral with great expectations on my first visit twenty years previously) rather overshadowed my feelings during that stay. But I enjoyed the organ, despite a few problems which the tuner did his best to deal with, and the youngster who turned the pages was suitably astonished by the sounds my programme was able to conjure from the instrument.

Then on to Australia and Brisbane, in the sultry State of Queensland. Once again I played in the spacious St Andrew's Presbyterian Church, and also once again Robert Boughen the Cathedral Organist came to the console to greet me as on previous occasions. The evening before I was taken to a very enjoyable Symphony concert by my hostess Pat – Shostakovich's First Cello Concerto (played by the Orchestra's section leader) and Mahler's Fifth Symphony, the first Mahler Symphony (apart from The Song of the Earth) that I got to know some fifty years earlier on the Bruno Walter LPs with the Vienna Philharmonic Orchestra. I have always found Mahler an extraordinarily interesting personality – as a composer, as a conductor and as a man – since I read Alma's book *Gustav Mahler – Memories and Letters* published in English in 1946. My copy is dated 1948 and it was given to me by Sonia, my then girlfriend in Warwick.

Next came the most important venue for this tour – Newcastle NSW where I was to be the Artist-in-Residence at the Christ Church Cathedral Annual Festival. This was my first visit to Newcastle since Michael Dudman's death in 1996, and for me was a somewhat sombre return after three very joyous previous visits. Philip Matthias had been Cathedral Organist for some ten years and I knew him well from each of my previous visits. The main feature of my Residence would obviously be an organ concert, and we eventually decided upon this programme: the 'Dorian' Toccata and Fugue of J.S. Bach, my transcription of Mussorgsky's 'Pictures', Lemmens' Grand Fantasia in E minor – 'The Storm' and 'The Fenlands' Suite. The inclusion of the Lemmens piece was entirely due to the obsessive liking for this piece of the Matthias' infant son. Philip had acquired the LP – 'Full Stops' which I had recorded on the Ely organ in 1978 (later transferred to CD) on the Meridian label, a popular programme which concluded with 'The Storm'. Once heard the child didn't want to hear anything else! Perhaps Philip thought that a live performance might serve to exorcise this unhealthy passion!

The week began with a visit to the Conservatoire to give a two-hour lecture on Improvisation. This not often taught systematically, except in France perhaps, and it is rare to encounter it in Conservatoire timetables, even in England. The next day was the Media launch day and we were all required to be present in the Cathedral for Radio and TV interviews. Wednesday was a day free for practice for me – not just for my recital programme, but for my appearances on Sunday also – at the Eucharist in the morning, at the afternoon Hymn Festival and finally at Evensong. On Friday morning I gave the Festival 'Tyrell' Lecture on 'My experience as a Composer and Director of Cathedral Music, over a period of 32 years.' This was copiously illustrated by CD recordings. That evening there was a concert of 'Baroque Classics' with the 'Calisto' Ensemble and the Cathedral Choir. On Saturday morning at 8.00 a.m. I attended the traditional Festival Breakfast at the Pepperina Restaurant, and spoke about my thoughts on my working life based on the church, and the possible direction and future of church music – all this from 'off the cuff'.

The main Festival Performance on Saturday evening was Bach's Mass in B minor conducted by Philip Matthias. The

Chorus consisted of 140 singers from the augmented Cathedral Choir, the Conservatorium Choir, and notably the Jacobean Singers from Sydney who were directed by Walter Sutcliffe and also sang with the Cathedral Choir at the Sunday Eucharist. I had not seen Walter since my first visit to St James' Church in Sydney in 1980, and I imagine that his Jacobean Singers arose from the sad demise of the choral tradition at St James. At the Bach rehearsal it was touching to meet the contralto Katherine Capewell again, whom Michael Dudman would surely have married had he not suffered that final heart attack. At the Eucharist I played the hymns, the improvisations and the final Voluntary, Mulet's Carillon-Sortie, while the Cathedral Assistant Organist played continuo with the orchestral Missa Sancti Nicolai by Haydn.

The Great Hymn Festival was a regular and favourite feature of the afternoon. There was a compere: Michael Blaxland, a brass ensemble, and the Tudor Singers heard in four of Bach's extended chorales including 'Awake thou, wintry earth', which I accompanied along with most of the other items. Two of my organ pieces were included, attached to the appropriate hymn tunes – Carillon on Orientis Partibus and 'The New Millenium Rag' based on three tunes: (1) 'O God our help in ages past' (2) 'God moves in a mysterious way' (3) 'A safe stronghold our God is still'. The Festival then concluded with an Evensong which began with my anthem 'Behold now, praise the Lord'; continued with the Canticles Noble in B minor, (Noble was at Ely before he went on to York Minster) the anthem being by Grayston Ives, an Ely Chorister who showed great promise as a composer from his early days in the Choir – Canticle of Brother Sun. I played the Bach Prelude and Fugue in E flat as the closing Voluntary. Then we all met in the Vestry for a closing al fresco supper.

After that very pleasant and settled week in Newcastle the next week was a great contrast – three venues in seven days and then the flight home. First then, the flight from

Newcastle to Melbourne where I was met by John Rivers, the Organist of Holy Trinity Cathedral, Wangaratta. He drove me there by car in two-and-a-half hours, where I was accommodated in the Deanery with Fr Ray and Glenis McInnes. Interestingly, John's father was well acquainted with Michael Howard in years past and had sung in the Renaissance Singers in the late 40s–early 50s period. At the Reception after my concert (on a very good three-manual organ) I had an interesting chat with him about those fascinating days – involving as they did fresh scholarship concerned with the provision of more accurate editions of early music and possible performance practice, and also the somewhat hectic alcoholic and sexual socialising which appears to be an essential aspect of the bonhomie associated with that repertoire throughout the ages. Though a brief visit, it proved to be a very enjoyable experience, and the furthest North I had travelled in the State of Victoria.

The next morning John drove me back to Melbourne and deposited me at St Paul's Cathedral where June Nixon was awaiting my arrival. This was my third concert at St Paul's, and always a favourite venue of mine, with excellent acoustics and Victorian High Church ambience, and a four-manual Harrison organ – well upholstered both in console fittings and sound. As Sidney Campbell was wont to say – they always feel comfortable! It was an early evening concert and it attracted a rather small audience – but then in ample compensation a nice party afterwards with some of June's pupils present. June has this year (2003) completed thirty years as Organist at St Paul's, and her Choirmen appropriately organised a celebratory dinner in her honour. I was asked to contribute a message, and in it I recalled my first visit to the Cathedral in 1980 when I attended Evensong, and then was Speaker at a RSCM Dinner afterwards. In this I spoke of my admiration for her work with the Choir, as demonstrated in that Service I had heard, and all of that tribute was certainly richly deserved.

The next morning I flew on to Adelaide for the last concert of the Tour, scheduled for Sunday afternoon in the Town Hall. Adelaide is very much an 'organ town' with many cognoscenti of the instrument, and the arrangements for the Town Hall concerts (nine each year) are overseen by an Organ Panel. The Town Hall has excellent acoustics, and its (relatively) new organ was very well voiced by J.W. Walker & Sons. From the player's point of view the mechanical action is rather too heavy for much modern repertoire, and even the availability of electrically assisted manual coupling only partially alleviates this problem. But the range of tonal colours available, and the projection of sound throughout the Hall, makes the instrument a delight to play.

The concert was extremely well attended, and I imagine that this Sunday afternoon series has over the years produced its bountiful crop of enthusiastic and knowledgeable aficionados. For me it was perhaps the most discerning audience of this tour. I had in the programme invited those present to visit my web site. One did – to congratulate me on a 'memorable occasion' but also to mention that some of my left-hand rapid fingerwork was not always ideally clear (not his precise words perhaps, but the gist). I forget my exact words in reply, but I'm sure it made mention of such matters as tiredness at the end of the tour, not as much practice time as I would have ideally liked, and (lamely in every possible sense) the sciatica I had already endured for the last three months. I had explored the possibility of going on to conclude my tour in Western Australia with concerts in St George's Cathedral in Perth, and St Patrick's Roman Catholic Cathedral in Fremantle.

Perth was especially attractive because Simon Lawford was the Director of Music – he was the son of Timothy Lawford – one of my room-mates at Canterbury in that far-off year of 1948/49. Both welcomed the idea, but I had also been offered a concert in Tewkesbury Abbey on the Saturday following my Adelaide appearance, so on the basis that I had already been away from home quite long enough (and suffered agony quite long enough), I decided to fly back on the Monday, arriving at Heathrow first thing on Tuesday morning, allowing me two days at home, before driving to Tewkesbury on Thursday, to begin practice that evening. The concert had been arranged by Christopher Regan as one in a series of two, to also include the very fine performer David Titterington. It seems that his concert was not as well attended as Christopher has hoped, so he decided to make my concert designated for attendance by the Gloucester Organist's Association – always a good move – and on this occasion it secured a Nave virtually full in appearance – and appreciation.

Tours have their merits in the concentration of the mind on performance over a sustained period, and in the enjoyment of travel, but some single concerts stay in the mind perhaps even more – an especial historical venue and distinctive instrument perhaps. Alkmaar, with its Schnitger organ inspiring a Prelude and Fugue from me is a good example from 1971, and the Basilica of Notre-Dame de Paris in 1975 perhaps even more so. After all, beyond the German baroque school, and the group of English composers who made an especial appeal to me, it was the French School – both pre and post Revolution that really excited me about the organ as an instrument. Its colour, in harmony, texture and sonority, really captured my imagination – just the sound it made! Intellectual ponderings about its intrinsic value simply as music did not bother me for many years (see below for Martin Cooper's views on the French organ school). And then the whole Gallic cultural tradition in painting, sculpture, literature and architecture simply riveted my interest. And perhaps the Impressionistic school in painting and music – Debussy and Ravel – in youth one simply swam in it! So that it was inevitable that I should eventually play a concert in Notre-Dame.

So Mary and I left Heathrow for Charles de Gaulle Airport on Friday 22nd February, arriving in time for a meal and a late evening practice in the Cathedral. Practice was only permitted when the building was closed – understandably in the light of the swarm of visitors throughout the day. The following morning we took the opportunity to visit the Rodin Museum – an unforgettable experience, and that evening was my last opportunity to practise for the concert timed for 17.45 on the afternoon of Sunday. The entrance to the organ gallery is outside the building, and from below the organ gallery appears to be placed just under the roof. The tutti is ear-shattering and the reverberation apparently endless. But there was some sense of anti-climax in the condition of the instrument at that time – the touch uneven, and the odd note missing here and there… it reminded me quite a bit of the Ely organ in the fifties! This was the programme – Bach: D major Prelude and Fugue, Widor: Moderato-Cantabile (Symphonie 8), Wills: Variations on 'Amazing Grace', Guillou: Toccata.

That morning we had attended Mass at Jean Guillou's stamping-ground, the Eglise Sainte Eustache – mainly to hear his improvisations – but the Sortie was his Toccata! Fascinating and compelling – and quite useful in the circumstances! But I must confess that the main shock of my recital for me was not the immense size of the audience (estimated at around 5000, and it being mainly made up of young people – I couldn't actually see anything clearly from that great height – I was told later) but the complete absence now of any reverberation in that huge edifice! Really – they should warn you! But all went well, and Pierre Cochereau then appeared to bestow his congratulations, and hand over the tape of the concert. In a flash twenty years fell away and I recalled that it was Cochereau's recordings on this organ that first inspired me to learn Vierne's 2nd Symphony and the Liszt Fantasia and Fugue on 'Ad nos salutarem', and then to go on to record in 1963 the 3rd Symphony of Vierne –

myself also possibly the first English Cathedral Organist to record a complete Vierne Symphony? A truly fascinating experience. But I must say that, since the time of my visit to play a concert in Notre-Dame, Paris has completely lost its attraction for me. Then, Picasso was but two years dead, Messiaen was still at La Trinité, and the whole atmosphere of the previous hundred and fifty years of artistic brilliance still permeated Montmartre. When I last visited the City, in the late Nineties, it reminded me of a brightly burnished coffin.

And then St Paul's Cathedral in 1986. Another 'must' venue with its challenging acoustic ambience, and tremendous audience attendances. The 'right' programme for that awesome combination simply cannot fail – Bach: E flat Prelude and Fugue, Franck: Cantabile and Piéce Hèroïque, Wills: Tongues of Fire, Mussorgsky/Wills: Pictures from an Exhibition. And unlike Notre-Dame the building doesn't appear to lose any of its resonance – however large the attendance. Of course some concerts stay in the mind because of unexpected problems, as did this recital at the Pro-Cathedral in Dublin, 23rd October 1975. I quote from the *Irish Times Newspaper* – 'Thursday night's recital at the Pro-Cathedral very nearly did not take place. The main motor of the organ broke down just before the recitalist, Arthur Wills of Ely Cathedral, was due to start. It refused to respond to first-aid and rather than abandon the evening, Dr Wills presented a modified recital on the smaller, chancel organ, an instrument he had never played before. It is a tribute to his musicianship and mental composure that he was able to give us a first-class recital, which under the circumstances was a tour-de-force. He altered the programme to suit the one-manual instrument but this did not detract from the enjoyment of the occasion. In all, an evening that turned from potential disaster into a triumph. I hope that we shall have the opportunity of hearing Dr Wills again soon.'

Finally, to end on a lighter note, I recall having a phone call from Sidney Campbell (mid-morning, early-60s so far as

I remember) – "Arthur, I'm booked to play a concert in Nottingham this evening on a Hammond Organ, and I'm not well enough to go – could you do it for me?" How could I refuse such a request from the man without whom I probably would not have been in Ely to hear his request for help?

I left after an early lunch, met the Hammond technicians at the Albert Hall, and played the programme (my own choice of course) to very reasonable effect. But of course that was not the end of it. Having successfully substituted for Sidney, the Hammond organ representatives were agog to know whether I might consider doing further engagements for them. I knew that Sidney was rather dubious about his involvement with the company and I shared those views, but their fees in the early 60s were then somewhat in excess of those in the 'theological market' as the Hammond people liked to so label their potential customers, and I was young (as I thought) and still avid for new and fresh experiences.

So I drove around the country in whatever unreliable car was available in the British market at that time. One such experience has stayed in my mind. I played a concert in Bolton – the Parish Church I think, and the following morning had to leave fairly sharpish to get to Swansea for a concert in St Andrew's Church that evening. The Hillman Minx (aptly named, I think!) I had recently taken delivery of got me down the M6 as far as Keele Service Station where it promptly refused to start again. (It had already given some indications of its temperamental nature.) Explaining my predicament to the garage mechanics led to my hiring an ancient Ford – a car which I had not driven before – but it was the only available means of transport. So I set off towards Wales, and eventually realised that I hadn't discovered how to reverse this wretched vehicle. Fortunately I had an engrossing drive through the remarkable scenery of the Welsh Valleys, which largely helped to dissipate my irritation with my predicament, and got to Swansea in time for lunch, pulled into the first garage I encountered for petrol

– and an explanation of how to reverse my hire car. The concert was reviewed by B.J. in *South Wales Evening Post*, sent to me by D.E. Jones of Port Talbot with this comment: "Just a few lines to say how much my wife and I enjoyed your recital last Tuesday evening."(etc.) One might decide that B.J.'s review had decidedly something of a Welsh lilt to it: 'The recital given by Dr Arthur Wills, organist at Ely Cathedral on a Hammond organ at St Andrew's Church, Swansea, was an event that left a deep impression on a not too large an audience.

The mechanics of organ-playing revealed a cultural concept, born of long experience. The programme was a demanding one. Bach's Prelude and Fugue in G was expounded with marked attention to the poetical in the initial section with its 'beauty suggested theme' and almost pensive the impact. The rhythmic fluency created a floral picture; the fugal development had an economy of treatment, one was ever aware of the fugue as a language that was eloquent. Gigout's 'Scherzo' with its fairy-like lilting rhythms was as light of tread as a butterfly. Franck, a prolific composer of piano music, could never resist the temptation to deviate from a mood of tenderness to a massive dominant chordal construction. This was noticeable in a brilliant exposition of his Pièce Héroïque.

The organist's own composition 'Deo Gratias' is a well designed work revealing vivid imagination and deep appreciation of the essentials that make for the classical. It was apparent that the composer had found a family of themes. Here was scholastic approach setting forth an idiom reflective of Bach.' Thoughtful language – if a trifle flowery, and no mention of the commercial aspect of the venture!

Boosey & Hawkes acted as an agency for the Hammond Organ Co. in the UK, and at a Dinner held in Blackpool I was featured as the Guest Speaker. For me a somewhat embarrassing occasion, but I was praised for my 'honesty' afterwards. The best aspect of the occasion was sitting next to Ralph Hawkes and him telling me that he wished he could find another Benjamin Britten for his Company – Britten at this time of course was becoming disenchanted with B&H and about to move to Faber Music. My involvement (and Sidney Campbell's) was a comparatively brief affair of the 60s. The use of a Hammond organ for practice purposes had its merits, but if any American organists turned up at No. 2 The Almonry their noses quickly followed suit when they saw the Hammond. Time to repent – but there had been some interesting locations and travel involved.

Of all solo instruments, the organ is both the most immediately comprehensive and impressive in its vast dynamic range and variety of colour, and yet the least readily communicative in the sense of audience involvement in the playing process. This is for obvious reasons, such as the invisibility of the performer when the console is out of sight behind choir stalls, or placed in a loft, or visible but still somewhat remote in a concert hall, with the player's back to the audience. Going back to the start of this chapter with its narration of an American recital tour, there were many places where the organ console could be moved into the chancel, and if easily placed on a slant, then much of the playing process could be observed and visual contact engaging the attention of the listeners. This situation also enables the organist to move to the front of the Chancel or stage with more easy rapport with the listeners then possible. I have mentioned Martin Neary's appreciation of my ability to draw the audience into the music with introductory comments at the Beverley Hills concert, and this is certainly reflected in their obvious reaction to the pieces they heard. Beginning a concert with 'Wondrous Machine!' or a similar work is a very useful gambit, which should help to alert the ears of the listeners to the colours used in the rest of the programme. Many concert halls place the organ console high at the back of the orchestral and choral forces, as in the Albert Hall in London, and the Sydney Opera House in Australia, and the use of television screens placed in strategic positions in such vast halls and also in cathedrals (as in Sydney Episcopal Cathedral) can be a very useful procedure. In the future such technical advances will be seen as essential, of that I am certain. But its also true that no one needs to be distracted by the sight of the organist at the console during a liturgical Service – here the 'mystique of the organ loft' is a help, not a hindrance.

The planning of a programme is also crucial to the success of a concert. During my career of fifty years or so it has been interesting to see how tastes and fashions have revolved. The one constant name since the revival of his music in the early 19th century is of course J.S. Bach, and the resultant desire to play his music and the pieces by all the Romantic composers influenced by Bach eventually led to the gradual introduction of pedal departments in organs all over the world. In my early teens I played as many of Bach's works as I could manage technically, as well as those of Mendelssohn, Liszt and Franck. A seminal influence on my developing taste in organ performance was a shellac recording of Franck's Choral in E major, played by Albert Schweitzer on the organ of Strasbourg Cathedral. I must have been aged around fifteen (1941 perhaps?), and on the two-manual organ of St Paul's, Warwick, I struggled to make the same kind of sounds I so relished on that recording. It was the same with those visiting recitalists from abroad that I heard in broadcast concerts – especially fascinating for me were those from Westminster Cathedral. Even Bach sounded compellingly different under those visitors' hands, and no doubt I was beginning to anticipate the 'wind of change' that only ten years or so later was to lead to the Ralph Downes revolutionary instrument at the Royal Festival Hall. But I also remember greatly enjoying Percy Whitlock's pieces – full of colour and fresh imagination. And then the French School – the Vierne pieces for manuals first of course – very strict in form, and with a harmonic language which galvanised me. It was Franck, but coloured by Debussy, and disciplined with Ravel's strictness of form. From there to the Fantasy Pieces and then to the Symphonies. I recorded No. 3 in the 60s and broadcast Nos 2, 4 and 6 in the 60s/70s.

And so to Dupré and Messiaen, the culmination of the modern French School which began with Franck. Again in Messiaen especially strictness of form rules with a strong reliance on repetition to move the music along with contrasting and ever varied blocks of material. (Boulez summed this up with some wit when he remarked "Messiaen is not a composer – he is a juxtaposer!") All this Francophile material featured regularly in my programmes until the late seventies – and then I turned towards the classics of the repertoire – Bach, Handel and Haydn pieces for manuals, Mozart, Mendelssohn, Schumann, Franck, Elgar, Messiaen and my transcriptions of Bach, Mussorgsky 'Pictures' and other colourful pieces such as movements from Holst's 'Planets Suite' and my own 'Fenlands Suite' together with some of my own compositions for organ. This move was audience-driven I suppose, with a strong desire to link the organ repertoire with mainstream composers. And for an encore my 'Etheldreda Rag' which first began life as a piano piece. I haven't mentioned the usefulness of page turners for recitalists – often my wife Mary would act in this capacity, later on in her career suggesting that a ten per cent fee would be appropriate for this essential activity!

How does one prepare for concert performances? My book *Organ* in the *Yehudi Menuhin Music Guides* series (Kahn & Averill, London) gives many useful hints and ideas. For a cathedral organist with daily services, the regularity of playing voluntaries at the conclusion of Evensong is one very useful way to keep technical competence alive and well, and the programmes of forthcoming concerts provide much of the material to be practised and played as voluntaries. Then, at home, retaining and developing technical facility on the piano with Chopin Etudes and pieces by Brahms such as the fearsome Paganini Variations is both refreshing and useful. From the mid-nineteenth century onwards the pedal-piano was and still is a useful adjunct to organ and piano practice, and in the last years of the twentieth century small pipe organs and large electronic instruments are commonly and increasingly in use.

Technical demands have increased in organ music, often suggested by those in piano music, from the Romantic period onwards. The practice procedures of such pianist composers such as Rachmaninoff are well worth considering, such as starting at half-speed with the help of a metronome. Also useful is the habit of not always starting work at the beginning of the piece, but tackling a persistent technical challenge as a warm-up. Although it is interesting to note that in the case of Messiaen, although his manual writing is every bit as technically challenging as in his piano compositions, his pedal parts are not as demanding. For the ultimate technical challenge of pedalling virtuosity we have to turn to Jeanne Demessieux's Six Etudes, dedicated to her teacher Marcel Dupre. These are intended to be the equivalent of the Piano Etudes of Chopin and Liszt. Technically they certainly are, but noticeably lacking in the other rather essential matter – quality of inspired invention. I can testify to one other useful aspect of these Etudes – when I was afflicted with a bout of sciatica, and eventually began to recover from this extremely painful disability, I found the Etudes more effective than any other treatment in helping to clear up residual discomfort in my knees, simply by practising them on my home pedalboard! Even today I begin practising with an Etude, first worked on at half speed, then as near to the indicated metronome mark as I can manage. Whilst on the value of these Etudes one commentator, Martin Cooper (*French Music From the death of Berlioz to the death of Fauré,* OUP 1951), has dismissed the entire French organ school as a 'rather doubtfully musical sphere' – not a very pleasant phrase and with little detailed commentary offered to justify it even when he applies it to the whole organ repertoire after 1750. Admittedly his book ends with the death of Fauré, for many years Choirmaster at the Madeleine Church, who in any case professed a definite preference for the piano and left no organ compositions. Saint-Saens, who was Titular Organist there for many years, left a number of fine organ pieces for the organ, and by no stretch of the imagination could be described as a 'doubtfully musical' composer. Cooper's remit does not extend to an assessment of Messiaen, which might have been of some interest. He does quote some words of Saint-Saens on the organ – (it) 'furnishes a harmonious noise rather than precise music'. But he ignores Franck's twelve organ pieces except to quote Liszt's assertion that the Six Pieces (1862) had 'their place beside the masterpieces of Bach'.

It is the organist's challenge to produce as precise music as the given instrument and the acoustical ambience allows. Consideration of Cooper's views on the organ and its performers leads to the topic of critical consideration of organ concerts and recordings. Apart from the specialist magazines devoted to the organ it is rare to find organ concerts reviewed at all in the arts section of any serious newspapers today. And it is equally rare to find orchestras programming organ concertos. The situation here has parallels with another solo instrument – the guitar. There is only one concerto normally programmed in either genre – in the case of the guitar, the Rodrigo, and for the organ, the Poulenc. This prevalent attitude to the organ and its concert repertoire needs to be considered by all serious performers. Undoubtedly it is a potent reason for the burgeoning of transcription material during recent years, and I have certainly played some part in this. Now all the Beethoven Symphonies (even No 9? – after all Wagner did a piano version!), Mahler's 5th, and Ravel's Second Daphnis and Chloe Suite have been transferred to the sonorities of the organ, to mention just a few of the many works now on offer.

Transcriptions of recorded improvisations have also made their appearance on recordings and in concert. These may be of great value for their intrinsic merit and also as an inspiration to organists who have many brief liturgical opportunities to indulge in this art.

NOTE

'Rough paths my feet have trod' comes from a poem by J.S.B. Monsell. 1811–1875, to be found in *Songs of Praise* No. 272 – 'I hunger and I thirst'. It is a passionate and moving text and I set it as an anthem/communion motet as a result of a commission from the Choir of Louisville Cathedral, Kentucky USA.

Chapter 10

The Praises that Come too Slow

It is well to steel yourself against unfavourable criticism whatever area of public life you embark upon – and also try to take favourable comments in your stride. You will do what you have to do, in spite of either scorn, indifference or praise from whatever quarter.

Robert Browning puts this very well in the two poems I chose for Dramatis Personae: Abt Vogler and Rabbi Ben Ezra. The versions of these songs for baritone and piano that I instrumentalised for solo organ in Diptyque show the strength of Browning's ideas in these two 'Songs without Words'.

Abt Vogler

(After he has been extemporizing upon the musical instrument of his invention)

(1)
Would that the structure brave, the manifold music I build,
Bidding my organ obey, calling its keys to their work,
Claiming each slave of the sound, at a touch, as when
    Solomon willed
Armies of angels that soar, legions of demons that lurk.
Man, brute, reptile, fly, – alien of end and of aim,
Adverse, each from the other heaven-high, hell-deep
    removed, –
Should rush into sight at once, as he named the ineffable
    Name,

And pile him a palace straight to pleasure the princess he
    loved!

(VI)

All through my keys that gave their sounds to a wish of my
    soul,
All through my soul that praised as its wish flowed visibly
    forth,
All through music and me! For think, had I painted the
    whole,
Why, there it had stood, to see, nor the process so wonder-
    worth:
Had I written the same, made verse – still, effect proceeds
    from cause,
Ye know why the forms are fair, ye hear how the tale is told;
It is all triumphant art, but art in obedience to laws,
Painter and poet are proud in the artist-list enrolled:–

(VII)

But here is the finger of God, a flash of the will that can,
Existent behind all laws, that made them and, lo, they are!
And I know not if, save in this, such gift be allowed to man,
That out of three sounds he frame, not a fourth sound, but a
    star.
Consider it well: each tone of our scale in itself is naught;
It is everywhere in the world – loud, soft, and all is said:
Give it to me to use! I mix it with two in my thought:
And, there! Ye have heard and seen: consider and bow the
    head!

(VIII)

Well, it is gone at last, the palace of music I reared;
Gone! and the good tears start, the praises that come too
    slow;
For one is assured at first, one scarce can say that he feared,

That he even gave it a thought, the gone thing was to go.
Never to be again! But many more of the kind
As good, nay, better perchance: is this your comfort to me?
To me, who must be saved because I cling with my mind
To the same, same self, same love, same God: ay, what was,
    shall be.

(IX)

Therefore to whom turn I but to thee, the ineffable Name?
Builder and maker, thou, of houses not made with hands!
What, have fear of change from thee who art ever the same?
Doubt that thy power can fill the heart that thy power
    expands?
There shall never be one lost good! What was, shall live as
    before;
The evil is null, is naught, is silence implying sound;
What was good shall be good, with, for evil, so much good
    more;
On the earth the broken arcs; in the heaven, a perfect round.

(X)

All we have willed or hoped or dreamed of good shall exist;
Not its semblance, but itself; no beauty, nor good, nor power
Whose voice has gone forth, but each survives for the
    melodist
When eternity affirms the conception of an hour.
The high that proved too high, the heroic for earth too hard,
The passion that left the ground to lose itself in the sky,
Are music sent up to God by the lover and the bard;
Enough that he heard it once: we shall hear it by-and-by.

(XI)

And what is our failure here but a triumph's evidence
For the fulness of the days? Have we withered or agonized?

Why else was the pause prolonged but that singing might
  issue thence?
Why rushed the discords in but that harmony should be
  prized?
Sorrow is hard to bear, and doubt is slow to clear,
Each sufferer says his say, his scheme of the weal and woe:
But God has a few of us whom he whispers in the ear;
The rest may reason and welcome: 'tis we musicians know.

(XII)

Well, it is earth with me; silence resumes her reign:
I will be patient and proud, and soberly acquiesce.
Give me the keys. I feel for the common chord again,
Sliding by semitones, till I sink to the minor, – yes,
And I blunt it into a ninth, and I stand on alien ground,
Surveying awhile the heights I rolled from into the deep;
Which, hark, I have dared and done, for my resting-place is
  found,
The C major of this life: so, now I will try to sleep.

This marvellous poem long fascinated me and I set this
choice of verses in 1993, and had already set in the previous
year my choice of verses from Rabbi Ben Ezra (Grow old
along with me!) followed by a version for male voice chorus,
and then I composed an organ solo version of both –
Diptyque: Two Poems for Organ – in 1994. Abbé Georg
Joseph Vogler (1749–1814), German composer, organist,
theorist, teacher and noted extemporiser, had been the master
of John Relfe, Browning's music teacher. He is virtually
unknown today, apart from this poem and his invention of
the 'orchestrion' – a large organ with presumably a
specification of stops which were strongly orchestral in
colour. Browning clearly empathises with this sensitive soul,
and the creative instinct which even perhaps was denied the
courage to produce compositions for close critical
examination and 'the praises that come too slow'.

Perhaps every artist will tend to think themselves undervalued in their life-time – as some undoubtedly are – even if their work has become well known and achieved some recognition in the tangible form of sales and performances – we will not consider the fires of critical estimation just yet! But the unique opportunities the profession of a cathedral organist offers in the combination of liturgical performance and composition is a most satisfying occupation for a composer – inasmuch that you do not feel obligated to please anyone but yourself and God – in the sense of the highest judge imaginable. You write within (just!) the known capabilities of your Choir, you pay no heed to the artistic perceptions (if any) of your Dean and Chapter, and you write just what your appreciation of the text in hand demands of you. And then for additional inspiration – the wonderful example of the medieval craftsman lavishing all his best efforts on some carving that will always be out of sight from ground level, or even entirely – without young legs and a ladder to climb. But today the market is always there, beckoning its victims along the primrose path that leads to material success. If that has always been true how much more so today, when image and fame are blatantly offered and brandished as an essential goal for those susceptible to this 'celebrity-media' temptation. So it is all the more satisfying that the broadcast and televised Services and concerts from cathedrals often result in letters of appreciation which are the more immediate because there is no thought of celebrity-profession involved and only the ear must judge. Here are two such:

"I would like to thank you for the really thrilling Evensong from Ely. I am getting rather old now, & more & more critical. I suppose I judge everything by Boris Ord's standards, it is rarely that I listen to Evensong & find that any Cathedral Organist meets Boris & King's – you do." (Mus.B. Cantab. Ipswich, 3rd June, 1970.)

And this, on the same broadcast:

"I was bitterly disappointed that I was not able to hear the whole of your broadcast service today but what I did, may I say was superb. The Psalm was just exquisite. (The only thing I did not like was the final 'eds' in some words but I am sure you have a very good reason for so doing). What a time you must have spent working on this psalm but it was most beautiful in every way. The blend and balance was first rate and the tone of the boys was such that I have seldom heard better (do tell them). I think the words meant so much indeed to your choir and everything was brought into focus, so much so that I felt I was taking part in the service and not listening to a concert. After the Psalm I was not able to listen to anything else until the anthem which was vigorous and full-blooded and not drowned by the organ." (Morecambe, Lancs.)

(The final 'eds' mentioned I retained from Michael Howard's regime. They are essential in the plainchant usage, and the archaic phrasings of such, and the consistency of treatment in Anglican chant obviously appealed to Michael, and also to me – as less conversational in style for liturgical use.)

(This was the music sung: Preces and Responses: Smith of Durham. Psalm 18: chants by Goss Mornington and Stanford. Office Hymn: E.H. 60 – Plainchant Mode ii: Canticles: Wills in D. Anthem: Exultate Deo – Samuel Wesley).

Then there are the broadcast organ recitals, with the responses more usually from those with some knowledge of the organ repertoire and the historical background of the instrument, though not necessarily so – witness this effusion which came to me via the Dean Patrick Hankey (without any comment):

"I have just listened to a broadcast performance on your organ. I can only call it a performance, there was no music, just a series of noises. It may have been clever technique, but its complete absence of beauty made it seem quite out of place in a place of worship. I have listened to, and enjoyed hundreds of organ recitals in my 64 years including most cathedrals and large churches in London & the Alexandra Palace (Mr Cunningham). But these items seemed more suitable for the accompaniment of a horror film than to enhance a cathedral. I have no doubt of your organist's ability to play, but he cannot be really musical to make such noises, even if they are fashionable – I have heard similar rows recently from St Alban's Cathedral." (March 11th 1965)

The main work in this programme was Messiaen's Combat de le Mort et de la Vie from his Suite: Les Corps Glorieux. This suite was published in 1942 and may be considered fully representative of its composer's mature idiom, which does require rather more from the listener than a knee-jerk reaction. But what can you say to a reaction such as this? 'You should have used the off switch'? Though it's true to say that such comments were very rare, I'm sure that most of the Great British Public with similar opinions did just that.

A different view of this broadcast came from E.H.C. (Worthing, 12th March) – "Your recital... was absolutely superb. The work by Messiaen was terrific, and must have been very difficult to play, I should imagine."

Most communications after broadcasts came from organists or aficionados of the instrument. I broadcast three of Vierne's Six Symphonies – the Second, Fourth and Sixth, each generally eliciting appreciative comments in letters from listeners such as this: (11.9.1970)

"My sincere thanks for the Vierne II, Radio 3 today. Glorious! – my son recorded it on my hi fi equipment and it will be added to your other superb recordings – of Vierne III etc on Alpha – THE finest organ record I have yet experienced; and the EMI disc (Franck's Final in B flat). Why is not more Vierne broadcast and committed to disc?" (C.A.B. Wimborne, Dorset).

The EMI disc mentioned was recorded in 1966 and was generally well received, in spite of the fact that the wind pressures were unreliable under the strain of the last chord of Messiaen's Dieu parmi nous.

Once the BBC have accepted you on to their list of recitalists you then have to get used to the idea of being 'produced'. This does take a few engagements to get used to, especially with regard to the matter of your favourite registrations! Following the composer's indications is not always sufficient, and it is quite normal to be told that "That melodic line doesn't come through at all in bars..." This necessitates considerable tinkering with the composer's registrations that sometimes seem quite wrong at the console. But if you wish for further engagements, it is as well to buckle down as requested. (And it can prove a useful learning experience!)

Press reviews of recorded performances always offer much food for thought, including reflections on the reviewer's motives. I include a varied selection of views on the same performances, but start here with one mainly concerned with the changing critical evaluation of myself as a composer.

'The Praises of the Trinity' Herald HAVPCD (1997) Choral and Organ music by Arthur Wills:
Ely Cathedral Choir – Paul Trepte (Director) Sean Farrell (Organ) and Arthur Wills (Solo Organ)

"In the 1960s Arthur Wills was looked on as cathedral music's Angry Young Man. [!] Some found his non-triadic, neo-Hindemithian harmony somewhat limited in expressive range and predicted a limited life span for his compositions."

(But this was a period in which only a neo-Howells idiom was considered 'liturgically correct' and I had no intention of going on down that path.) This was from D.W. in the *Choir Schools Today* magazine. But he then goes on: "It would be good if every composer whose idiom appears forbidding at the outset were given the opportunity for a revaluation a generation or so later and we rejoice at the opportunity given to Arthur Wills, after a period of comparative neglect." There follows a generally laudatory discussion of the items included.

My first exposure to the international critical world was not entirely unpleasing... in the Summer Term of 1958, at the conclusion of which I was appointed Organist and Master of the Choristers, Michael Howard directed the Choristers and the Men of the Renaissance Singers in a recording for the Argo Record Company of 'Music for the Feast of Christmas' drawing on repertoire from the 15th/17th century. As an afterthought, finding a spare three minutes or so and a couple of days to spare, Michael asked me if I would like to add 'Les Anges' from Messiaen's La Nativité du Seigneur – a truly brilliant idea, demonstrating the innate spiritual link between the ethos of 'Early' music before the classical period and that of some of the 20th century. This unusual repertoire was generally well received, but the USA *Music* magazine had fairly usual reservations about the limited choice of repertoire, and remarked of the choral pieces – "sparkle seems to be lacking. The one exception I found was the stunning performance of the Messiaen 'Les Anges' which, on direct comparison with the composer's own recording, is remarkably authentic in style and even in sound; if the organ lacks the ultimate lean brilliance of that at La Trinité, on the other hand it is squarely in tune." (In the re-build of the mid-seventies it did attain that lean brilliance, and was still in tune! But more of this later).

Possibly the worst review I ever received for a gramophone record was from K.L. – of 'Victimae Paschali'

(1964) – a recording of music for the seasons of Lent, Passiontide and Easter, which I had planned and hoped to be a worthy successor to Howard's Christmas programme. This vicious attack ends – "certainly it is impossible to recommend this record." But A.R. in *The Gramophone* concludes "This finely designed recital is beautifully sung and played and well recorded. It has an excellent acoustic... I warmly recommend the disc to all lovers of church music and above all to those who can enter into its devotional spirit." *The Musical Opinion* reviewer opines "...the Choir have clearly been well trained and well rehearsed. They sing with strength and even passion, as in Haec dies (a Plainchant), in Terra tremuit and Woefully arrayed." Truly, beauty is in the ear of the listener! It is also perhaps worth recalling to mind some words of Christopher Campling (then Vicar of Pershore Abbey) who told me that every Good Friday, after his Services were over, he would go home and play the recording of Cornysh's Woefully arrayed.

I received this letter from Benjamin Britten after he had attended Evensong on Palm Sunday, 1964. I saw him briefly after the Service (at which we sang Wood's Glory and honour and laud) and then sent him the recently issued Victimae Paschali recording. He responded on 2nd April as follows:

Dear Mr Wills,
I was very pleased to get your nice letter, and touched that you should send me the record. I have not frankly had time to play it yet, but remembering the Choir's splendid singing on Palm Sunday, and seeing what excellent music you perform, I much look forward to hearing it. I very much hope to see you when we come over for the Requiem performances in June, and to hear your excellent Choir many times in the future.
Best wishes to you all,
Yours sincerely,
Benjamin Britten

An interesting venture on the part of the BBC was the series: 'Britain's Cathedrals and their Music' (1965) in which John Betjeman talked about the buildings and their history followed by a twenty-minute recital of music associated with the Foundation. After the broadcasts these programmes were then made available on LP recordings with a different Cathedral on each side. This was the Ely programme:

Kyrie Eleison (Orbis factor plainchant) – Christopher Tye
Teach me thy way, O Lord – William Fox
O Lord, we beseech thee – George Barcroft
Organ: Chorale Prelude: Christ unser Herr zum Jordan kam – J.S. Bach
Choir: The Praises of the Trinity – Arthur Wills

I was able to choose the choral items entirely from Ely organist/composers, and few other provincial cathedrals could make up such a programme. Ely has indeed been fortunate in having such a heritage of composers from the Reformation onwards – the Tye Kyrie eleison for example is an absolutely astonishing piece. Betjeman's script, delivered in those inimitable tones, was remarkably informative about the history and character of Ely, and after the last choir piece he bids us farewell with reflections about Ely Minster towering over the cowering Fen town which necessarily came into existence to serve the medieval monastery and then continued as a farming community after the Reformation. Not his exact words perhaps, but certainly the gist of his thinking. Listening to him again, some forty years on, I think that the character of Ely has changed hardly at all. Fortunately it has managed to retain the most complete collection of monastic buildings in this country – still in use by the Cathedral and the King's School. The residential areas of Ely have greatly expanded as it has attracted commuters who work in either Cambridge or London (or both, as I did for much of my professional life) and the size of the cathedral congregation has greatly benefited thereby – and not necessarily to the disadvantage of the Parish Church. Also, in common with other cathedrals Ely has developed its attractiveness as a place of quasi monastic pilgrimage, offering shops, restuarants, 'Ely Experience Weekends' – and if the climate continues to warm, perhaps even eventually its own wine label.

Reviews of recordings done on the rebuilt Harrison organ in 1975 are of special interest, given the somewhat mixed reception my ideas were accorded in some academic and other critical circles. I was at that time especially (and still am to some extent) very concerned with the performance of the pre-Revolution French school, and longed to have the tonal resources to do ample justice to the Couperins, Clerambault and Marchand et al, as well as English music from Purcell onwards, and of course the Baroque music of the German school. The most important disc I did with this in mind was the two volumes devoted to Daquin's Book of Noels and several of Louis Marchand's Livre d'Orgue. The American *High Fidelity* magazine's reviewer demonstrated his appreciative perception of my aims as follows (October 1977):

"The newly rebuilt organ in England's Ely Cathedral has proved to be a musical medium of rare versatility, with a chameleon-like ability to sound persuasive (and even wholly authentic) in a surprising range of literature. It has (as does organist Arthur Wills) a special affinity for French music, and rarely can a modern organ have captured so definitively the sounds of the eighteenth century French instruments." (S.C.) Bravo! – I couldn't have put it better myself.

In the *Gramophone* magazine S.W. wrote: "Having now heard a second record on the rebuilt organ in Ely Cathedral, one cannot but feel that the dense textures of the old instrument did less than justice to Arthur Wills' powers as a recitalist. He now has at his command an organ completely responsive to the exceptional finesse and subtlety of his playing which has captivated audiences all over the United States as well as in Europe." Exactly!

But the academic historians do not want 'historic' organs developed in response to changing ideas on the interpretation of the classical repertoire, or the demands of contemporary composition, and they certainly do not want the ideas of one executant (with the help of a sympathetic advisor, who is also able and willing to assist financially) to be allowed to 'do his own thing' without let or hindrance. Maybe I shall be seen to have been the last cathedral organist to have that freedom and opportunity to ignore contemporary 'historical correctness'.

Organs are of their time and reflect the general aesthetic of the compositions of that particular period. The Harrison organ of 1908 was a logical outcome of the Romantic orchestra of the post-Wagnerian aesthetic – reflected in the works of Mahler, Richard Strauss and Elgar. It also necessarily reflected developments in the Town Hall organs of the period with that particular repertoire of transcriptions, and earlier music registered in an orchestral style. One hears this aesthetic, in reverse as it were, in Elgar's orchestration of the Bach Fantasia and Fugue in C minor (BWV537). Ten years or so after my retirement the 'dense textures' were largely restored with the wind pressures of the 1908 instrument (the Great and Pedal reeds now blot out the foundation work – in my version they coloured it) and the restoration of the Tuba – a sound I cordially disliked. All this at a cost of £500,000.

Nevertheless, somewhat emasculated versions of my added sonorities such as the entire Positive division remained and are still fairly useful in the older repertoire. When the rebuilt organ was finished (not quite as it turned out) the old thickness of sound had returned, and the lack of balance between the various divisions really disturbed me, but I was not prepared to be truthful at that point – Paul is a dear friend, and I think he valued my opinions – he certainly felt that he ought to ask. But where art is concerned everyone is an individual, and there is no point in being difficult, unless of course you are being hired to be just that!

From the time when Sidney Campbell and I arrived in Ely, the state of the organ was always a matter of some concern. Mr Jack Hind was the tuner, based in Cambridge (and most Cambridge organs were from the Harrison stable in that era) and on almost every visit he would report on the deteriorating state of the instrument, although Sidney would tend to ascribe this simply to a vein of neuroticism in his character, and not worry overmuch. I think that Sidney knew that his years at Ely would be few, and any organ problems could be safely left to his successor. I have mentioned Michael Howard's re-arrangement of the Choir Organ pipes – very imaginative; these were incorporated into the rebuild of 1975, with further additions, and now remain, though in a rather more chastened voicing, in the 2001 rebuild. The gradual deterioration of the instrument of course continued, and it was clear that the Dean and Chapter would not be able to finance any substantial repairs for the foreseeable future. Some notes disappeared from speech, and I well remember the astonishment of Hans Vollenveider, when he came to record an LP of Bach repertoire for HMV in the mid-1950s (having been recommended to Ely by Ralph Downes – who well knew the then state of the organ) when he first became aware of this deficiency voicing his opinion to me, as his page turner, in no uncertain terms. But somehow he made it all work in the end, and I found him a most convivial companion over several drinks at 'The Lamb' Hotel. "I'm an L.B.E.," he assured me – "Likes beer!"

By the early sixties the state of the organ could no longer be ignored, and some basic remedial action in respect of the bellows was urged upon the Chapter by Cuthbert Harrison. In view of this decision I took the opportunity to discuss the possibility of removing some of the 'fat' from the Great and Pedal chorus reeds. As always, Cuthbert listened sympathetically and said, "I can't give you open shallots, but we can put them on the voicing machine for a bit more bite," – or words to that effect – and so it was agreed. The increased 'bite' was accompanied by a much greater intensity of sound – to a degree noticeable even by Dean Hankey: "Arthur, the organ is so much louder now!" As quick as a flash and there was the answer – "It's the repaired bellows, Mr Dean. We are not losing all that wind now." This organ was ready in 1963 for my recording of Vierne's Third Symphony and the Choir recording Victimae Paschali – both on the Alpha label. (The Vierne recording was eventually transferred to the Saga label.) There was notably a short vogue for 45 Extended Play Mono recordings in the sixties – Argo, Ryemuse and Abbey were amongst the leaders in this field, seeing the gentle rise of the Cathedral Shop from one table discreetly placed at the Crossing as a potential ally in these ventures. Argo in 1960 issued a ghostly return of the Ely Choristers from the Howard regime which was very welcome: Byrd's 'An earthly tree' was transferred from Music for the Feast of Christmas, but the other items were of fresh compelling interest: the plainchant Missa Cum Jubilo and Lallouette's O mysterium ineffabile (then unpublished). Both were very convincing displays of Howard's way with boys in this repertoire. Ryemuse issued this organ programme from Ely, typical of the genre – Bach: In Dulci Jubilo BWV 729, Bach: Fugue in G minor BWV 579, Vierne: Impromptu (a great favourite of mine then) Wills: Deo Gratias.

Four years later in 1967 the E.M.I. recording in the Great Cathedral Organ series was issued – a programme of French composers plus my Introduction and Allegro (which might have come from France, and was in fact composed as something of a reaction and homage to Messiaen's Dieu parmi nous). It is clear from the conclusion of the Messiaen piece that the winding of the instrument was still far from secure, although the placing of the microphones largely overcomes this, except for the most sharp-eared of listeners. *The Gramophone* reviewer (S.W.) was not entirely happy with the organ and his comments are perceptive: "At Ely, the organ represents a state of transition between, say, the traditional Harrison in King's College, Cambridge, a few miles away, and such recent Harrison organs as those at St Albans Abbey and St George's Chapel, Windsor. All the pieces are brilliantly played by Dr Wills; the limitations on complete effectiveness are imposed by the organ itself. The great new voice in French organ music is Messiaen and, paradoxically enough, his famous 'Dieu parmi nous' (from La Nativité du Seigneur) comes off extraordinarily well on this record. The impact in the building itself must have been absolutely stunning."

Another reviewer (*Records & Recording*, G.C.) was even more enthusiastic: "...one of the best in the Great Cathedral series. Of course it is the excerpt from Messiaen's great work La Nativité du Seigneur which provides the greatest artistic satisfaction... a brilliantly flamboyant account of Franck's Final" and so on. But no mention of the winding problem at the end of Dieu parmi nous. Even my one review (so far as I know!) in *Woman* magazine homes in especially on the Messiaen – "one of the most breathtaking recordings I know. – those with a taste for the way-out will thrill to all the ear-searing discords of French composer Messiaen, played by the virtuoso organist Arthur Wills."

The following year Abbey issued a 45 'stereo playable mono' of Bach, Couperin and Wills – here again Couperin's Dialogue sur les trompettes, clarion et tierce du Grand clavier et le bourdon avec le larigot du positif (4th couplet from Gloria, Messe a l'usage des Paroisses) demonstrated that my love of the French Baroque organ school still awaited to be assuaged. The last 78 recording before the complete rebuild of 1975 was done by Michael Smythe on his Vista label and issued by RCA in 1972. This included D'Aquin's Noel X – thereby demonstrating my continuing interest in the 18th century French School – eventually to be consummated in the D'Aquin/Marchand double record issued by Saga on the rebuilt organ in 1976.

It was now imperative for Dean Michael Carey to launch his appeal based upon the restoration of the West Tower, and the Organ. Of the two causes, the Tower was a clearly visible imperative and the Organ could clearly cling to its coat-tails for support. In the event a single donor offered the original estimated sum for the organ of £70,000; but of course the seventies was a period of high inflation, and money throughout the decade was extremely tight. I suggested that the Chapter Advisor should be Cecil (Sam) Clutton, whose interest in the project sufficed to indicate that he would not charge for his services, and this offer was gratefully accepted. The scheme was agreed and accepted, when Sam had a final inspiration – a five-rank Cornet on the Great. I had to point out that we had spent all the available appeal money, but Sam then spoke like a true Advisor – "Leave it to me – I'm in the Isle of Man for the weekend, and I'll talk to some of my friends." Sam's powers of persuasion worked as powerfully as ever, and this expensive stop was duly added. My only regret was that its compass stopped at Middle C – for true usefulness the five additional notes down to G were essential – but too expensive even for Sam to procure. Coupling the Positive Cornet séparé was a possible way out of this though, and this rank can still be heard to good effect in Purcell's Voluntary for double organ in the CD recording entitled 'Full Stops'.

The Organ Festival Programme mounted in 1976 ran from May 1st to July 28th. The opening Concert was given by the Richard Hickox Orchestra with myself as Organ soloist, and consisted of Organ Concertos by Handel, Poulenc and Wills, with Elgar's Serenade for Strings as a more gentle interlude. I had asked Richard to provide the orchestra and also conduct in view of our recent Cambridge academic connections, and I was not at all pleased when on the day of the concert his Orchestra turned up – but he didn't, sending instead a message that he was unwell! Fortunately, even at this very short notice, we were able to obtain the services of Neville Dilkes, who had conducted the World Premiere of the Concerto with myself and the English Sinfonia on the 22nd July at the 1970 Nottingham Festival in Southwell Minster. Without Dilkes' willing availability at that shortest possible notice I don't know what we would have done – the Hand of God only works through human hands!

Philip Ledger conducted Mendelssohn's 'Elijah' with the Cambridgeshire Choir founded by David Willcocks; there was the annual Diocesan Festival of Praise, but for this occasion augmented by a Brass Ensemble and further enlivened by the first performance of my new solo organ piece – 'Resurrection'. This was an even more extreme (in its musical language) successor to my 'Tongues of Fire' of a couple of years before, and it was most aptly named, both for its celebration of the rebuilt organ, and also for its prominent usage of the revoiced chorus reeds.

Celebrity recitalists included George Thalben Ball and Peter Hurford, and both concerts were broadcast by the BBC. Hurford's was a typical Bach programme, but Thalben-Ball's very varied choice included my Elevation for Strings. We also welcomed Fred Swann from the Riverside Church and the Manhattan School of Music. Fred had often hosted me at Riverside and it was a great pleasure to hear him in Ely. Before the concert he professed to feeling nervous, but I'm sure he was only 'pulling my leg'. He included my Scherzetto in his programme which began with the Organ Solo from Janacek's Festival Mass. My Organ Concerto is dedicated to Fred and he gave the USA premiere on July 6th 1971 at a Convention of the American Guild of Organists held in Honolulu. It was conducted by Paul Calloway, another good friend of mine, from Washington Episcopal

Cathedral – how I wished that I might have been there in Honolulu! Fred was soon to move to The Crystal Cathedral, Garden Grove, California where he assured me that untold riches and musical opportunities awaited – and abounded – "As a matter of fact, I have – IN RESIDENCE – a symphonic band, and various wind ensembles, as well as a full symphony orchestra – at the Cathedral." Wow! (I was hoping that I might introduce 'The Fenlands' Suite to the Californians, but it didn't work at that point in time.)

Gerald Gifford was the very talented Assistant Organist at this time, and he played two concerts in the Festival – one for the Ely Former Choristers Festival, at which I talked about the organ, and another with the Cathedral Choir to demonstrate the Organ's accompanimental capacity in music from Byrd to Wills. He also played solo pieces by Tomkins, Blow, S.S. Wesley, Harwood and Mathias. I did two solo recitals – one on the occasion of a Visit from the United Reformed Church – Eastern Province, and a lecture recital for a Visit by Members of the Organ Club of Great Britain. This programme included the first performance of my Symphonia Eliensis, based both on the Etheldreda Sequence Plainchant and the structure of the Cathedral. And each of its structural sections was mirrored in a characteristic sonority of the rebuilt instrument.

It was good to welcome Harold Britton for a Lunch Hour recital. He occupied one of the few remaining Borough Organist posts for the Walsall Corporation, and played a virtuoso programme of Bossi, Bach/Dupré, Mozart, Reger, Franck and Vierne. There was also a welcome visit from Roger Judd who was my Assistant from 1968 to 1972 before becoming Master of the Music at St Michael's College, Tenbury. His programme included Reubke's Sonata on the 94th Psalm. Finally, on July 28th, the Festival culminated in a visit by the Royal Liverpool Philharmonic Orchestra conducted by Sir Charles Groves, who readily agreed to the inclusion in his programme of Handel's Organ Concerto in F

– 'The Cuckoo and the Nightingale'. In this work Handel gives an opportunity for an improvised Andante movement by the soloist, which I relished 'with both hands' as it were. Thus was consummated a truly memorable and most worthy Organ Festival.

I quoted above from a review of the Saga Daquin/Marchand recording by S.W. in the *Gramophone* magazine. But as a critical assessment of the rebuilt organ as heard on the first recording to be issued, and of course the possibility of many repeated hearings thereafter, the review by S.W. in the magazine issue of August 1976, based on a varied programme of music from the 18th century to the 20th century must carry even more weight, and I quote this in full:

"The first record I ever reviewed for *Gramophone* was of Arthur Wills at Ely Cathedral in 1967. One would not think from this new disc that one was listening to the same organ, so wide-ranging are the changes in the tonal design made in the Harrison restoration completed this year, and now being celebrated by a series of summer concerts by eminent recitalists. It is thus timely and topical to have the means at hand to study its new graces in detail.

Dr Wills claims on the sleeve that Ely now has 'arguably the most fascinating and comprehensive cathedral organ in this country'. It is certainly one of the most versatile. The Arthur Harrison organ of 1908 was a masterpiece but with very dense textures; now they are transparent without sacrificing in any way the essential grandeur of a large instrument in a huge building. The first concern in the rebuild was to provide the tonal resources capable of interpreting the German and French idioms of the eighteenth century. How well this has been done is indicated by the glitter given to the Bach Weimar Prelude and Fugue in D major, and the two classical French pieces, the Marchand Basse de trompette (a nasal reed against a light background) and the Couperin

Chaconne. A new positive section (played from the choir manual) contributes to the brightness of these effects.

Thence Dr Wills moves easily into the Romantic nineteenth century with two pieces which reflect the organ's basic character, Liszt's Prelude and Fugue and Franck's Choral No. 2. The big sounds are all there, but they are contrasted with an exquisite family of string stops on the solo organ – in the hushed harmonization of the notes B-A-C-H before the immense final chords of the Liszt, and in the mysterious prayer-like passage which Franck conceived for the voix humaine in his Choral. Finally, Dr Wills, a prolific composer as well as a formidable academic and executant, gives us his own Carillon on the Christmas carol Orientis Partibus, first performed in 1973, a dazzling show piece. The fidelity achieved by Michael Smythe's recording is the best of this month's batch of organ records."

Michael Smythe – there's a name to conjure with. His Vista label was at the forefront of organ recordings at this time along with EMI, and well before Saga, Meridian and Hyperion. He thoroughly deserves that tribute from S.W. above, but regrettably he died in mid-career, and so never achieved the fullness of success that would undoubtedly have been his. Possibly his finest envisaged project was a recording of Widor's Ten Symphonies on the organ of Coventry Cathedral involving three performers – myself, Jane Parker-Smith, and Graham Steed from Canada. This was an ambitious project for the mid-seventies, but an enticing one for me – Coventry being my home-town, and the organ that was designed by Sidney Campbell and built by Harrisons in the sixties. The Symphonies were to be issued in two box-sets of five for the RCA label, but in fact only Symphonies 1–5 eventually appeared, in 1976. My recording sessions in 1972 were scheduled for the end of the Summer holiday and ran from Tuesday, August 29th to Thursday 31st, and had to cover Symphonies 1, 4, 6, 8, and 10. I had spent the previous four weeks caravanning with the family in France, of course visiting many of my favourite Cathedrals, but also finding time for some relaxation in the Midi. The Lay Clerks began singing the Michaelmas Term Services on the following Saturday after the mid-week recordings. This hectic time-tabling seems to be quite pressurised in retrospect, but it was clearly the accepted norm of life then! We certainly needed those three evenings to get the five symphonies down, but my memory is of satisfaction with both playing and recording. Nevertheless, four years later, some critical reception was quite hostile, to my performances especially, and I think that Michael must have found this quite upsetting – Browning's 'the praises that come too slow' were certainly in evidence here – and S.W.'s tribute to his new Ely recording must have been all the more welcome.

John Shuttlesworth's new label Meridian (spawned from Saga), and still in partnership at this time with Ted Perry, were now interested in a popular miscellaneous programme from Ely, and I was delighted to oblige. The then Master at the Choir House, James Tilly, suggested the title 'Full Stops' and Ted Perry accepted it with alacrity and delight as 'witty'. This was the programme: (1) Marche Pontificale (5th movement from Widor's Symphony No. 1) – the use of this title clearly demonstrates that the French Symphonic School of composers after Franck thought of their pieces as suites of contrasting movements, rather than the 'thought-through' symphonic designs of the Austro-German School. (2) Adagio in G minor – Albinoni-Giazotto – an overtly 'pop' number of some emotional drama, especially in the version for organ and strings; (only the bass line is by Albinoni). (3) The Ride of the Valkries (the opening of the third act of Wagner's opera Die Walküre) arranged by Lemare – the texture of this orchestral writing readily translates into the French organ toccata style. (4) Variations on 'Amazing Grace' – Wills – the popularity of this melody ensures its ready comprehension by most listeners throughout a kaleidoscopic

257

variety of organ colours. (5) The Storm – Lemmens – a dramatic piece of 19th century programme music, though mostly quiet! This record was accorded an (A:1) by *HI-FI News & Record Review* – March 1979, with the comment: 'A good buy, if you happen to like the contents.' This seems to have been the prevailing critical opinion, but W.A.C. writing in the *Gramophone* Magazine was much more positive:

"The title "Full Stops" given to this record suggest showmanship ...but it is showmanship of the very best kind and incidentally only possible on comparatively few organs, whoever is playing. The organ of Ely Cathedral matches the vast building perfectly. It was completely restored about three years ago and, as this record demonstrates, it is now a superb and highly versatile instrument: Dr Wills, who has known it for more than 20 years (that is before and after its restoration), is its complete master. As a sampler, my choice would be the Marche Pontificale, which is one of the movements from Widor's First Symphony. Organ, soloist, building and recording staff combine to invest it with all its magnificence. The brilliance of the Ride of the Valkries is tremendously exciting and to set against these showpieces there is the rich opulence of the Albinoni/Giazotto Adagio. To call the Grand Fantasia in E minor Storm has always been a misnomer. The storm section has long been the most popular of organ storms but the bulk of the work is very different in mood. This leave's the soloist's own Variations on 'Amazing Grace', and very happily it lives with its companions. The earlier and simpler variations lead up to a finale which taxes the resources of all concerned, including the recording engineers, and all come out of the exercise with flying colours."

Re-issued on CD in 1995 it accumulated (not entirely suitably) three pieces by Purcell and Blow from the Meridian

LP Anthems by Purcell and Blow (1978). But it appears reasonable enough not to waste good recorded material!

My three organ recordings for Ted Perry's Hyperion label were all very different – the transcription of Mussorgsky's Pictures from an Exhibition was chosen by Ted as the opening recording for his own new label in 1980. This was a considerable vote of confidence in me, and he did his best to demonstrate that with special sleeves and signed copies. It was then transferred to CD in 1988 with these sleeve quotes: 'The most spectacular digital recording'. 'The digital recording is clear, atmospheric and thunderously realistic'. 'An overwhelming aural experience'.

Music for Organ and Brass Band was recorded in 1982, and followed on from the premiere in October 1981 of my commission from the Cambridge Co-operative Brass Band – 'Symphonic Suite: The Fenlands', which was broadcast by the BBC. On the second side of this LP were the following pieces: Elgar – Pomp and Circumstance Marches No.1 and No.4, and 'Nimrod' from the 'Enigma Variations'. Walton – March: Crown Imperial and 'Touch her soft lips and part' from 'Henry V' – all with organ parts arranged by myself. M.M. in the *Gramophone* Magazine (June 1983) concluded: "To some of the sounds on this record there is a touch of apocalyptic quality, which would not have been possible without a recording quality equal to the very best of today's. This, too, is on offer; in total this record is a winner." This recording also was transferred to CD in 1988. Broadcasts and recordings do make a difference! As soon as January 1983 I was asked to perform the work in Huddersfield Town Hall with the Huddersfield Technical College Brass Band conducted by Phillip McCann.

In January1994 the first movement of 'The Fenlands' – 'The Vikings' was recorded by the Dallas Wind Symphony with Paul Riedo, Organ. This movement achieved wide currency in the USA through its many broadcasts, which also then led to requests for music scores for various brass ensembles, which in due course I did my best to satisfy.

And in that year of 1994 I also made a transcription for organ solo of three movements from 'The Fenlands' – 'The Vikings', 'Oliver Cromwell' and March: 'City of Ely', which I and others have played many times in organ concerts here and abroad. Even this was not the end; in 1992 Jennifer Bate performed the Suite in Truro Cathedral with the Bodmin Band, and then approached me about a version of the 'City of Ely' March for Military Band, for a performance in Hereford Cathedral in October 2002. The thought crossed my mind – 'this is all getting too much!' The Army Band in question was the Band of the Light Division based in Winchester, with the Director of Music Major Calum Gray. To my utter amazement he offered to rescore the March for this Fundraising Event (no small labour of love), and I gratefully gave him permission to do so. I was to be on tour in the USA that October, and therefore unable to attend the Hereford Concert.

There have been a good number of live performances of the complete Suite with Band in which I have been the organ soloist, and one very noticeable aspect of these has been the temperamental character of many of the E flat cornets I have encountered. It is a high solo instrument, and not doubled, therefore the player is on his own, and if he is absent so is his part. At a performance by the Brighouse and Rastrick Band in the Peterborough Festival held in July 1987 the player was late arriving for the rehearsal. One of his colleagues commented adversely on this, and the player immediately walked out, leaving me to supply the part on the organ, as requested by the conductor. Even at the St Albans Organ Festival of 1991, with the highly esteemed Grimethorpe Band, the E flat cornet did not manage to be present for either the rehearsal or the first part of the concert – once again I had to supply the part. The more prestigious the band it seems, the more temperamental the solo E flat cornet is apt to be. On the other hand, as part of the Leeds Summer Festival 1995, I played 'The Fenlands' with the Sellers Engineering Band, conducted by Philip McCann (who had played cornet in the Grimethorpe Band for the 1991 St Albans performance). This is an accomplished youthful Band, mostly trained by Philip himself I should imagine, and certainly no one was missing this time!

Besides commissioning many works from me, David Salter has played a leading part in the setting up of performances of many of my large-scale works in the Leeds area – the world premiere of my 'Symphony in A minor' for instance. This was my 'Exercise' for the Durham D.Mus. examination, composed in the mid-1950s. Few candidates are given the chance to hear their examination work performed at all, and the Sinfonia of Leeds, conducted by David Greed, gave an excellent account of the piece in 1991 at the Clothworkers Hall. University of Leeds.

My third and last recording for Hyperion as a solo organist was Bach at Ely – a set of my Bach transcriptions for organ solo, recorded at Ely in November 1983. There were of course already many complete recordings of his organ works, but I felt that a group of pieces which Bach did not actually transcribe himself could make an enjoyable programme of his work. The final piece of the programme – the famous Chaconne from the Partita for solo Violin has proved to be the most absorbing for many listeners, and has inspired several keyboard transcriptions, the best known being those by Busoni and Brahms (this for left-hand alone!). I played it as the final voluntary after a Choral Evensong broadcast from Ely on the 11th April 1984, when it aroused much comment: "If I may say so, the Chaconne this afternoon was simply marvellous. Thank you very much." B. F-W. Malvern. "That Chaconne was splendid. The whole Service was excellent, but the Chaconne was magnificent." A.R. Leamington Spa. "If the Chaconne has not yet been recorded, may I suggest its inclusion in a record or cassette of other works by Bach..." G.L.M. Eltham. The Bach LP was not transferred to CD – most probably because there was no compatible material to add to its duration. Its content was published by Oecumuse as *The Arthur Wills Bach Book* in 1985 and it does stand up as a complete recital programme, as was successfully demonstrated when Anne Marsden Thomas invited me to play it at her St Giles Church, Cripplegate on the afternoon of Easter Day 1992.

My last important recording was for the PRIORY Label Great European Organs Series which I did in April 1988, and this review by Robert Lawrenson appeared in the August 1989 edition of *The Organist's Review*:

"Arthur Wills has been at Ely for more than thirty years. He and the Harrison organ seem such a part of one another that it is difficult to imagine one without the other. [Prophetic words – with the year 2002 in mind!] The French influence on both has been strong, along with the English cathedral tradition. In this recording all these strands are brought together. Wills offers a mature and remarkably authentic-sounding performance of Widor's late Symphonie Romane. Quite unlike most Widor, this has the spirituality of Vierne or Messiaen with much tonal language in common with Tournemire.

Wills' own Symphonia Eliensis is clearly related in style to the works of the influential Jean Guillou, whose rather brutal Toccata opens the programme. His symphony is concerned mainly with organ sonorities and thus displays the Ely organ to perfection. Its eight conjoined movements (some very short) are only definable as separate sections through a change of mood. There is little thematic relationship until the last section, but sufficient imaginative devices keep the listener interested until the end." (In fact the work is based on the Etheldreda Sequence plainchant melody, and the eight sections all refer to the architectural design of the Cathedral – that shouldn't have been missed.)

Widor's Symphonie is based on the plainchant melody Haec Dies – the Gradual for Easter Day – another important element in my planning of the programme that deserved to be mentioned. But he is correct in pointing out the stylistic links between the Toccata and my Symphony.) The reviewer goes on – "It may not be your cup of tea, in which case turn to the Parry. (Three Chorale Preludes) Here I am a little disappointed as the two fast preludes are rather thrown away, especially 'The Old 104th', though 'Christe Redemptor' is nicely atmospheric." Yes, I agree with the reviewer here – I was looking for some English organ music of the early 20th century to match the Widor, but Parry wasn't the composer for that task, and probably there wasn't one to be found – the two national organ traditions were quite out of any significant or useful comparisons at that point in time, and I had little experience or sympathy with the required style. The review concludes: "The organ is well-caught by Priory, the only occasional problems of balance being its own." Possibly, or perhaps simply my less well judged choice of registrations!

As time went on there began to surface some references to the 1975 re-build that were critically less positive, and demonstrated a growing stance on organs as instruments to be preserved, rather than critically appraised and then developed for their greater usefulness in the repertoire to be performed. This essential usefulness – one frequently overlooked meaning of 'organ' is 'tool' (!) – is especially important in the case of the English cathedral organ which has to be capable of accompanying repertoire from the 16th to the 21st centuries, as well as giving a convincing account of the solo organ repertoire from a diverse range of European cultures – not the easiest of requirements!

Praises not too slow, but totally absent, and referring both to my supposedly absent abilities both as a composer and performer – and possibly also to my choice of collaborator – may be relished in these excerpts from a review by Simon

Cargill of the first performance of my Concerto for Guitar and Organ: 'Of Innocence and Experience' premiered at Christ Church, Harrogate in the 1990 Harrogate Festival. "This is the sort of thing which gives modern music a bad name... The pity of it was that such notable composers as Dowland, Scheidt and Rodrigo (not to mention Bach) were also treated to such mostly lacklustre playing." (*Yorkshire Post* 30 July 1990). But in the *Harrogate Advertiser*, David Andrews managed at least some rather less slow praises – "The last section, Reflection, contained the most satisfying music. The guitar writing was more obviously idiomatic with its gentle spread chords in three-time against a sustaining organ. In the Rodrigo Concerto Fiona Richardson played with style and confidence..." And so on.

There are a few significant landmarks towards the later stages of a life in the arts, and I mention but two here as food for thought. In his article for the *IAO Millennium Book, The Rise and Rise of the Recording Industry* Terry Hoyle manages a ten-page resume without mentioning either myself as composer or performer – or any of my recordings. But in his book *British Organ Music of the Twentieth Century* published in 2003 Peter Hardwick gives my music a quite deep and thorough consideration, comparable in length and estimation with that given to Francis Jackson, nine years my senior. Artistic criticism is indeed a very subjective occupation.

But of course it is very true that the only real satisfaction in a life devoted to 'high'? art is to be found in the creation of it. Composers who can earn a living as performers can also remain relatively indifferent to the financial success or otherwise of their music. In my case it was only when I reached my mid-sixties and retired from the Cathedral and my RAM teaching that I really began to take an interest in the possible benefits of a promotional approach to my output. Commissions were usually adequately funded, and the sheer interest in fresh creativity amounting to a compulsion to get on with it at all costs easily override second thoughts about the long-term fate of all the labour involved. It's also true that some composers are not readily accepted during their lifetime, and especially perhaps if they already have a considerable reputation based on their prowess as performers – Liszt, Rachmaninoff and Mahler come to mind in this connection. The case of Mahler is of especial interest. In 1955 the first scholarly account in English of his music appeared in the Master Musicians series. The writer Hans Redlich coupled Mahler with Bruckner – thus both these composers were given only half the space given to Bizet and Fauré. Mahler had died in 1911. Redlich could not have anticipated that within another ten years both composers were well on the way to being accepted as comparable masters with Brahms and Sibelius – or of even greater significance for later composers.

But it's not all over yet, though it's impossible not to take note of the increasing frequency of the obituaries of one's near contemporaries in the musical scene. The praises may still be slow in some quarters, but the appreciation in others has far exceeded the nay-sayers. My conclusion here and now has to come from Browning's Rabbi Ben Ezra in the second of my two Dramatis Personae settings (now available either in its original solo song version, or in a version for Male Voice Choir done at the request of The Saint Louis Chamber Chorus, St Louis, MO USA):

(1)

Grow old along with me!
The best is yet to be,
The last of life, for which the first was made:
Our times are in his Hand
Who saith 'A whole I planned,
Youth shows but half; trust God: see all nor be afraid!'

(2)

Then, welcome each rebuff
That turn's earth's smoothness rough,
Each sting that bids nor sit nor stand but go!
Be our joys three-parts pain!
Strive, and hold cheap the strain;
Learn, nor account the pang; dare, never grudge the throe!

(3)

Youth ended, I shall try
My gain or loss thereby;
Leave the fire ashes, what survives is gold:
And I shall weigh the same,
Give life its praise or blame:
Young, all lay in dispute; I shall know, being old.

(4)

So, take and use Thy work:
Amend what flaws may lurk,
What strain o'the stuff, what warpings past the aim!
My times be in Thy hand!
Perfect the cup as planned!
Let age approve of youth, and death complete the same!

Browning's last line now brings to mind my last
compositions – to date! In October 2004 Mary and I enjoyed
a short holiday in Ibiza – now increasingly relished for the
unusual beauty of its sunsets, and even more so – regrettably
– known for the atrocious behaviour of its young British
holiday-makers during the peak seasons of the year. (Age
certainly cannot approve of youth in that connection!) On
returning home, a suitable musical response to the sunsets
soon nagged me into a search for a sufficiently compelling
text, and eventually only Tennyson's 'Crossing the Bar'
seemed appropriate. The work, for solo treble (preferably)
choir and organ, eventually achieved its finished state and is

certainly well qualified for inclusion in my funeral service if the choral forces (or perhaps a recording) is available. In that same year 2004 Ely Choral Society (of which I'm President) asked me for a work for their annual Carol Concert to be held in St. Mary's Church the following year. "That Wondrous Birthday" – a sequence of four Christmas texts was the outcome, premiered in December 2005. In that same year Gordon and Cecilia Barker commissioned a thirty-two bar organ piece for Ron Barker's 70th Birthday – a meditation on 'Adore Te devote'. The result was thirty-six bars – for the same fee! January 2006 saw sketches for Remembrance: 'the world of light!' – this brings together a collage of four poetic texts, concluding with 'in Paradisum' – and resulted from the deaths of two dear friends way back from the 1940's – Jim MacChesney and Michael Fleming. It was completed in March and dedicated to Scott Farrell and the choir of St. Nicholas Cathedral, Newcastle upon Tyne.

A sad way to start this year – but my 80th birthday in September beckons! – And now another commission – a second from St. Stephen's Church, Bournemouth; this time a communion Motet for their May Festival in 2007. 'Any standard text will do' said Ian Harrison, organist and director of Music. But I found that it wouldn't; a perusal of all the Communion texts in the English Hymnal failed to ignite the spark, except 'O food of men wayfaring' and that was already finely wedded to its 18thc. German chorale melody 'In allen meinen thaten'. A trawl through one of my many books of English verse fetched up on George Herbert yet again – 'Love'. I don't know any setting of this text but immediately I could hear it as a choral recitative – alternating in a fascinating dialogue with upper and lower voices and culminating in 'O food of men wayfaring' – either just the first verse for choir in my harmonization attempt to outdo Bach, or all three with the congregation entering at verse two – literally a gift from heaven! – and ideally suited to accompaniment with the chamber organ at the West End of St. Stephen's Church.

A final thought: could a life-story similar to the one I have here be enacted today? I'm sure that many would say – 'No'! But I am far from certain about this. The world of the Church and the Arts is fertile ground for one's gaining of attention and subsequently being valued, and the rest is then down – or up to you. 'Say not the struggle nought availeth!'

Appendix 1

Worklist to date

(Most manuscripts are now in Cambridge University Library.)

Novello/Music Sales – www.musicroom.com
RSCM publications are available on print-to-order –
    e-mail: musicdirect@rscm.com; web: www.rscm.com
For fagus-music.com – e-mail: sales@fagus-music.com
Anglo-American Music Publishers –
    www.worldwidemusiconline.com
Ely Cathedral -e-mail:
    Shop.office@cathedral.ely.anglican.org
OUP – e-mail: music.enquiry.uk@oup.com

Circa 1953

Rhapsody (Unpublished, but see 1960)

1958

Short Holy Communion Service for Men ATB (fagus-Music.com)
Missa Eliensis SATB Organ (Novello/Music Sales – www.musicroom.com)

1959

Postlude for Organ N/MS
Elevation (Included in 'The Colours of the Organ') N/MS
Introduction and Allegro (Included in 'Six from the Sixties' – Organ Music for the Recitalist 1985) N/MS

Evening Canticles for Men ATB
Shop.office@cathedral.ely.anglican.org

1960

Two Motets for Trebles (Latin) 1. Ave verum corpus 2. O
quam gloriosum N/MS
Fanfare (Included in 'Fanfares and Processionals' for Organ)
N/MS
Eucharistic Suite for Organ (This had as its 3rd movement
the Rhapsody of 1953, now entitled 'Sortie'. The first two
movements – 'Introit and Communion' were re-published
in a volume entitled 'Arthur Wills Select Organ Works'.
N/MS
'Sortie' is published separately by fagus-Music.com)
Missa Brevis for Unison Voices N/MS
Deo Gratias for Organ N/MS

1961

Missa Passionis Christi SATB unaccompanied.
Shop.office@cathedral.ely.anglican.org
Elegy for Organ (First composed in 1955, published by
Novello in 1961 and now published by fagus-Music.com)
Alla Marcia for Organ (First published by Novello in 1961
and now published by Anglo-American)
Five Pieces for Organ – 'Procession – Ariosos – Intermezzo
– Requiem aeternam – Finale' N/MS
Let this mind be in you SATB N/MS

1962

A Wedding Anthem: Blessed are all they that fear the Lord
SATB N/MS
Magnificat and Nunc Dimittis in D SATB N/MS
Fantasy Toccata for Piano Unpub.
Trio Sonata in B minor for Organ Anglo-American
Music for Noah Unpub.

1963

Psalm 150 SATB and Organ N/MS
Waltz Caprice for Two Pianos Anglo-American
Prelude and Fugue for Organ N/MS
Sonata for Organ fagus-Music.com

1964

Two Introits SATB (1. O Saviour of the world. 2. O Lord,
how manifold are thy works) N/MS
Behold now praise the Lord SATB RSCM
The Praises of the Trinity SATB Unacc. N/MS
Psalm 98 (Sing a new song to the Lord) Unison (Brass parts
available) N/MS
Fanfares for a Bishop's Enthronement (The Arthur Wills Ely
Organbook) fagus-Music.com

1965

Let God arise SATB Unacc. N/MS
Jubilate Deo SATB N/MS
Two Anthems for ATB (1. By the waters of Babylon
2. Their sound is gone out) N/MS
Three Carols SATB (1. I sing the birth 2. Sweet was the song
3. Chanticleer) N/MS
Variations on a Carol 'I sing the birth' N/MS

1966

O praise the Lord of heaven SSA Unacc. N/MS
Carol: 'The Christ-Child lay on Mary's lap' Unison voices
and Piano N/MS
Psalm 130 (From the depths of my distress) Unison N/MS
Preces and Responses (for Parochial Use) Unison voices and
Organ or Choir Unacc. N/MS

1967

O praise the Lord SATB N/MS

The Carol of King Canute SATB Unacc.N/MS

Te Deum Laudamus (With optional descant) Unison voices
and Organ N/MS

Christmas Meditations (Five pieces for Organ) N/MS

1968

Festival Fanfare for Brass and Organ N/MS (Hire library)

Congregational Communion Service fagus-Music.com

Magnificat and Nunc Dimittis for Trebles
Shop.office@cathedral.ely.anglican.org

1969

Boot and Saddle (Browning) Unison Voices and Piano fagus-
music.com

Concerto for Organ and Strings fagus-music.com

1970

Communion Service for SATB, Unison voices and Organ
RSCM

Magnificat and Nunc Dimittis for SATB, Unison voices and
Organ (NEB text) RSCM

1971

Trio Sonata for Organ fagus-Music.com

Hymn Tune 'Ely Minster' The Arthur Wills Ely Choirbook
fagus-Music.com

Sing joyfully, God's power proclaim fagus-Music.com

An English Requiem (Soprano and Baritone solo, Chorus,
Strings, Harp, Timpani, Two Pianos and Organ)
(Hire only) N/MS

Prelude and Fugue 'Alkmaar' for Organ fagus-Music.com

1972

I hunger and I thirst Anthem for SATB and Organ N/MS

Hymns: (1) Draw near with faith (2) Let festive sounds of
 praise
(The Arthur Wills Ely Choirbook) fagus-Music.com
Let all men everywhere rejoice Anthem for Unison voices,
 SATB, Brass and Percussion
Guitar Sonata fagus-Music.com
Carillon on 'Orientis Partibus' for Organ (Included in 'The
 Bristol Collection' Vol.3 Novello – Music sales
'Sherwood' for Female voices and Piano Unpublished
The Lord's Prayer for Men's voices Unpublished

1973

The Celtic Monk's Carol for Tenor and Harp (Unpub. but see
 'The Child for Today' for an SATB version)
The Child for Today – Carol Sequence for SATB and Organ
 N/MS
Magnificat and Nunc Dimittis (The Verse Service) SATB
 and Organ – OUP
'Bitter-Sweet' Anthem for SATB and Organ RSCM
Mass of St Mary and St Anne SSA and Organ Opt. Trumpets
 – fagus-Music.com
Pavane and Galliard for Guitar – Ricordi
The Art of Organ Improvisation (Eventually incorporated
 into the book 'ORGAN' Menhuin Music Guide Series
 1984).
In 1973 I also provided an organ part for Arthur Bliss's 'The
 World is charged with the Grandeur of God' for N/MS.

1974

'Prayer' Anthem for SATB and Organ N/MS
Homage to Ravel for Guitar OUP
Tongues of Fire for Organ – Joseph Weinberger Ltd.
I sing of a Maiden S.S. OUP
The Song of Songs – Six Pieces for Manuals – fagus-
 Music.com
'Homage to John Stanley' for Manuals – fagus-music.com

Scherzetto (For the Duchess of Kent – Patron of the RCO) – Cramer

Three Poems by e.e. cummings for Tenor, Oboe and Piano – fagus-Music.com

Saraband Sacrae for Organ – Cramer

Welcome Yule! Anthem for SATB and Organ with Optional Brass OUP

There was a Boy ATB fagus-Music.com

Variations on 'Amazing Grace' for Organ (also includes 'Toccata' which was first included in 'The Art of Organ Improvisation' of 1973) N/MS

1975

Love's Torment (Three Elizabethan Love Songs) for Countertenor and Guitar/or Piano) See 1980.

Eight Pieces for Wind Instruments: Aria for Oboe & Piano – Dance Piece for Clarinet & Piano – The Brontë Country and Bucolics for Bassoon & Piano – September Gold for Horn & Piano – Pageant for Trumpet & Piano – ABRSM Publishing.

Ramayana for Oboe & Piano – Fjords for Trombone & Piano – fagus-Music.com

Moods and Diversions for Guitar – Edizioni Berben (Ancona Italia)

Magnificat and Nunc Dimittis on Plainsong Tones – Banks Music Publications

When our two souls for Soprano, Clarinet and Piano – Spartan Press Music Publishers Ltd.

1976

Resurrection for Organ – Joseph Weinberger Ltd.

'Bells' for Organ Manuals – OUP

'Dreams' for Baritone and Piano Unpub.

Symphonia Eliensis for Organ – fagus-Music.com

The Light Invisible – Anthem for Double Choir, Organ, Harp and Percussion – Joseph Weinberger Ltd.

Le Joie de Vivre for Solo Trumpet – fagus-Music.com
There is no Rose of such Virtue – for S.S. Choir and Piano or
Organ – Basil Ramsey Banks Music publications
Fanfare and Processional for Organ (The Arthur Wills
Organbook) – fagus-Music.com
Nativity – Anthem for Double-Choir – fagus-Music.com

1977

Responsorial Psalms for the ICEL Roman Communion
Service Rite A Text Unison Voices (For the USA
Seminary of the Southwest.) G.I.A. Publications, Inc.
Chicago Ill. USA
Mass In Memoriam Benjamin Britten – RSCM
Two Carol Preludes: 1. In the bleak midwinter
2. This endris nyght – fagus-Music.com
Trinity Sunday – Anthem for SATB and Organ – RSCM
Ave verum corpus – Anthem for SATB and Organ – Animus
Think on these things – Anthem for SATB and Organ –
RSCM

1978

Responsorial Psalm 27 – ICEL
Versets on 'A solis ortus cardine' – The Modern Organist –
Banks Music Publications
Sing Nowell – fagus-Music.com
Carol of the Foal – SATB –
Shop.office@cathedral.ely.anglican.org.
The Contemporary Guitarist (With Hector Quine) – Ricordi
Glory to you – Anthem for SATB and Organ – RSCM

1979

Missa Ad Hoc – Organ – fagus-Music.com
A Woman in Love – Song-Cycle for Mezzo-Soprano and
Guitar – fagus-music.com
Three Responsorial Psalms 46, 84, 121 – RSCM
Toccata for Two – Duet for Organ – Anglo-American

Sad and Glad – Guitar – OUP

On Christmas Day – SATB and Organ (Anglo – American)

1980

Love's Torment – Four Songs for Counter-Tenor and Guitar
or Piano/Harpsichord – fagus-Music.com

Missa Brevis for Trebles and Organ (Auckland Boys Choir)
– fagus-Music.com

Transcription for Organ: 'Pictures from an Exhibition' –
Mussorgsky – fagus-Music.com

1981

Symphonic Suite: 'The Fenlands' for Organ and Brass Band
– fagus-Music.com.

Canticle (Let us give thanks to the Father) and Magnificat or
Trebles and Organ – RSCM

1982

The Brecon Mass (For Diocese of Swansea) – Banks Music
Publications

Lullaby for a Royal Prince – fagus-Music.com

New Year Music for Flute, Horn, Bassoon and Piano –
Anglo-American

I wonder as I wander Arr. for SATB – RSCM

J.S. Bach – Chaconne in D minor for Violin Solo Arr. for
Organ (see The Arthur Wills Bach Book) – fagus-
Music.com

Elgar – Sospiri Op.70 arr. for Organ – fagus-Music.com

Psalm 99 - RSCM

1983

Overture: 'A Muse of Fire' for Brass Band with Opt. Organ –
fagus-Music.com

Homage to Howells – Postlude for Organ – fagus-Music.com

The Arthur Wills Bach Book – Eleven transcriptions for
Organ – fagus-music.com

My beloved spake – Anthem for SATB and Organ – RSCM

Away in a Manger – Carol arr. for Two-part Trebles and
Organ – RSCM

Jerusalem luminosa (Light's abode, celestial Salem) –
Anthem for SATB and Organ (Anglo-American)

1984

Etheldreda Rag for Organ and Piano – fagus-Music.com

Toccata-Finale on 'Marienlyst' for Organ – Anglo-American

'Ely' for SS and Piano –
Shop.office@cathedral.ely.anglican.org

The Spirit of Elgar: Three Pieces for Organ – fagus-
Music.com

'Africana' – Three Pieces for Guitar – OUP

'The Year of the Tiger' for Guitar – fagus-Music.com

Piano Sonata '1984' – Anglo-American

Book 'Organ' (Yehudi Menhuin Music Guides) Macmillan –
see 1993

1985

'Caedmon' – A Children's Cantata Sopranos and Piano –
fagus-Music.com

In Honour of Etheldreda – Anthem for SATB –
Shop.office@cathedral.ely.anglican.org

Praise Him in the sound of the Trumpet (or Tuba or
Whatever) for Organ – Anglo-American

Sweet Spring – SATB – fagus-Music.com

At break of day – SATB and Organ – Anglo-American

'Music' A Madrigal of Love and War – SATB – fagus-
Music.com

Benedicite – SATB and Organ – fagus-Music.com

When the Spirit comes – Four Poems of Emily Brontë –
Mezzo-Soprano and Piano – fagus-music.com

Bread of Heaven – Communion Motet for SATB and Organ
– RSCM

1986

Mozart: Fantasia in F minor K.594 Trans. for Organ – OUP

The Spiritual Railway – SATB –
  Shop.office@cathedral.ely.anglican.org

Icons – for Organ – fagus-Music.com

The Dark Lady – Eight Shakespeare Sonnets for Baritone
  and Piano – fagus-Music.com

The Lord is my Shepherd – Anthem for the Royal Maundy –
  SATB and Organ

Symphony for Orchestra – (Exercise for Durham D.Mus
  degree) fagus-Music.com

1987

Let all the World – Anthem for SATB and Organ – Anglo-
  American

Sacrae Symphonie: Veni Creator Spiritus for Woodwind and
  Brass ensemble – fagus-Music.com

Oliver Cromwell's March for Brass ensemble, Perc. and Opt.
  Organ – fagus-Music.com

Concerto Lirico for Guitar Quartet – Anglo-American

1988

Soft Guitar – fagus-music.com

Preces and Responses for SATB (Unpub.)

Concerto for Guitar and Organ – Anglo-American

Opera: '1984' (Piano Score) Unpub.) In abeyance due to
  extension of copyright from 50 to 70 years.

1989

'Christmas' (Betjeman) – SATB – Goodmusic

'Agricultural Caress' (Betjeman) – Tenor and Piano –
  Goodmusic

A child like me – Anthem for SATB and Organ – Anglo-
  American

1990

Missa Sanctae Etheldredae – fagus-Music.com

High Hills and Stony Rocks – for Organ – fagus-Music.com

The Hound of Heaven – for Counter-tenor and Piano – fagus-Music.com

A Shepherd Boy – Carol for SATB and Organ – RSCM

The Holy Child – Carol for SATB and Organ – fagus-Music.com

1991

Remembrance of Things Past – Suite in three movements for Organ – fagus-Music.com

'On this Rock' – Fantasy for Organ on Byrd's motet – 'Tu es Petrus' – Anglo-American

While shepherds watched their flocks: Trad.Yorkshire melody: 'On Ilkley Moor' arr. SATB with Organ and optional Percussion. – fagus-Music.com

Psalm 8 and 13 for Soprano and Organ/Piano – Anglo-American

Etheldreda Rag arr. Solo Guitar – fagus-Music.com

Peach Blossom Rag – Piano – fagus-Music.com

1992

Choral Concerto: 'The Gods of Music' for Solo Organ, Brass and Percussion – Anglo-American

'Eternity's Sunrise': Three Poems by William Blake for Contralto and Organ or Piano – Anglo-American

A Carol for Sark: 'Love came down at Christmas' – Animus

Rabbi Ben Ezra – Epilogue: 'Grow old along with me' (Robert Browning) – Song for Baritone and Piano – fagus-Music.com

1993

'A Toccata of Galuppi's' – Scena for Counter-tenor and String Quartet – fagus-Music.com

Oriental – Three Variants for Organ' – fagus-music.com

Oration for Trombone and Piano – Warwick Music

Kahn & Averill: Book 'Organ' Second Edition, (Yehudi Menuhin Music Guides) London

'Betjemania' – Four Songs for Tenor and Piano (Fentone) De Haske Music (UK) Ltd.

Abt Vogler – Prologue: 'Would that the structure brave' (Robert Browning) – Song for Baritone and Piano – fagus-music.com

1994

Scherzo-Fantasy: 'The Ely Imps' for Organ – fagus-Music.com

'The Shining Sea' (Sketch)

Symphonic Suite: 'The Fenlands' (Transcription for Organ Solo) 'The Vikings' – 'Oliver Cromwell' – March: 'City of Ely' – fagus-Music.com

Song Without Words – for Organ – (Fentone) De Haske Music (UK) Ltd.

At the round earth's imagined corners – Anthem for SATB and Organ – fagus-Music.com

Diptyque: Two Poems for Organ after Robert Browning: Prologue – Epilogue – fagus-Music.com

Six Ely Aphorisms – for Organ – fagus-music.com

Transcription of 'Venus' and 'Jupiter' from 'The Planets' (Holst) for Organ N/MS (see 1998)

1995

Celebration of Life for Organ – (Fentone) De Haske Music (UK) Ltd.

Valediction: Drop, drop slow tears – for Organ (Included in the Kenneth Leighton Memorial Album - Banks Music Publications)

'The Shining Sea' – Cantata for Solo Tenor, Chorus and Orchestra – fagus-Music.com

Symphony-Bhagavad Gita for Organ (Published in 2000) fagus-Music.con

1996

Versicles and Responses for Knaresborough Parish Church –
    fagus-Music.com
Prelude to Act Three: Die Meistersinger – Wagner
    Transcribed for Organ – (Fentone) De Haske Music (UK)
    Ltd.

1997

'Wondrous Machine' – Variations on a Theme by Henry
    Purcell for Organ – (Fentone) De Haske Music (UK) Ltd.

1998

Transcription of Holst's 'Mars' to complete 'The Planets'
    Triptych requested by Novello/Music Sales.

1999

The New Millennium Rag (Divine Comedy) – fagus-
    Music.com
Buddha-Song for Bass and Piano – fagus-Music.com
'The Vikings' (from Symphonic Suite: 'The Fenlands'
    Transcribed for Brass ensemble, Percussion and Solo
    Organ. – fagus-Music.com
'Easter to Pentecost' two Organ Interludes for the
    Millennium Festival Service in Salisbury Cathedral -
    Unpub.

2000

Missa Sancti Stephani for SATB and Organ – for
    St Stephen's Church, Bournemouth – Anglo-American
Toccata, Adagio and Fugue on BACH – fagus-music.com

2001

Missa Incarnationis for SATB and Organ – for the Church of
    the Incarnation, Dallas, Texas USA – Anglo-American

2003

'Have mercy, Lord, on me' – St Matthew Passion – Bach –
Transcribed for Organ Solo – Animus

Rabbi Ben Ezra (From Diptyque for Baritone and Piano)
Trans. for Choir: S.A. or T.B. fagus-Music.com

2004

'That Wondrous Birthday' – Three Carols and a Coda for
SATB and Organ for Ely Choral Society – fagus-
Music.com

Crossing the Bar (Tennyson) – SATB and organ –
Shop.office@cathedral.ely.anglican.org

2005

Meditation on 'Adore te devote' for organ fagus-Music.com

Communion service for A.T.B. (St.Thomas Church, New
York) fagus-music.com

2006

Nine Responsorial Psalms: 24 67 68 93 96 108 114 118 148
fagus-Music.com

Remembrance : 'the world of light!' fagus-Music.com

Recordings

1958

The Argo Record Company Ltd

Music for the Feast of Christmas – (Choristers of Ely Cathedral – The Renaissance Singers – William Jermiah and Richard Swabey (solo trebles) – John Whitworth (counter-tenor) – Arthur Wills (organ) – Director: Michael Howard

1. Rejoice in the Lord alway – Causton
2. This is the record of John – Gibbons
3. O ye little flock – Amner
4. Les Anges – Messiaen
5. Dominus dixit – Plainsong mode 1
6. Dies Sanctificatus – Palestrina
7. Hodie Christus natus est – Sweelinck
8. An earthly tree, a heavenly fruit – Byrd
9. Resonet in laudibus – Handl
10. Eya martyr Stephene – Anon
11. O quam gloriosum – Victoria
12 Vox in Rama – Plainsong mode vii
13. Salvete flores Martyrum – Plainsong mode 1 with faux bourdon by Dufay
14. The Coventry Carol – Anon

The Choristers of Ely Cathedral (Issued 1960) – 45 R.P.M. Extended Play Record – William Jeremiah (solo treble) Arthur Wills (organ) Director: Michael Howard

1. Missa Cum Jubilo – Plainsong
2. An earthly tree, a heavenly fruit – Byrd
3. O mystrerium ineffabile – Lallouette

1963

Audiovision Developments (Oxford Ltd)

Arthur Wills (organ)
Louis Vierne:
Symphony No.3 Op. 28
Cortège, Berceuse, Divertissement, Carillon (Op. 31)

1964

Audiovision Developments (Oxford) Ltd

Victimae Paschali A sequence of music for Lent, Passiontide,
and Easter – The Choir of Ely Cathedral
Michael Dudman (Organist) Director; solo organ Arthur Wills

1. O Lord, we beseech Thee – Barcrofte
2. Durch Adams Fall – Sweelinck (organ)
3. O Jesu, look – Kyrbie
4. Salvator mundi – Blow
5. Vexilla regis prodeunt – Dufay
6. Agnue Dei – Morley
7. Herzlich thut mich verlangen – J.S. Bach (organ)
8. Hosanna to the Son of David – Weelkes
9. Ave verum corpus – Byrd
10. Woefully arrayed – Cornyshe
11. Haec Dies – Plainsong
12. Terra tremuit – Byrd
13. O fili et filiae – Dandrieu (organ)
14. Surgens Jesus – Philips

1965

Ryemuse Productions Ltd. 45 Extended Play

Organ Music at Ely Cathedral – Arthur Wills – Organ

1. J.S. Bach – Chorale Prelude: In dulci jubilo BWV 729
2. J.S. Bach – Fugue in G minor BWV 579
3. Louis Vierne – Impromptu (Pièces de Fantasie)
4. Arthur Wills – Deo Gratias

BBC – Britain's Cathedrals and their Music, with John
  Betjeman – No.3

Conductor and Solo Organist Arthur Wills
Choir: Christopher Tye – Kyrie eleison (Orbis factor)
William Fox – Teach me thy way, O Lord
George Barcrofte – O lord, we beseech thee
Organ: J.S. Bach – Chorale Prelude: Christ unser Herr zum
  Jordan kam (S.684)
Choir: Arthur Wills – The Praises of the Trinity

1967

E.M.I RECORDS (The Gramophone Company Ltd)

Great Cathedral Organ Series (No.13) Arthur Wills Organist
1. Messiaen – Dieu Parmi Nous (from La Nativité du
   Seigneur)
2. Gigout – Scherzo (No.8 of 10 Pièces)
3. Gigout – Toccata (No.4 of 10 Pièces)
4. Franck – Final in B flat, Op.21
5. Dupré – Variations sur un Noël, Op.20
6. Vierne – Naïades (from Pièces de Fantaisie, Op.55)
7. Wills – Introduction and Allegro

1968

ABBEY RECORDS EYNSHAM OXFORD

Ely Cathedral Organ – Arthur Wills 45 Extended Play
1. J.S. Bach – Prelude and Fugue in E minor S.533
2. F. Couperin – Dialogue sur les trompettes, clarion et tierce
   du Grand clavier et le bourdon avec le larigot du positif,
   (4th couplet from Gloria, Messe a l'usage des Paroisses)
3. Arthur Wills – Postlude

The Choristers of Ely Cathedral conducted by Arthur Wills –
45 Extended Play; Organist Stephen Carleston

1. Warlock – Adam lay ybounden
2. Viadana – Agnus Dei (Missa Dominicalis)

3. Fauré – Salve Regina
4. Nares – (1) The souls of the righteous
5.   (2) In the sight of the unwise
6. Wills – O quam gloriosum

1972

RCA LTD. RECORD DIVISION

The Organ of Ely Cathedral – Arthur Wills

1. Daquin – Noel X
2. Dupré – Berceuse (From Suite Bretonne)
3. Vierne – Scherzetto (Twenty-four Pieces in Free Style)
4. Franck – Pièce Héroique
5. Wills – Prelude and Fugue
6. Schumann – Study in B minor (From Six Studies for Pedal Piano)
7. Brahms – Chorale Prelude: 'Es is ein Ros entsprungen'
8. Reger – Introduction and Passacaglia

1973

CHANDOS RECORDS LTD

The Choir of Ely Cathedral – Director Arthur Wills,
Organist Gerald Gifford

1. Wills – The Carol of King Canute
2. Brahms – How lovely is Thy dwelling place
3. Bain arr. Humphries – Brother James' Air
4. Stanford – Te Deum in B flat
5. Stanford – Jubilate in B flat
6. Attwood – Turn Thy face from my sins
7. Bizet – Agnus Dei
8. Mendelssohn – Hear my prayer
   including:
9. O for the Wings of a Dove
10. Mozart – Ave Verum K618

11. J.S. Bach – Jesu, Joy of Man's Desiring

(This programme was transferred to CD 6519 and 6603, together with recordings by the Choirs of Westminster Abbey and Worcester Cathedral))

1976 (The Organ was rebuilt with extensive tonal changes the previous year.)

VISTA VPS 1030 STEREO

The Organ in Ely Cathedral – Dr Arthur Wills

1. J.S. Bach – Prelude and Fugue in D major BWV 532
2. Marchand – Basse de Trompette
3. Liszt – Prelude and Fugue on the Name of B.A.C.H.
4. Louis Couperin – Chacone in C
5. Franck – Choral No.2 in B minor
6. Wills – Carillon on 'Orientis Partibus'

SAGA RECORDS 326 Kensal Road, LONDON W.10

Louis Daquin – Book of Noëls and organ works by Louis Marchand – Arthur Wills Organ of Ely Cathedral
(Two Records)

Louis Daquin

Noël No. 1 – Sur les jeux d'anches, sans tremblant
Noël No. 2 – En dialogue, duo, trio, sur le Cornet de Récit
    les Tierces du Positif et la Pédalle de Flûte
    Lentement, et très tendre.
Noël No. 3 – En musette, en dialogue et en duo.
    Très tendrement
Noël No. 4 – En duo, sur les jeux d'anches, sans tremblant
Noël No. 5 – En duo
Noël No. 6 – Sur les jeux d'anches, sans tremblant et en duo
Noël No. 7 – En trio et en dialogue, le Cornet de Récit de la
    main droite, la Tierce du Positif de la main
    gauche. Très tendrement.

Noël No. 8 – Noël étranger, sur les jeux d'anches, sans
        tremblant et en duo.
Noël No. 9 – Sur les flûtes. Très tendrement.
Noël No. 10 – Grand jeu et duo.
Noël No. 11 – En récit en taille, sur les Tierce du Positif,
        avec la Pédalle de Flûte et en duo. Lentement
        et tendrement.
Noël No. 12 – Noël Suisse. Grand jeu et duo. Pesamment.

Louis Marchand

Plein jeu
Fugue
Quatuor
Tierce en taille
Dialogue
Grand jeu
Basse de Cromorne
Duo
Dialogue

SAGA RECORDS (Later issued on Saga Classics SCD 9006
(Sound-Products Holland BV)

William Boyce – Anthems and Voluntaries – Choir of Ely
Cathedral with Gerald Gifford (organ) Directed by Arthur
Wills (organ solo)

Anthem: O where shall wisdom be found?
        Soloists: Andrew Wigley and Mark Turner
        (trebles)
        Anthony Ransome (alto)
        Colin Flanagan (tenor)
        Kenneth Burgess (bass)

Voluntary I

Anthem: Turn thee unto me, O Lord
        Soloists: Andrew Wigley and Ross Thain (trebles)

Voluntary II

Voluntary IV

Anthem: By the waters of Babylon
Soloists: Andrew Wigley and Richard Wigley (trebles)
            John Aitchison (alto)
            Colin Flanagan (tenor)
            Kenneth Burgess (bass)

Voluntary X

Anthem: I have surely built Thee an house
            Soloists – John Aitchison (alto)
            Colin Flanagan (tenor)
            Kenneth Burgess (bass)

1977

EMI Records Ltd.

Paul Patterson – Kyrie – Gloria – Pieces for Organ
The London Chorale – Conductor Roy Wales – Dr Arthur
    Wills (Organ)
(Organ works recorded in Westminster Cathedral, London)

Kyrie
Gloria
Trilogy for Organ: Intrada – Interludium – Jubilate
Visions
Fluorescences

RCA RED SEAL 4 Record Set

Symphonies 1–5; Widor Performers: Arthur Wills – Jane
    Parker-Smith – Graham Steed
Organ of Coventry Cathedral

Symphony No. 1 in C minor Op. 13 (No.1) – Arthur Wills
Symphony No. 2 in D major Op. 13 (No.2) – Jane Parker-Smith
Symphony No. 3 in E minor Op. 13 (No.3) – Jane Parker-Smith
Symphony No. 4 in F major Op. 13 (No.4) – Arthur Wills
Symphony No. 5 in F minor Op. 42 (No.1) – Graham Steed

ABBEY Records LPB 781

Rejoice – A live recording of highlights of the Jubilee Service held in the Royal Albert Hall, London, on 30th June 1977, in the presence of Her Majesty Queen Elizabeth the Queen Mother. This notable occasion deserves inclusion in that my Anthem: 'The Light Invisible' received its first performance conducted by Lionel Dakers. The words were chosen by Canon Joseph Poole from T.S. Eliot's 'The Rock' and I was able to use harp and percussion in addition to the organ (which I played). I also played before the Service – Bach's Prelude and Fugue in D major and Liszt's Prelude and Fugue on BACH. 'The light Invisible' which uses a semi-chorus in addition to the main choir may be performed with organ alone, and is included so in a recording by the Ely Choir in 'The Praises of the Trinity' a Herald CD of 1996 listed below.

1978

MERIDIAN Records

E77014

Full Stops – Arthur Wills: Organ of Ely Cathedral

Marche Pontificale – Widor
Adagio in G minor – Albinoni-Giazotto
The Ride of the Valkries – Wagner
Variations on 'Amazing Grace' – Wills
The Storm (Grand Fantasia in E minor) – Lemmens
(Transferred to CDE 84305 in 1995 with the addition of three organ pieces from Anthems by Purcell and Blow)

MERIDIAN Records

E77013

Anthems by Purcell and Blow – Choir of Ely Cathedral with Stephen le Prevost (organ).
    Directed by Arthur Wills (organ solo)

Purcell:

I was glad when they said unto me
Jehova, quam multi sunt hostes

    Soloists: Colin Flanagan (tenor) Kenneth Burgess (bass)

Voluntary for Double Organ
Benedicite:

    Soloists: John Aitchison (alto) Ross Thain (treble)
    Colin Flanagan (tenor) Kim Clarke (treble)
    Christopher Gove (bass) Steff Scott (alto)

Blow:

Let Thy hand be strengthened
O pray for the peace of Jerusalem

    Soloist: Ross Thain (treble)

Voluntary in A
Salvator mundi
Echo Voluntary in G
Evening Service in G

    Soloists: Richard Wigley (treble) Ross Thain (treble)
    John Aitchison (alto) Steff Scott (alto)
    Colin Flanagan (tenor) Adrian Goss (tenor)
    Kenneth Burgess (bass) Christopher Gove (bass)

(Some items transferred to CDE84276)

1980

HYPERION Records Ltd. (Digital Recording)

Pictures at an Exhibition – Mussorgsky: A new transcription
    for Organ by Arthur Wills
Arthur Wills – Organ of Ely Cathedral
(This recording was used by Ted Perry to initiate his new
label Hyperion. It was given a special silvered cover, and I
signed a hundred copies for its launch.) It was transferred to

CD in 1988 and again in 1999 – see Organ and Brass CDH55003)

HYPERION Records Ltd.

'Service High and anthems clear' Choir of Ely Cathedral with Stephen le Prevost (organ). Directed by Arthur Wills

Samuel Wesley: Exultate Deo
Samuel Sebastian Wesley: Blessed be the God and Father
    Treble solo: Dickon Stainer
Stainer: Evening Canticles in B flat major
Attwood: Come, Holy Ghost
    Treble solo: Simon Ellis
Parry: I was glad
Stanford: Evening Canticles in G major
    Treble solo: Simon Ellis Baritone solo: Kenneth Burgess
Wood: O Thou, the central orb

1982

HYPERION Records Ltd.

Music for Organ and Brass Band – Arthur Wills (Organ)
The Cambridge Co-operative Band
David Read (Conductor)

Symphonic Suite: The Fenlands (Arthur Wills)
1. The Vikings 2. Wicken Fen 3. Oliver Cromwell
4. March: City of Ely
Pomp and Circumstance March No. 1 Op. 39 No.1 (Elgar)
Nimrod, from the 'Enigma' Variations (Elgar)
Pomp and Circumstance March No. 4 Op. 39 No.4 (Elgar)
Touch her soft lips and part (From 'Henry V' Walton arr.
    Wills) Cornet solo David Reed
March: Crown Imperial (Walton)
Transferred to CD 1988, and transferred again to CD 1999
plus Mussorgsky – Pictures at an Exhibition but minus Elgar
– Pomp and Circumstance March No. 1.

1983

HYPERION Records Ltd.

Bach at Ely – Ten Transcriptions by Arthur Wills
Arthur Wills (Organ)

Sinfonia from Cantata BWV 29, 'Wir danken dir, Gott'
Air, Gavotte and Gigue from Orchestral Suite No. 3 in D
    BWV 1068
Sarabande and Bouree from Suite in C for solo Cello BWV
    1009
Jesu, Joy of Man's Desiring – Chorale from Cantata BWV
    147
Sheep may safely graze – Aria from Cantata BWV 208
Subdue us by thy goodness – Chorale from Cantata BWV 22
Chaconne from Partita in D minor for solo Cello BWV 1004

1984

MERIDIAN Records Ltd.

Music of Six Centuries – Choir of Ely Cathedral, with
Stephen le Prevost (Organ), Directed by Arthur Wills

Carol: Eya, martyr Stephane – Anon. 15th century
    Soloists: Anthony Barthorpe (alto) Peter North (tenor)
Christe, qui lux es et dies – Robert Whyte c. 1538–1574
O sing unto the Lord a new song – Hinde c.
    early 17th century
    Soloists: Benjamin Stainer and William Morgan (trebles)
    Anthony Barthorpe (alto) Peter North (tenor)
    Paul Smith (bass)
Ascribe unto the Lord – John Travers c. 1703–1758
    Soloists: Benjamin Stainer (treble)
    Anthony Barthorpe (alto)
    Peter North (tenor) Paul Smith (bass)
Tu es sacerdos – Samuel Wesley 1766–1837
O Lord my God – Samuel Sebastian Wesley 1810–1876

Lead, kindly light – Sir John Stainer 1840–1901
   Soloist: Benjamin Stainer (treble)
Hail, gladdening light – Charles Wood 1866–1926
Evening Canticles in C – Charles Villiers Stanford
   1852–1924

(Some items transferred to CDE842176)

1986

PRIORY RECORDS

The Choral and Organ Music of Arthur Wills – Choir of Ely
Cathedral, directed by Arthur Wills
Stephen le Prevost (Organ) Solo organ – Arthur Wills

1. O Praise God in his holiness
2. In Honour of Etheldreda
3. Ave verum corpus
4. Tongues of Fire (Organ Solo)
5. Missa Eliensis
6. The Praises of the Trinity
7. Benedicite omnia opera
8. Etheldreda Rag (Homage to Scott Joplin – Organ Solo)
9. Magnificat on Plainsong Tones
10. Nunc Dimittis on Plainsong Tones

Christmas Eve at Ely Cathedral – Directed by Arthur Wills
Organ: Stephen le Prevost

1. Office Hymn: Veni Redemptor genitium – Plainsong
   Mode 1.
2. Hosanna to the Son of David – Weelkes
3. The Holly and the Ivy – trad. arr. H. Walford Davies
4. O little Town of Bethlehem – English Traditional
5. In the Bleak Mid-Winter – Harold Darke
6. Ding Dong merrily on high – Malcolm Williamson
7. O come all ye faithful – J.F. Wade (Ascribed.)
8. The Carol of King Canute – Arthur Wills

9. Carol of the Foal – Arthur Wills
10 Once in Royal David's City – H.J. Gauntlett
11. The Three kings – Peter Cornelius
12. Welcome Yule! – Arthur Wills
13. Hark! the herald angels sing – Felix Mendelssohn
14. Dismissals (at the Carol Procession) – Arthur Wills
15. Organ: Christmas Meditation No.3 'And suddenly there was with the Angel' – Arthur Wills

1987

CHRYSALIS RECORDS LTD.

The Art of Noise – In no sense nonsense. Written and performed by Anne Dudley & J.J. Jeczakik.
Recorded and mixed by Ted Hayton – Ely Cathedral Choir directed by Dr Arthur Wills.

SIDE ONE	SIDE TWO
Galleons of Stone	Ode to Don Jose
Dragnet	A Day at the Races
Fin du Temps	Counterpoint
How Rapid?	Roundabout 727
Opus for Four	Ransom on the Sand
Debut	Roller 1
E.F.L.	Nothing was going to stop them, anyway
	Crusoe
	One Earth

THE ABBEY RECORDING COMPANY LTD.

Music for a Royal Year in Ely Cathedral 1987

1. Music from the distribution of the Royal Maundy by H.M. The Queen

Ely Cathedral Choir – Director: Arthur Wills – Assistant Organist: Stephen le Prevost

The Children and Gentlemen of Her Majesty's Chapel Royal, St James Palace

The Organist, Choirmaster and Composer of Her Majesty's Chapel Royal – Richard Popplewell

Psalm 138 – Chant by C.H. Lloyd
Preces and Responses – Richard Lloyd
Anthems: The Lord is my shepherd – Arthur Wills
                    Lord for thy tender mercies' sake – Hilton
                    Zadok the Priest – Handel
Hymn: All my hope on God is founded – Howells

The National Anthem: Arr. Wills

2. Evensong in the Lady Chapel on the occasion of the opening of the Festival of Flowers, in the presence of Her Royal Highness The Princess of Wales

Preces and Responses – John Reading
Psalm 47 – Chant: Beckwith
Canticles – Purcell in G minor
Anthem – Rejoice in the Lord alway – Purcell (Strings and Organ)
Hymn: For the beauty of the earth – Geoffrey Shaw
Voluntary – Church Sonata in C K. 336 – Mozart (Strings and Organ)

1988

PRIORY RECORDS

PTCD 246

Great European Organs No. 9 – Arthur Wills plays the Organ of Ely Cathedral.

1. Toccata – J. Guillou

Symphony No. 10 (Romane) – C.M. Widor
2. 1st Movement: Moderato
3. 2nd Movement: Chorale

4. 3rd Movement: Cantilene
5. 4th Movement: Final

Three Chorale Preludes: C.H.H. Parry
6. The Old 104th
7. Christe Redemptor
8. Crofts 136th

Symphonia Eliensis – Arthur Wills
9. Galilee Porch
10. St Catherine's Chapel
11. Lady Chapel
12. Nave
13. North Transept
14. South Transept
15. Octagon

(This was my last complete recording as Director of Music at Ely Cathedral.)

1996

HERALD AV Publicatios – HAVPCD 197

'The Praises of the Trinity' – Choral and Organ music by
    Arthur Wills
The Choir of Ely Cathedral – Sean Farrell organ – Arthur
Wills solo organ – The Choir of the King's School, Ely –
Instrumental ensemble – Paul Trepte director

1. O praise God in his holiness – with instrumental ensemble

Verse Service:

2. Magnificat
3. Nunc Dimittis
4. Their sound is gone out
5. The Light Invisible
6. The Praises of the Trinity
7. By the waters of Babylon
8. Elegy

Solo organ (Arthur Wills)

9. I hunger and I thirst

Missa Sanctae Etheldredae:

10. Kyrie eleison
11. Gloria in excelsis Deo
12. Sanctus
13. Benedictus
14. Agnus Dei
15. Office hymn for Christmas Day
    Choristers and solo organ (Arthur Wills)
    The Fourth Service:
16. Magnificat
17. Nunc dimittis
18. Let all men everywhere rejoice – with instrumental
    ensemble and the Choir of the King's School, Ely

2000

GUILD MUSIC LTD GMCD 7225

Wondrous Machine! – Organ works by Arthur Wills –
Jeremy Filsell – The Organ of Tonbridge School Chapel

1. Carillon on 'Orientis Partibus'
2. Song without Words (In Memoriam Sergei Rachmaninoff)
3. Prelude and Fugue (Alkmaar)
4. Scherzo fantasy 'The Ely Imps'
5. Wondrous Machine! A Young Person's Guide to the
   Organ – Variations and Fugue on a theme
   by Henry Purcell
6. Arioso (from Five Pieces)
7. Intermezzo (from Five Pieces)
8. Scherzo 'High Hills and Stony Rocks'
9, Variations on a Carol
10. The New Millennium Rag
11. Postlude

2004

LAMMAS Records – LAMM 168D

Sounds of Arthur Wills – ICONS
Robert Crowley plays the music of Arthur Wills on the
Organ of Ely Cathedral

Icons
1. Very broadly
2. Lively
3. Very slow
4. Turbulent: As at first

5. Lullaby for a Royal Prince

Trio Sonata

6. Allegro
7. Adagio alla Siciliana
8. Vivace

Symphony Bhagavad Gita

9. Andante – Allegro feroce – Mesto – Allegro trionfante
10. Adagietto
11. Leggermente – Tenebroso – Con fuoco – Leggero
12. Molto adagio
13. Homage to Howells

Diptyque

14. Prologue
13. Epilogue

– Remembrance of Things Past
Robert Crowley plays the Music of Arthur Wills on the
Organ of Ely Cathedral
(A projected recording for issue 2008)